# Just Liberal Violence

## Off the Fence: Morality, Politics and Society

The series is published in partnership with the Centre for Applied Philosophy, Politics & Ethics (CAPPE), University of Brighton.

### Series editors:

**Bob Brecher, Professor of Moral Philosophy, University of Brighton**
**Robin Dunford, Senior Lecturer in Globalisation and War, University of Brighton**
**Michael Neu, Senior Lecturer in Philosophy, Politics and Ethics, University of Brighton**

*Off the Fence* presents short, sharply argued texts in applied moral and political philosophy, with an interdisciplinary focus. The series constitutes a source of arguments on the substantive problems that applied philosophers are concerned with contemporary real-world issues relating to violence, human nature, justice, equality and democracy, self and society. The series demonstrates applied philosophy to be at once rigorous, relevant and accessible – philosophy-in-use.

*The Right of Necessity: Moral Cosmopolitanism and Global Poverty*,
Alejandra Mancilla

*Complicity: Criticism between Collaboration and Commitment*,
Thomas Docherty

*The State and the Self: Identity and Identities*,
Maren Behrensen

*Just Liberal Violence: Sweatshops, Torture, War*,
Michael Neu

# Just Liberal Violence

## Sweatshops, Torture, War

Michael Neu

ROWMAN & LITTLEFIELD
INTERNATIONAL
London • New York

Published by Rowman & Littlefield International Ltd
Unit A, Whitacre Mews, 26–34 Stannary Street, London SE11 4AB
www.rowmaninternational.com

Rowman & Littlefield International Ltd. is an affiliate of Rowman & Littlefield
4501 Forbes Boulevard, Suite 200, Lanham, Maryland 20706, USA
With additional offices in Boulder, New York, Toronto (Canada), and Plymouth (UK)
www.rowman.com

**British Library Cataloguing in Publication Data**
A catalogue record for this book is available from the British Library

ISBN: HB 978-1-7866-0064-6
PB 978-1-7866-0065-3

**Library of Congress Cataloging-in-Publication Data**
ISBN 978-1-78660-064-6 (cloth : alk. paper)
ISBN 978-1-78660-065-3 (pbk. : alk. paper)
ISBN 978-1-78660-066-0 (electronic)

∞™ The paper used in this publication meets the minimum requirements of American
National Standard for Information Sciences – Permanence of Paper for Printed Library
Materials, ANSI/NISO Z39.48–1992.

Printed in the United States of America

Meinen lieben Eltern, Anne und Karl-Josef –
und in Erinnerung an die beste Oma der Welt,
Antonie Gastreich

# Contents

# Acknowledgements

I would like to begin by thanking three colleagues who have made the most significant intellectual contributions to this book: my lovely mentor and favourite dinner companion, Bob Brecher; my unsurpassable ale-tasting and writing partner, Robin Dunford; and my 'most awesome' running and future writing partner, Vicky Margree. You are the best friends and colleagues anyone could wish for. I thank you for being the people and friends you are; incomprehensibly generous and equipped with a degree of intelligence and integrity I wish I could match. You are also fun to be with (a characteristic I *can* match). Thank you, to all three of you, for having helped me so incredibly much. If and insofar this book has any virtues, we have produced them together. Its mistakes and shortcomings, however, are my own.

There are many other colleagues who have directly or indirectly contributed to this book. Paddy Maguire, our Head of School, has given me a substantial amount of teaching relief. Mark Devenney, our Humanities Programme leader for so many years, has always been supportive and ingenious; we and I owe him a lot. Cathy Bergin has advised me on my conclusions and has been giving me a generous portion of mirthful verbal abuse for several years now; Lars Cornelissen's company is always lovely, and our conversations have never failed to inspire me; Andy Knott has provided insightful feedback on a couple of chapters and is slowly turning me into a Brighton & Hove Albion fan; Zeina Maasri has been a fabulous walking companion and friend, and has also designed a lovely present that made me start writing this book in the first place; Vicente Ordóñez read and commented on two chapters and was a terrific visiting scholar during his time at the Centre for Applied Philosophy, Politics and Ethics (CAPPE); Becca Searle quite simply embodies the ethos shared by colleagues in Pavilion Parade; and Ian Sinclair is a brilliant CAPPE administrator and a great friend. We have a remarkable academic community, including our superb admin and student support team: Clare Baker, Amira Driscoll, Tanya Gujral, Martina Knight, Jason Porter, Louise Ranger, Mel Searle and Lol Stein Johnson. I hope that we can keep things going in the years and decades to come, taking pleasure in what we do. I would also like to express my gratitude to the student community in Pavilion Parade and let you know how much you mean to me, and how much of *you* is in this book. I feel privileged to be surrounded and supported by you.

More thanks are due. My PhD supervisor, Garrett Brown, is an outstanding academic and exceptional person. I am very grateful for his integrity and for everything he has done for me over the years. Sarah Campbell, Rebecca Anastasi and Elaine McGarraugh from Rowman & Littlefield International are never anything but a pleasure to work with. Maeve McKeown offered thoughtful comments on the sweatshop chapter and has strengthened it enormously as a result. Robb Somerton-Jones kindly read the chapter on just liberal violence. I would also like to thank two anonymous reviewers for Rowman & Littlefield International, whose thorough comments were very helpful. Moreover, I would like to express my gratitude to Sharla Cute from the State University of New York Press for allowing me to quote extensively from Uwe Steinhoff's book *On the Ethics of Torture* (Albany: Suny Press, 2013). Some of the arguments I present in chapter 5, 'War', draw on material I have previously presented in the following publications: Michael Neu, 'The Tragedy of Justified War', *International Relations* 27, 4 (2013): 461–80; 'The Supreme Emergency of War: A Critique of Walzer', *The Journal of International Political Theory* 10, 1 (2013): 3–19; and 'Why McMahan's *Just* Wars Are Only *Justified* and Why That Matters', *Ethical Perspectives* 19, 2 (2012): 235–55.

My arguments have developed though, and if and insofar as what I write *now* differs from what I wrote *then*, it is always the more recent arguments that should be attributed to me. Some of the thinkers whose work I target with these arguments are people I have met in person. Brian Orend hosted me very kindly during a research term at Waterloo in 2007; Uwe Steinhoff has been an excellent conference companion; Michael Walzer took the time to talk to me for a long afternoon at Princeton; and Jeff McMahan gave me generous advice on a paper I once wrote, and responded to another one. But the fact that I have experienced all of these individuals as very generous, well-meaning and supportive does not mean that I should abstain from criticizing their work. I do hope that I have written this book in a way which – despite the severity of the critique offered – enables, rather than shuts down, dialogue.

There is no way I could envisage my life without the Linsmeier family: Felix, Gabi, Hannes and Lisa. They are wonderful friends, and a pure joy to be with. Felix has helped me magnificently by shrewdly commenting on drafts, cooking delicious meals for me, teaching me how to 'chill', among many other things, and curbing my occasional enthusiasm for being inappropriately polemical. Afxentis Afxentiou is the most loyal, dedicated and affable friend one can imagine, and his critical input into this book has been invaluable. Dominik Feldmann is the most impressive thinker and critic I know and friend I have. Vasilis Leontitsis commented on an earlier draft of my sweatshop chapter and has, more importantly, been the most consistent source of trust and friendship since the day we met. Ross Sparkes has been tremendously and tirelessly supportive throughout. Not only did he manage to persuade me that I *might* have something worthwhile to say; but he also gave me the most crucial advice: 'Remember to relax, don't exhaust yourself writing a book you've already written a thousand times in conversation with friends'. Lucas Schneider came to see me when the book was done, making sure that I reverted back to my bouncy self and got rid of any remaining exhaustion – we simply whisked it away. These friends have, on countless occasions, shared their thoughts with me on what I was trying to do in this book – it would be nice if we could write something together in the future (it is generally a good idea, I think, to co-author books with people who are far cleverer than oneself). Other friends have not only enabled me to pull through with this book; they have also – in their very different ways – given me the chance to enjoy the moments in-between. There have been many such moments, whether in Brighton, Brighton Beach, Rottingdean, Rottingdean Beach (thank you for everything, JF), the South Downs, the Plough and Harrow, the Pyrenees, Rome, Norway, the Pyrenees *again*, Iceland, Măgura, the Transylvanian Alps, Köln-Kalk, Olpe, Rhode, Kreuztal,[1] Villabunt, Ottfingen, Nürnberg, Passau, München, Cornwall, the Plant Room and – in anticipation – the Peaks. I would also like to thank my godchild Anna and her sister Charlotte for giving me some hope in the world, and their parents Daniel and Nadine for making me feel at home in it. But I do not want just to create a list of friends who I have shared these moments with. I will thank them in person when I see them next – including my dear 'old' school friends Simon Lixfeld, Peter Menne and Benedikt van Bömmel, who never cease to be loyal regardless of how much I neglect them.

Finally, and most importantly, I would like to thank my family, the foundation of my life: mum, dad, Daniel – with Jessica and Mia – and Oliver. Mum and dad always make everything possible, with complete dedication. There is no other family quite like us, but I do not need to engage in a public celebration of this fact, so I shall just leave it there.

Let us all try to continue living in peace and respect – and friendship.

Michael Neu

# Chapter 1

# A Plea for Defiance

This book is a critique of contemporary defences of 'just liberal violence'. I use this term in two senses. First, just liberal violence is violence purportedly committed in defence of human rights and/or in order to minimize human suffering. It is those intentions that are said to render violence in their pursuit just; to make such violence the morally right thing to do. Second, just liberal violence is *just* that: liberal violence. While allegedly serving just goals, it is undertaken in practice, and defended in theory, by ignoring considerations which disturb the liberal framework governing the use of just violence.[1] When those considerations are made explicit, it is clear that just liberal violence is *mere* violence, violence without adequate justification. In this book, I aim to offer a critique of liberal moral defences of such violence, focusing on sweatshops, interrogational torture and war. I argue that these defences share fundamental assumptions and methods of argument that are mistaken.

*Just Liberal Violence* does not, however, impose a *rigid* unifying lens through which to evaluate and reject these defences. I do not put forward the claim that moral defences of sweatshops, interrogational torture and war are all exemplars of *exactly* the same sort of thinking. Rather, I claim that they share a set of common features, which often play out in different ways. The critiques I offer are thus intended to stand on their own, as well as form part of an extended argument; they are critiques both of the works of individual authors and of the wider literature of which these authors' works are emblematic. This book is an invitation to resist ways of thinking that justify violence morally within a narrow framework of unexamined liberalism. But of course we need to *do* something about mere violence, rather than just think about it. So this is not only a philosophical intervention; it is also a political one. In developing it, I am not putting forward a particular conception of

1

justice; I merely argue that contemporary defences of just liberal violence
are inadequate.

Since this book is also an attempt to persuade people of something they do
not believe already, it carries the risk of failure. My hope is that the authors
whose work I engage with will find reasons to pause for a moment before
continuing to steamroll their theoretical defences of violence across a landscape inhabited by people often largely indifferent to, or obsessed with, the
*practice* of violence. Be that as it may, I am hoping that some of those readers
who sympathize with arguments in defence of just liberal violence will come
to reconsider their views. I am not just talking about academics here, but
about *everyone* who follows political matters, makes judgements about them,
debates and criticizes. The most important audience I address, however, is
the community of students, broadly construed; all those who are open to
argument, have not made up their mind, and have not invested their careers
in certain forms of intellectual inquiry and/or political practice, including
the practice of complicity.[2] There is no doubt that my analysis is limited, but
I hope that it can nonetheless help people *re*think, or at least recognize that
there *might* be something to be rethought. I also hope that 'better minds than
mine'[3] – but minds perhaps inclined to agree with some of the basic contours
of the arguments offered – will correct, improve and expand on my case
against just liberal violence. Their most important task, however, will be to
make this case *politically effective.*

In the next chapter, I introduce the key features of moral defences of sweatshops, interrogational torture and war. I begin by identifying three common
reductions: (1) a reduction of violence, (2) a reduction of moral agency and
(3) a reduction of perspective. For example, defenders of sweatshops reduce
all violence to merely *physical* violence, arguing that sweatshop workers
are not subjected to violence unless they are physically coerced into doing
their job; just war theorists reduce moral agency to *reactive* agency, focusing
exclusively on the moral rightness or wrongness of waging war in response
to an act of unjust aggression, rather than thinking about how agency could
prevent purported 'just war situations' from arising in the first instance; and
torture defenders take a reduced perspective on the world, dividing it, neatly,
into a world of evil villains and complete innocents.

I then show that these reductions point towards two foundational problems.
The first is a neglect of interconnectedness, which I refer to as 'analytic atomism'. Defenders of just liberal violence assume a world that is neatly sepa-
rable through analysis. They are concerned with the morality of individual
and/or communal conduct, but they neglect the way in which individuals
and political communities are interconnected in social structures, including
structures of global reach. And/or they fail to see that any attempt analytically
to separate their philosophical arguments from the politics of their time – the

attempt, essentially, to engage in apolitical moral philosophy about matters of politics – renders these arguments at once invalid and dangerous. The second foundational problem is a tacit 'moralistic realism'. Defenders of just liberal violence appear to be challenging the political realist position according to which the world of politics is a world of selfishness, fear of death and pain, as well as lust for power and domination. And yet their apolitical prescriptions are oriented – even if unwittingly – towards maintaining precisely that violent status quo.

Taken together, the reductions and foundational problems identified constitute the unexamined liberalpolitik of just liberal violence. Defenders of just liberal violence are effectively trying to square the circle in their respective attempts to build their defences of violence on the basis of the choices, rights and/or liabilities of specific, isolatable agents. For their moral case turns out not only to justify way too much to be able to justify anything at all; it also inevitably collapses into an argument about *consequences* whenever the attempt to square the circle has failed. And while I am not making the case in this book that consequentialism is mistaken as a moral outlook, I will argue that contemporary defenders of sweatshops, torture and war – within their narrow framework of unexamined liberalism – are attentive only to *some* consequences of their respective moral prescriptions, but not to others. This, I argue, is a mistake.

Lots of people have written in moral defence of sweatshops, torture or war. I focus – in chapters 3, 4 and 5 – on the defences offered by a limited number of authors whose work I take as emblematic of a wider literature. There would not have been much to gain from throwing in a great number of thinkers who, for all the differences of emphasis, are all engaged in projects that have key features in common.[4] After all, this is a reflective book intended to 'irritate and stimulate discussion',[5] not a textbook designed to give a detailed and comprehensive overview of three contemporary strands of literature. Suffice to say that my critique applies to the work of *all* those thinkers – and there are plenty of them – who frame their moral inquiries in similar ways.[6]

So whose work to focus on? In the case of sweatshops, the topic of chapter 3, I reject arguments made by economist Benjamin Powell and philosopher Matt Zwolinski. Powell has written an entire monograph devoted to the cause of defending sweatshops – published by Cambridge University Press. Since his argument lacks philosophical sophistication, however, it is important also to deal with the more erudite – but no less flawed – defence offered by Zwolinski. Conveniently, these two authors have even joined forces and produced a co-authored defence in addition to their single-authored ones. I argue that their defence is based on a narrow understanding of violence, one that fails to recognize the structural violence which forces people to subject themselves to working under atrocious conditions; it reduces human agency

to, for example, a woman's ability to choose between greater and lesser risks
of being sexually assaulted at work – with financial compensations varying
in accordance with associated levels of risk;[7] and it reduces perspective by
shrinking the material world into an economic marketplace, inhabited by
disconnected rational choosers – a place devoid of historical and political
location. The choice-based argument in defence of sweatshops embraces
analytic atomism by way of making a moral case that treats transactions
between sweatshop employers and employees as isolated events in space and
time. Not only does it have the inadvertent side effect of functioning perfectly
well as a defence of existing slavery in the contemporary world; it also offers
prescriptions that, if followed universally, can serve only to perpetuate an
extremely hierarchical global system of exploitation. The liberal case for
sweatshops fails.[8]

And so does the case for interrogational torture, as I proceed to argue in
chapter 4. Alan Dershowitz's case for legalizing interrogational torture would
have been my obvious target here, had Bob Brecher not already offered a
thorough critique of it in *Torture and the Ticking Bomb*.[9] I have chosen to
focus instead on defences of interrogational torture put forward by Fritz Allhoff and Uwe Steinhoff, whose writings on the matter represent two poles
of the torture-defending position.[10] The former is overtly *political* in that
Allhoff defends interrogational torture not just in theory but also with explicit
reference to the political context in which the defence is articulated: the
'war against terror'. The latter, by contrast, is purportedly *apolitical* in that
Steinhoff defends interrogational torture analytically, separating this analytic
defence, indeed explicitly distancing it, from the context of contemporary
politics. Different though they may be, however, both Allhoff's and Steinhoff's defences suffer from similar reductions. In particular, they both reduce
the violence of interrogational torture to singular acts, failing to recognize the
violence of a society in which such acts are morally, legally and institutionally possible; they reduce agency to reactive agency, that is, to making sure
that the innocent and virtuous are *in the right* when resorting to torture in
response to some villain's aggression; and they eliminate alarming features of
liberal-democratic politics from the moral perspective they offer.

As regards moral defences of war, which I attend to in chapter 5, there
is little doubt that Michael Walzer and Jeff McMahan are the most widely
read and cited contemporary just war theorists. Their writings differ a lot,
however. While Walzer aims to make a 'moral argument with historical
illustrations',[11] McMahan does the sort of abstract and relentlessly analytic
philosophy we also encounter in Steinhoff. He often presents the reader with
a multitude of intricate thought experiments designed to figure out, in strictly
binary fashion, what is right and wrong, and who may be killed and who may
not. That both McMahan and Walzer have used just war theory as a critical

tool to condemn war, such as the war against Iraq in 2003,[12] is one of the reasons why I have chosen to engage with their work: as the sort of work that – because of its having been used as a critical tool – exemplifies the strongest possible intellectual opposition to the argument I make. I will argue that just war theory – even in its most thoughtful and 'critical' articulations – fails to give us the sort of critical instrument needed to confront the political moralists of our time. For there is something that unites Walzer's and McMahan's moral defences of war: a reduction of the violence of war to – predominantly – killing; of agency to the merely reactive agency of doing right when it is too late; and of perspective to one that assumes the binary divisibility of the complex and messy political world of war into right and wrong.[13] These reductions render both Walzer's and McMahan's accounts, for all their differences, guilty of the same unexamined liberalpolitik.

The sixth and final chapter is on the question of intellectual complicity. I revisit arguments in defence of just liberal violence through the lens of Kazuo Ishiguro's novel, *Never Let Me Go*, suggesting that defenders of just liberal violence are complicit in maintaining a moral climate in which violence is not just taken for granted but considered *just*. They thus have a responsibility fundamentally to revise their current intellectual practices, and to stop being complicit. But the answer, in times of Trump, cannot just be for these thinkers – indeed for anyone – to withdraw from public life. As colleagues and I have written elsewhere, 'To be non-complicit is an exercise in self-defensive psychology; the aim is to avoid blame. To be anti-complicit is to be defiant, in collaboration with others, in the face of structural wrongdoing'.[14] *Just Liberal Violence* is a plea for defiance – in theory and in practice.

## Chapter 2

# Just Liberal Violence

In this chapter I introduce the core features of just liberal violence, thus laying the ground for my critiques of moral defences of sweatshops, torture and war. I will go through these core features later in the book: first, the three reductions of violence, agency and perspective – reductions which *must* be made for the moral defences to work; second, the foundational problems of analytic atomism and moralistic realism to which these reductions point; and, third, the unexamined liberalism that these reductions and foundational problems, together, constitute. In the chapters that follow I offer elaborations of these claims in relation to defences of sweatshops, torture and war.

One of the claims I make in this book is that defences of just liberal violence turn out on closer inspection to be question-begging: their field of analysis is reduced in such a way that they assume what is to be demonstrated, namely that certain forms of violent conduct can be just. Just violent conduct includes granting people the option of subjecting themselves to atrocious working conditions so that they need not prostitute themselves to be able to stay alive; engaging in interrogational torture to uncover information that might prevent a metropolis from being blown up; and bombing an evil regime to stop it from engaging in aggressive warfare and/or committing genocide. The only alternative to the enactment of just violence in such situations is always depicted as even worse, indeed as *much* worse. Liberal arguments for the justice of violence are articulated with a view to prevent those even-much-worse alternatives, giving action-guiding advice to those in a position to enact such violence. What is assumed is that it *must* be morally possible for just agents to do the right thing in situations whose production they have, as is also assumed, played no part in.

These defences of liberal violence reduce the variables which have been marked out as relevant for moral judgement. They focus on specific moral

7

*agents* – individual or collective – and eliminate from the scene of analysis the complexity of the social *structures* within which real-world agents are located.[1] The obliviousness to complexity thus functions as an enabling condition for defences of just liberal violence to get off the ground, making it possible for theorists to develop their analytic arguments within a simplistic framework of right and wrong. In this configuration, violence can be divided – neatly – into vicious and virtuous violence. The former is used by those who *break* the law, the latter by those who *defend* and *restore* it. Indeed, there is a sense in which those who write in defence of just liberal violence see their intellectual contribution as an exercise in virtue. Not only do they provide us with a framework through which to criticize those who enact violence unjustly; they also come to the rescue of, and to empower, the morally troubled warriors of liberal justice.

## REDUCTION I: VIOLENCE

A constitutive feature of defences of just liberal violence is their being narrowly concerned with solely *physical* violence. Defenders of sweatshops, for instance, do not think that sweatshop labourers are treated violently unless they have been physically coerced into doing the job; hence they would not even conceive of their moral case as a defence of violence. Uwe Steinhoff, a torture defender, thinks there is no such thing as *psychological* torture.[2] The United Nations (UN) economic sanctions imposed on Iraq between 1991 and 2003, which led to the deaths of some 500,000 Iraqi children, would not be categorized by authors contributing to the just war discourse as an instance of the UN – or the United States and United Kingdom, who had led the process – waging war on Iraq.[3] It is only direct, physical assaults that count as violence; physical assaults on life, liberty and property. Just war theory in particular often focuses exclusively on direct, physical *killing* as the sort of thing it tries at once to prevent (as far as the unjust aggressor's killing is concerned) and justify (as far as the just defender's killing is concerned). It is entirely obsessed with such killing.

There is another dimension to this reduction of violence, which plays out in different ways. This is a lack of concern with a violence 'built into the structure', as Johan Galtung writes, a violence that 'shows up as unequal power and consequently as unequal life chances'.[4] Sweatshop defenders, for example, would not regard as violent the broader economic conditions in which it is possible for people to choose to subject themselves – or indeed their children – to labouring under atrocious conditions. Similarly, defenders of just war give no indication of considering the possibility that violence can be structural, let alone that purportedly just war wagers might be implicated in producing and reproducing such violence.[5] Rather, the focus is on aggressive villains who enter the tranquil scene out of the blue and attack the innocent – physically, perversely – thus breaking the good order that it could reasonably be expected to be everyone's responsibility to uphold. The basic parameters of the material world, and the structural forms of violence that operate within it, never enter the analytic picture.

A parallel to this can be found in defences of torture, where the call for the legalization of interrogational torture fails to recognize the structural implications that such legalization would yield; the development of what Brecher calls a 'torturous society'.[6] Such a society would be a *violent* society, and its violence would affect not just those subjected to torture. As Galtung writes, 'A violent structure leaves marks not only on the human body but also on the mind and the spirit'.[7] I argue that Uwe Steinhoff's call for legalizing torture is – albeit unwittingly – a call for a torturous society that leaves such marks. Steinhoff genuinely believes that we can legalize torture without institutionalizing it and that law, if adopted and implemented within a liberal framework, will serve to prevent irresponsible conduct. But this is not the case. Laleh Khalili points to 'the differential application of law in line with the contours of power' and argues 'that contrary to claims that places like the Guantánamo Bay detention center are lawless or legal black holes, their very creation and reproduction has been steeped in legal argument and definition'.[8] Thus, 'in situations structured by racialized hierarchies, law can simply become another malleable tool'.[9] Far from being a bulwark against irresponsible conduct, modern law functions,[10] as Scott Veitch has demonstrated, to *organize* irresponsibility and to legitimate human suffering on a mass scale.[11] In the case of the above-mentioned UN sanctions against Iraq, 'the law, our "cherished instrument" – not simply the bad or misguided policy of reckless or self-seeking politicians – has been complicit in achieving the absolutely worst sorts of outcome. Here precisely, then, is a case of an "excess" – the deaths of half a million innocents – carried out under the dark light of the law'.[12] While this *is* violence, it was redescribed by former US Secretary of State, Madeleine Albright, as a 'price . . . worth it'.[13] In a similar register, Peter Hain, the then UK Foreign Office Minister, defended these measures by pointing out that 'Britain has a duty to play its role, as a supporter of the UN, as a defender of human rights and an opponent of aggression' in the containment of Saddam Hussein's regime.[14] This is a typical example of a political statement in which, as Mahmood Mamdani writes, 'Labelling performs a vital function. It isolates and demonizes the perpetrators of one kind of mass violence, and at the same time confers impunity on perpetrators of other forms of mass violence'.[15]

This can be seen in the case of Iraq. One theorist, Brian Orend, has put forward the view that 'the 2003 Iraq attack was much better justified *not* as an anticipatory attack of pre-emptive self-defence but, rather, as an act of humanitarian intervention'.[16] On this view, the very agents who had already killed 500,000 Iraqi children *might* have acted justly in attacking Iraq had they done so for humanitarian reasons aimed at rescuing the Iraqi people from 'the rights-violating brutalities of Saddam's unjust dictatorship' (which they did not).[17] While Orend does not argue that the Iraq war was just, he insists that Saddam's regime 'could be counted as a serious danger' and had 'no right not to be attacked'.[18] He does *not*, however, raise the question here of whether or not the United States and United Kingdom, as drivers of the UN sanctions regime, should have been counted as serious dangers too. Did *they* not lack the right not to be attacked? They obviously *were* highly dangerous – indeed lethal. But the killing they were responsible for – through sanctions, rather than chemical weapons – would not count as *violence* within the reduced lexicon of just war. Only physical killing does.

But not all physical killing counts as violence, and not always. When Orend, in 2006, expressed his sympathies with the humanitarian intervention that the Iraq war might have been but was not, he did so from a place in history where '24,865 civilians [had been] reported killed' in the first two years of the war alone.[19] This killing – as opposed to killing through economic policies – is the sort of violence that *can* be captured within the liberal framework governing the defence of just war. But, as Orend's comment shows, this does not necessarily mean that it is. For violence that is not strictly intended by liberal warriors of justice – the sort of killing that is taken to be merely a side effect – becomes much harder to *recognize* as violence. Similarly, with the slapping of children in sweatshops; the sexual assaults; the crushing of more than 1,100 bodies when the Rana Plaza sweatshop collapsed in 2013: none of it is intended. While interrogational torture, by contrast, *is* intended, it is taken to be carried out with a pure and heavy heart – the just torturer does not *intend* to intend to torture. This is the *moral* reduction of violence or, as Butler puts it in *Frames of War*, 'a way of giving an account of whose life *is* a life, and whose life is effectively transformed into an instrument, a target, or a number, or is effaced with only a trace remaining or none at all'.[20]

## REDUCTION II: AGENCY

There is a second reduction, that of agency: the ability to act on rational, moral grounds, rather than merely to behave as part of some causal chain of events. Agency, for defenders of just liberal violence, is strictly reactive in the sense that moral agents are claimed to be able to do the right thing in situations where their options are severely limited. As far as broadly 'Western' agents are concerned, the options for them would be to exploit people in sweatshops (right) *or* allow people to scavenge on trash dumps or prostitute themselves (wrong); to torture the evil villain (right) *or* allow their innocent victims to perish (wrong); to wage war (right) *or* allow innocents to be killed at the hands of some unjust aggressor (wrong). Agency that might transcend such reactiveness is largely excluded from the field of analysis. I mean here the sort of agency that is directed towards constructing a world in which the binary choices just listed would no longer have to be made. This is the agency that matters though. As Brecher writes, 'We need to do what we can to eliminate the conditions which give rise to bombs, ticking or not. If we fail, then it is too late'.[21]

Why too late? The reactive agency we find in defences of just liberal violence explicitly allows for running roughshod over innocents: people who have done nothing that would render them liable to violent treatment in the sense that treating them violently would not be wrong. They may just happen to be in the way, blocking the road to justice (i.e., the argument about 'collateral damage' in defences of just war); or they are – despite their innocence – tortured by virtuous agents trying to prevent a great disaster (in hypothetical scenarios imagined and defended by Steinhoff); or they allegedly play, as children working in sweatshops, a necessary instrumental role in the economic progress of their country. If these people are harmed, if they are treated merely as a means to just ends, those who do the harming are not to be held accountable. They are perceived to be merely reacting.

So this is one paradox. In matters of violence, the virtuous only ever appear to be in a position to exercise their agency when it is already too late for them to choose in any meaningful way; when their agency has already been eliminated or at least severely compromised through corrosive forces seen to be beyond their rational control.[22] But to do what is taken to be the just thing *then* – when choosing is effectively off the table – is considered to be of supreme moral importance. The vehement insistence on the possibility and importance of moral agency is offset here by a complete denial that such agency could be put to use to change the very structure within which moral choices are to be made when it is already too late.

Let us look at some examples. Just war theorists will always safeguard reactive moral agency but will never think about the nature of the social structures within which their intellectual contributions appear to be required in the first place. In a similar vein, defenders of interrogational torture simply assume that we live in a world where evil lunatics keep popping up, placing virtuous liberals in a position where they *must* sometimes torture, lest a disaster occur. The question of *why* it is that these situations keep arising is located beyond the theorists' epistemic and moral concern. In other words, agency is not taken to be the sort of thing that could *avoid* 'just interrogational torture situations'. Perhaps unsurprisingly, in the case of moral sweatshop defences, it is *behaviour*, not *agency*, which is prescribed as the rational solution to the problem of underdevelopment; letting economic laws run their natural course without intervening too much, if at all. There is a second paradox here, located on the other side, as it were. Defenders of sweatshops celebrate the workers' autonomy in choosing to work in sweatshops, while categorically denying the possibility that workers could use their autonomy to transform the very situation in which they find themselves into one where they would no longer have to choose to subject themselves to atrocious working conditions in order to avoid a fate that is even worse.[23]

This reduction of agency points to a broader reduction of morality, which is taken simply to be a matter of good and evil, right and wrong. This is what I refer to as the 'binary' account of morality. Just conduct is not about changing the world so that one is no longer forced to make horrible choices, or at least not *as* horrible choices, or *as many*; it is about being *reactive* and doing what is just *regardless of how awful things get*. There is a virtue-ethical ambition to this too: even in situations where just agents are forced to torture innocent children or carpet-bomb whole cities when confronting an objectified evil, or where they open a sweatshop in which they know lots of children are going to be slapped and women sexually assaulted, it *must* remain possible for them to continue being who they, essentially, are: just liberal agents who are doing *right*.[24] I will argue that this sort of moral argument justifies way too much to be able to justify anything at all.

The agency of intellectuals pronouncing on these matters is perceived to be similarly limited. Theirs is not a responsibility to engage in a structural analysis and critique but rather to offer a set of necessary and sufficient conditions that determine when the threshold is crossed and violence becomes just. Some defenders of just liberal violence also deem it unnecessary and/or impossible to comment on violence that is actually being practised and defended on grounds – purportedly – of precisely the sort of argument they offer. As torture defender Fritz Allhoff makes clear, his task is to provide 'some sort of theoretical framework', not to input the facts.[25] When commentary *is* provided on real-world matters, it is shallow or radically inconclusive. Helen Frowe's comment on the justness of the 2003 Iraq war is both of these things: 'If it had been true that Saddam Hussein had weapons of mass destruction, his possession of which violated international agreements, Great Britain and the USA may well have had a just cause for the 2003 war in Iraq. But if the real reason that they invaded had not been to locate these weapons, but rather to topple the Ba'ath regime and help secure Western access to oil, the war itself would have been unjust'.[26] The Iraq war, and the mass killing that came with it, is reduced here to a heuristic device that, by enabling us to consider different hypothetical interpretations of why the war *might* have been waged, serves the strictly academic purpose of exploring the substance and implications of one's moral theory, and of clarifying what that theory *would* have to say on the matter if one knew what the matter were. To get one's theory right seems to matter more here than to stop people being bombed. There is a real sense, then, in which many of those who defend violence *in theory* are indolent or defeatist as far as their epistemic position in the world is concerned. They embrace epistemic illiteracy. Instead of being concerned with what is going on in practice, they are often engaged in a war of abstraction that effectively serves to obliterate their responsibility as public intellectuals.[27]

## REDUCTION III: PERSPECTIVE

A reduced perspective is a third feature of defences of just liberal violence. This relates to what defenders see – or fail to see, or imagine they see – when looking (or failing to look) at the material world. Many defenders of just liberal violence are not only disconnected from that of which they speak; they are also vividly imaginative in so being, concocting obscure hypothetical thought experiments that have very little to do with, and severely reduce and distort, the object of moral analysis. The concoctions are meant to isolate moral variables and help us gain clarity on the one single moral question asked about the world in which we live: whom may we kill or torture in a situation of forced choice? We have trains running 'towards a hundred people, who are stuck on the track and cannot get out of the way' – trains which can, however, be diverted in the direction of one other person who, while not being able to get out of the way either, can throw a grenade and destroy the switch that would need to be flipped to divert the train.[28] We have a fat man being pushed off a cliff, falling towards a picnicker who cannot move out of the way but has enough time to hoist their sun umbrella so as to impale the fat man and thus avoid their own death (rather than allow the fat man's fall to be nicely cushioned).[29] We have civilians who happen to know they are about to be killed collaterally by a just tactical bomber but 'have access to an anti-aircraft gun'.[30] We have sadists '[giving] a father of a twelve-year-old boy the option to either waterboard his son for 30 minutes or to have him executed'.[31] The sweatshop version of this reduction of perspective to forced choice concoctions is a reduction of the world to a radical economism. It is taken to be entirely rational, for example, for sweatshops operating in a competitive marketplace to offer women a higher financial compensation for a higher risk of being sexually assaulted at work – or a lower compensation for a lower risk.[32] Choosing one offer over the other is described, indeed celebrated, as an autonomous decision in the economic marketplace. Not only is the phenomenon under consideration understood in purely economistic terms; it is also defended morally on the basis of that understanding. To begin to imagine what is deleted from the picture here, one need only to take a brief look at the cover photo on *Out of Poverty*, Benjamin Powell's book-length defence of sweatshops. It features a bunch of happy, smiling workers, in a clean and safe sweatshop environment. What one does not see in this picture is death, devastation and despair.[33]

Such analytic mind games and reductions in perspective cannot, of course, play a useful role in furthering our understanding of the conditions that frame human action and interaction within global social structures. They also cannot tell us how these conditions have developed historically and are being maintained politically. Instead, they serve to suppress the sort of perspective by which – I argue in this book – they ought to be replaced. This is a perspective that not only takes a much closer look at the realities of slaughtering and suffering but also directly addresses today's global politics; that does not just look at *agents* but at *structures* too; and that does not shy away from engaging in political critique. The perspective I argue for would not take those agents out of any real context at all. Nor would it place them in a context that is declared realistic without consideration of the way in which it has come about and is being (re-)produced. We need to begin to imagine the apparently unimaginable; that the hegemonic mode of liberal moral thinking about violence needs to be transformed in its very orientation, away from abstract, binary dogmatizing towards formulating a political demand for beginning to reconstruct a world that is rotten at its very core. We need moral thought that is *political* and that does not just deal with symptoms.

It would be impossible to formulate such a demand without doing so from a particular angle. I cannot avoid this, being positioned as a white, male academic, at a liberal institution, in an English-speaking environment. And yet my criticism stands. Defenders of just liberal violence pay too little, if any, attention to the angles from which they look at the world, and to the ways in which their alleged moral universalism might be, and often is, epistemically parochial. For example, when just war theorists comment on real wars, the perspective taken is not only radically reduced in terms of the question asked – Is the war just? – but also, for the most part, by only asking whether *our* war is just: the war *against* Afghanistan, *against* Iraq, *against* Libya. The question of whether or not Iraq's defensive war against the U.S.-led aggression in 2003 was just would simply not be a perspective taken by most theorists; it is excluded more or less axiomatically.[34] Neither are the narrow terms on which the moral debate is entered put into question nor is any perspective usually adopted other than 'ours'.[35]

This is strange for a theory that is claimed to be universal. There is a tendency to assume that just wars are, if anyone's, the business of Western liberal democracies – or at least of 'minimally just' governments, as Orend writes.[36] Most torture defences – though not Steinhoff's – have the same bias built into them: the question raised is never about whether or not *they* may torture *our* soldier or politician in order to gain life-saving intelligence about the next drone strike, for example;[37] it is whether or not *we* may torture a terrorist who has hidden a ticking bomb in a metropolis. Compare the case of sweatshops, where the question is always what *we* may do to alleviate *their* misery. That *they* are agents too is not part of the story told; their autonomy is celebrated only in the sense that, thanks to *us*, they now have a choice in their lives, whereas previously they did not. The choice is to work under atrocious conditions or to scavenge on a trash dump.

What underlies this reduction of perspective in defences of just liberal violence is a belief not only in the intrinsic justice of Western liberal democracy and its position as the natural home of virtue, reason, progress, indeed agency, but also – and perhaps less consciously – in the inconceivability, or at least the negligibility, of its involvement in the production of large-scale suffering around the globe.[38] In fact, the whole point of just liberal violence is that it is reluctant and agonized, even heroic.[39] It is *laudable* violence. The *substance* of defences of just liberal violence reflects – however inadvertently – a radically differential attribution of worth to human lives, while its often clinical analytic *style* is emblematic of its failure to consider 'grievable' – as Judith Butler puts it – the lives of those who are subjected to such violence; to recognize, let alone to begin to imagine, their suffering. As Butler argues, what is '[a]t stake is the following sort of inquiry: whose lives are already considered not lives, or only partially living, or already dead and gone, prior to any explicit destruction or abandonment'?[40] Defences of just liberal violence do not offer this sort of political inquiry. Their failure to do so renders them, in the end, completely disconnected from that of which they speak. Not that this disconnection from lives that one has not taken the trouble to imagine is an unfamiliar phenomenon in the liberal tradition. As Domenico Losurdo demonstrates in *Liberalism: A Counter-History*, the fathers of liberalism were 'characterized by a peculiar tangle of love of liberty and legitimation or revindication of slavery'.[41] It was possible for them at once to celebrate equal rights *and* to exclude the overwhelming majority – whether Indians, slaves or women – from having any of them.

Liberal disconnectedness brings with it a reduction in the ability to imagine the possibility of a different future. For all their eagerness to offer action-guiding advice, defenders of just liberal violence have nothing to say on how a world could be built to which their moral theories would no longer have to speak; where they would have become a remnant of the past. Or, on the rare occasions that they do – as Powell does when he suggests that sweatshops will lead to forms of development that progressively improve working conditions – their analysis is inadequate. While agency *is*, in one sense, taken to be the sort of thing that can allow us to transcend the misery of the human lot, it does so strictly by way of providing all agents in the world with the option of making the rational decision to become civilized, follow reason and obey the law – that is to say, *our* law – rather than by demanding a transformation of the politico-economic structures within which these agents currently interact – structures which place many of them at the receiving end of radical inequality. It asks everyone, in effect, to become a liberal.

Let us now take a closer look at the two foundational problems of just liberal violence towards which the reductions of violence, agency and perspective point. These are a neglect of interconnectedness, which I call analytic atomism, and a tacit endorsement of a particular kind of political realism, which I refer to as moralistic realism.

## FOUNDATIONAL PROBLEM I: ANALYTIC ATOMISM

Defenders of just liberal violence see a world that is analytically divisible in all sorts of ways: into us and them; good and evil; right and wrong; violent and nonviolent; moral and political. There is simply no recognition of the complex material and ideational web that connects a multitude of agents and entities in the world, and that does so *prior* – both logically and temporally – to those eruptive moments of violent engagement which are the exclusive concern of defences of just war and torture. In defences of sweatshop labour, global social structures are reduced to a competitive marketplace, in which atomic self-interested individuals and entities appear out of the blue to enter a contractual exchange. What this approach fails to acknowledge is that social connections, at a structural level, *always already* exist. One does not need to be an expert in the history of (neo-)colonialism to see this; one has simply to try to imagine living one's life in a way which does not presuppose and/or affect the existence of others – including anonymous, distant others. This is not a possible life. Try to go shopping for clothes or mobile phones as a disconnected atom in the human universe. Try to pay tax. Try to cast a vote. Try to not cast a vote. Try, even, to be a Thoreau and live in the woods. As Butler writes, 'we need to understand and attend to the complex set of relations without which we do not exist at all'; this is so because 'no human creature survives or persists without depending on a sustaining environment, social forms of relationality, and economic forms that presume and structure interdependency'.[42]

Many of the thought experiments and historical-empirical accounts we find in defences of just liberal violence, however, presuppose exactly the opposite – complete *dis*connectedness. They feature, for example, evil aggressors and complete innocents. The villains are assumed to jump onto the stage, as it were, without there being any indication of an already-existing social connection between them and those they attack. Similarly, it is assumed that there is no connection between those who are scavenging on the trash dumps and those who grant them the opportunity to work in a sweatshop instead. To express this differently, neither history nor transnational politics make an adequate appearance in defences of just liberal violence. The reader is presented, rather, with 'rational choice' scenarios in which the question of *why* it is that these scenarios have come about, and how they are historically and politically situated, is not pertinent. In particular, there is no reflection on the complex social connections upon which increasing asymmetries in wealth, power and suffering are built. Nor is there any recognition of what Ramón Grosfoguel describes as 'the sexual, gender, spiritual, epistemic, political, linguistic and racial hierarchies of the modern/colonial world-system', where 'non-European people are still living under crude European/Euro-American exploitation and domination', and where '[t]he mythology about "decolonization of the world" obscures the continuities between the colonial past and current global colonial/racial hierarchies and contributes to the invisibility of "coloniality" today'.[43] The simple assumption is that there is a nonviolent normality among the just and civilized, a state of affairs regularly disrupted, from the outside, by irrational perpetrators of aggression. As Ikechi Mgbeoji puts it, 'The [barbaric other] is depicted as anarchic, primitive and in need of "pacification" and civilisation. The process of pacification and civilisation often involves military attacks and vilification of those believed to be uncivilised. Embedded in this narrative is the belief that the "savage" peoples of the global South, a diverse bloc of peoples, cultures and societies, are a menace and a threat to global peace'.[44] Even prospective sweatshop workers can be reconfigured as aggressors in this logic. After all, they refuse to do what they ought to be doing – developing rationally as self-interested atomistic individuals – which is why the only way to rescue them from their present state of misery is to make them suffer in a different sort of way. And *that*, in turn, appears to be quite an outrageous thing to have to justify oneself for.

What is lacking in accounts of just liberal violence, then, is an analysis of how those who are called upon to enact the violence, the morally advanced, might *themselves* be implicated, historically and in the present, in the production and reproduction of rights violations and/or human suffering in the world.[45] Their involvement is either not grasped at all or not grasped as *violent*. In particular, there is no analysis of how such conduct might in fact be causally connected to the recurring emergence of situations which, it is argued, legitimate or even demand violent responses.[46] Just war theorists, for example, do *not* engage in a critical analysis of the U.S. economy's dependence on continuing to have, and/or continuing to imagine having, enemies to fight.[47] Theorists might of course suggest that this is a fact from a different, *empirical* realm of human interaction, and that just war theory is concerned with the *moral* realm, and the moral realm *only*. But this is the problem: the assumption that we can think in neat little boxes; that we can take a narrow, singular perspective, speaking about one thing without considering another. There is, once again, a parallel in defences of interrogational torture, where there is a failure to recognize that moral philosophers pronouncing on matters of violence are structurally situated too; that they *cannot* articulate their moral defence of torture in a philosophical safe space, neatly separated from the politics of their time.

At the root of this failure lies an atomistic conception of the human individual and of the political entities that individuals build. What is imagined in defences of just liberal violence is a world of ontologically separate agents and entities who pursue their interests on a presumed level-playing field; and the notion of individual responsibility that defenders of just liberal violence subscribe to accords with this atomization of human conduct. The assumption here is that morality is captured, appropriately and exhaustively, within what Iris Marion Young calls the 'liability model of responsibility', under which 'one assigns responsibility to a particular agent (or agents) whose actions can be shown to be causally connected to the circumstances for which responsibility is sought', with responsibility to be attributed to agents *only* for the harmful outcomes of actions undertaken voluntarily and knowingly. This is different from a 'social connection model', according to which 'individuals [also] bear responsibility for structural injustice because they contribute by their actions to the processes that produce unjust outcomes'.[48] These processes are often global in scope; 'they connect people across the world without regard to political boundaries'.[49] Young explains that '[m]ost of the conditions under which people act are socio-historical: they are the products of previous actions, usually products of many coordinated and uncoordinated but mutually influencing actions'.[50]

Of course, people often contribute to processes that produce unjust outcomes without knowing that they do, and they do this both as individuals and as members of political communities. But I argue that it is the task of moral and political thinkers to contribute to generating knowledge about 'processes that produce unjust outcomes', rather than to suppressing it by way of embracing an atomistic conception of responsibility that turns a blind eye to interconnectedness. For a recognition of such interconnectedness is a necessary condition of moving towards a way of thinking and writing about violence that is not reliant on the reductions identified earlier. Only once interconnectedness is recognized, and once its implications are explored, will it no longer be acceptable for moral thinkers to endorse a radically reduced conception of violence and agency. Nor will it then still appear plausible for them to engage in binary dogmatizing about just violence as if reality were not in the way. But there is a long way to go. As things stand, defenders of just liberal violence refuse to engage with certain aspects of reality as much as they fail to offer any critique worth its name. They proceed, in Richard Seymour's words, 'as if there has been no history of centuries of white supremacy and racism, no colonial hauteur, no liberal collusion with a machinery of violent domination'.[51] Or as if these things belonged to some temporarily and morally distant past. This is not just a theoretical problem; it is a way of contributing to the reduction of imagination about possible futures. However inadvertently, defenders of just liberal violence embrace a quiescent form of political realism. To that second foundational problem I shall now turn.

## FOUNDATIONAL PROBLEM II: MORALISTIC REALISM

Just liberal violence defences are saturated with a particular variety of political realism: the notion, broadly, that the world is characterized by selfishness, fear of death and pain, as well as lust for power and domination, and that this is a fundamentally dangerous and difficult place to be (just) in. A plea to be realistic is thus woven right through the fabric of just liberal violence. Whatever moral arguments we make about sweatshops, they are guided by the economic laws that govern the global capitalist order. Whatever moral arguments we make about torture, they start from the premise that we live in a world where evil lunatics keep turning up, forcing us to torture them so as to prevent some moral disaster. Whatever moral arguments we make about war, we have to build them on the assumption that we live in a world where someone is – one day, probably soon – going to attack us. And yet there is also a sense in which political realism is *taken on* by defenders of just liberal violence. After all, the first chapter of Michael Walzer's seminal *Just and Unjust Wars* carries the title, 'Against Realism'.[52] How to explain this?

The relationship between defenders of just liberal violence and political realism is convoluted and contradictory, with such realism being at once opposed, misunderstood and inadvertently promoted.[53] Realism is, first, *opposed* in that defenders of just liberal violence prescribe *moral* political conduct. For example, one must not torture unless doing so is *morally* justified; torture would not be justified simply by virtue of cementing or augmenting one's position of power. Second, realism is *misunderstood* in the sense that realist conditions are located exclusively or predominantly on what is taken to be the barbaric side of the civilizational divide, while political agents on the brighter side are taken to have left the stage of barbarism behind. Or at least they have *started* leaving it behind. For example, just war theorists assume that liberal regimes have become addressable in moral language. While there is no guarantee that liberal agents will allow their political conduct to be guided by the constraints imposed by just war theory – they have not yet shaken off their previous mode of being *entirely* – there is a realistic chance that they might. A large number of other agents in the global arena still have not left the barbaric stage, however, and they are the prime candidates for committing the crime of aggression. Again, what is missing in this liberal picture is a recognition of interconnectedness. There is no analysis of how those who are taken to be addressable in moral language might themselves be implicated, structurally, in the production of precisely the realist conditions which, at least partly, make the world such a dangerous and difficult place to be (just) in.[54]

This leads to the third observation that realism is inadvertently *promoted*. The moral prescriptions given are not recognized as functioning, if implemented, to play their own role in reproducing the conditions which purportedly force liberal agents to engage in the sort of violent conduct for which moral justification is then sought. For example, sweatshop defenders prescribe building more sweatshops, and buying more clothes, as the free market solution to global poverty. If followed, however, their prescriptions would, as I suggest in the following chapter, work towards the constant reproduction of social structures in which people from the global South could forever be claimed to need rescuing from their horrible life circumstances. And such rescue would never cease to take the form of giving prospective workers the chance to subject themselves to atrocious working conditions. Or take the example of the 'Responsibility to Protect', where, as Mamdani writes, 'the depoliticizing language of humanitarian intervention serves a wider function; "humanitarian intervention" is not an antidote to international power relations, but its latest product. . . . It justifies interventions by the big powers as an antidote to malpractices of newly independent small powers'.[55] So this is what I mean by moralistic realism. Defences of just liberal violence are highly moralistic, but serve, whether inadvertently or not, to bolster precisely the sort of political world that realists consider the only possible one: a world characterized by selfishness, fear of death and pain, and lust for power and domination. Essentially a state of war, but very nicely talked about.

Perhaps this paradox is not all that surprising though. After all, realists cannot help but be highly moralistic in their attempt to be realistic; they prescribe the sort of conduct that, if followed, would be guaranteed to continue preserving what is assumed to be unalterable from the start. And defenders of just liberal violence fall into much the same status-quo-affirming trap. They do so by allowing the violence of sweatshops, torture and war to be cast in moral terms, and by failing to offer a critical analysis of the social structures and power hierarchies that provide the ideal habitat for such violence to be constantly reproduced, and forever cherished. Just liberal violence *makes* the world a dangerous and difficult place to be (just) in; it contributes to a violent moral climate.

The sort of political conduct that defenders of just liberal violence invite, by stipulating a set of necessary conditions for just violence against the evil, irrational other, is that of the self-righteous, publicly agonized political moralist. This is not to say that moral theorists do not produce their accounts with the best of intentions. They might in fact do so out of a genuine willingness to employ these accounts as critical tools, to *take on* the violent moralists of our time, rather than lend philosophical support to them. This is certainly at least in part the intention of three of the thinkers whose work I deal with: Uwe Steinhoff, Jeff McMahan and Michael Walzer. But being 'critical' in this manner does not lead them to question their being engaged in an intellectual practice of analytic truth-finding in the assumed safe space of a political vacuum and/or shallow historical narration. And this is where the problem lies.

But a potential solution is offered too, and that solution – whether or not suggested explicitly – is the civilizing of one part of the world by the other. This is to be achieved through an appeal to reason which, if it goes unheard, justifies righteous violence. Violence can be a civilizing force; after all, this is in part what renders it just – much like slavery, in liberalism's foundational period, was defended as 'an unavoidable means if one wished to achieve the end of civilizing blacks'.[56] The idea here is to bring everyone, over time, onto the civilized side of the civilizational divide, and thus eventually to escape the tight grip of realism on a global scale. Or not actually to escape it, but rather to loosen it, to dissolve the tension between what is *necessary* and what is *right*. Self-interest continues ruling the brighter side of the human world, but as a self-interest reconciled with reason and tamed by the law. There is no analysis of how those who are seen to be in a position to enact such violence are structurally implicated in the (re-)production of precisely the realist conditions which, it is suggested, could be overcome only if everyone were to make the rational decision of stepping onto the bright side of the civilizational divide.

Such a prescription is ill-considered, however. As Robin Dunford writes, ' "Western" modernity was and continues to be produced through global coloniality'. Specifically, 'Capitalism and liberal-democratic democracy were only possible through the colonial encounter, whilst enlightenment knowledge production, with its emphasis on disembodied universality, was bound up with the colonial imposition of particular perspectives set up as global designs'.[57] This has not changed – uneven, violent global structures still underwrite capitalism and liberal democracy in the contemporary world. And a violence-prescribing moral theory that is oblivious to these structures will serve only to bolster them.

## UNEXAMINED LIBERALISM

The reductions and foundational problems identified earlier constitute the unexamined liberalism of defences of just liberal violence. Proponents of unexamined liberalism are guilty of a number of things. They adopt an extremely narrow conception of violence as physical assaults, specifically on life, liberty and property; they reduce agency to reactiveness in a world of evil and irrationality; they reduce perspective by pressing the world into a binary moral straightjacket; they fail to recognize the way in which agents, whether individual or collective, are interconnected in global social structures; and they inadvertently endorse the political realism that some of them purport to eschew, by continuing to equip those who they take to be post-barbarians with the rhetorical tools to recast their realist conduct as morally virtuous, indeed heroic. The assumption is that while violence might be here to stay, it can at least be *just* if performed by the right sort of agents, for the right sort of reasons, exercising the right sort of constraint. This is the unexamined liberalism of just liberal violence.

In rejecting defences of just liberal violence, I am not necessarily committed to rejecting liberalism *per se*.[58] I reject a version of it that is unexamined and that, on account of being so, offers inadequate justifications of violence. They are inadequate because the analytic atomism on which they depend is untenable. Politics is taken to be a realm of otherwise disconnected entities, a realm in which entities are taken to connect only at moments of direct exchange, which are often moments of drastic and violent visibility. Morality is seen to be disconnected too, as something pure and sacrosanct that ought to speak to politics, but that cannot, and must not, be infected by it. And individuals are understood as self-interested atoms. They have a responsibility not to break the rules of engagement, but they are not taken to affect each other beyond those moments of direct engagement to which defences of just liberal violence speak. It turns out that we can neatly divide these individuals too: into those who are just and those who are not (yet). Defences of just liberal violence are thus characterized, fundamentally, by a systematic attempt to separate out what cannot be separated out; that which belongs – and those who belong – together constitutively. These defences *cannot* yield adequate justifications of violence because they are based on an inadequate understanding of the moral object of analysis. With complexity reduced to such a dramatic extent, there is never any need to vacate the academic comfort zone of binary dogmatizing.

I attempt in this book to expose and undermine the terms on which defenders of just liberal violence enter the moral debate. I argue that there are good reasons to reject these terms and begin to offer action-guiding advice of an altogether different and politically imaginative kind, namely one geared towards beginning a process of structural transformation. As soon as we understand that a simplistic framework of right and wrong fails to account for interconnectedness, and thus cannot appropriately capture the complexities of social structures – especially not of *global* social structures – the binary dogmatizing about violence which characterizes defences of just liberal violence will, quite simply, fail to apply. The framework needs replacing, urgently, with critical, structural, political analysis – the sort of analysis that does not beg the question of whether liberal violence can be just.

## Chapter 3

# Sweatshops

Sweatshops are awful places to work in.[1] As Benjamin Powell writes, they 'often have long and unpredictable working hours, a high risk of injuries on the job, and generally unhealthy working conditions. Sweatshops also sometimes deny lunch or bathroom breaks, verbally abuse workers, require overtime, and break local labor laws'.[2] Female workers have been reported to 'face sexual harassment ranging from verbal harassment to demands of sexual favors' (*OP*, 68). And children are abused so that they work faster:

> Consider the case of Halima. She is an eleven-year-old girl who clips loose threads off of Hanes underwear in a Bangladeshi factory. She works about eight hours a day, six days per week. She has to process 150 pairs of underwear an hour. When she falls behind, supervisors shout at her or slap her. She is only allowed to go to the bathroom two or three times per day, and it does not have soap or toilet paper. At work she feels 'very tired and exhausted,' and sometimes falls asleep standing up. She makes 53 cents a day for her efforts. (*OP*, 83)

Despite his knowledge and frankness about sweatshop conditions, however, Powell has written 'a comprehensive defense of sweatshops', arguing not only that it is in the workers' 'best interest' to work in them but also that they have chosen to do so 'voluntarily' (*OP*, 3). His defence, I shall argue, typifies defences of just liberal violence in that it is built on the basis of three reductions:[3] the reduction of all violence to merely physical violence, the reduction of agency to merely reactive agency, and the reduction of the perspective taken on the world to a mere economism. Defenders of sweatshops insist, first, that workers are not *violently* coerced into sweatshop jobs unless the coercion is *physical* (in which case they would no longer be sweatshop workers, but slaves).[4] Second, they celebrate the moral agency of both workers and 'multinational enterprises' (MNEs[5]) – though only the sort of moral agency that reacts to whatever is dictated by 'economic laws'. Third, they take a reduced perspective on the world that is preoccupied with the immediate 'transactions'[6] between sweatshops and their employees. Not only do they pay insufficient attention to the nature of the global social structures within which these transactions occur; they also straw-person the moral critic as someone who must be committed *to a certain way* of responding to sweatshop transactions taking place, namely, to demanding that such transactions be interfered with and blocked *immediately* through legal prohibitions, regulations and/or boycotts. They cannot imagine the critic as someone who would call for a broader structural transformation.

The defence of sweatshops, then, is a case of analytic atomism. It puts forward an argument that defends sweatshops in abstraction from the political context of their production, placing somewhere in the background what the critic ought to insist on locating in the foreground, such as the dispossession of peasants through land grabbing.[7] And it speaks about one thing – contracts between individuals and their employers – without considering another: the political context that leads to, and constantly reproduces, a socio-economic context in which individuals choose to subject themselves to atrocious working conditions. The abstract moral defence of sweatshops is intellectually irresponsible, then, as it occludes the coercion that precedes the only thing it is morally concerned with: the moment of contractual exchange. Indeed, the defence turns out on closer inspection to be virtually indistinguishable from a position of economic realism, because what is morally right, on this view, is *whatever* choices people make in situations dictated by purported laws of economics. Moral issues are thus treated as if they were economic ones. In fact, there are not any transactions that such a moral approach could plausibly fail to justify – in the sense of demanding that they not be interfered with – provided rational agents have chosen to enter them. The concealed paradox here is that the more atrocious sweatshops are, the stronger the force of their defence becomes, for it can always safely be assumed that the workers' alternatives must be *even more atrocious* (unless we deny the workers' rationality). I will argue that such a realist defence of sweatshops on grounds of voluntary choice is a bottomless pit. It collapses into an unsophisticated consequentialism that not only turns out to justify existing forms of slavery but also fails to attend to relevant features of the material world – a consequentialism, in other words, that is careless about consequences.

In developing this argument about the inadequacies of the liberal moral defence of sweatshops, I focus on the individual and joint defences offered by economist Powell and his philosophical confederate, Matt Zwolinski. I argue that their writings are systematic exemplifications of a wide range of such attempts, posing a serious challenge to those of us who think not only that it is impossible successfully to defend sweatshops but also that something is disturbingly wrong about the very attempt to do so. My aim is to refute Powell and Zwolinski's argument by subjecting to scrutiny two positions in the debate that they regard as uncontroversial:

> First, no one – not even the most ardent defender of sweatshops – condones the use of physical coercion to force individuals to work in sweatshops, or to prevent them from quitting once they have begun work. Forced labor is a serious moral wrong, and its status as such has been explicitly affirmed by almost every participant in the debate over sweatshops. Second, no participant in the current debate holds that typical workers are coerced into taking sweatshop jobs. That is, all of us reject the claim that individuals are 'forced' to work in sweatshops by 'the coercion of poverty'.[8]

We need to take a closer look at these two positions. According to the first, people are being physically coerced when they are threatened with violence *or* when they have their bodies forcibly moved. Powell and Zwolinski regard both of these things as instances of people having had an option *taken away* from them. Conversely, people are *not* being physically coerced when they have had an option *added*. But there are two problems with this. First, Powell and Zwolinski are in no position to condemn 'voluntary slavery'. When slavery is an added option, and when people choose it without being physically forced or threatened, then Powell and Zwolinski cannot help but condone that choice by demanding non-interference with it. As long as people evince the preference to enter slavery, and as long as they knowingly and voluntarily subject themselves to the coercion and threats of violence that are essential ingredients of slavery, we must regard their choice as 'morally transformative'.[9] To give an example informed by the material realities of the contemporary world, Powell and Zwolinski cannot – on their thin conception of voluntariness, and in an analysis that insists (as theirs does) on holding other conditions constant – coherently refuse to condone Bangladeshi farmers' choice to 'give themselves into slavery against a loan'.[10] The second problem is that Powell and Zwolinski fail to appreciate a crucial difference between the two understandings of physical coercion they employ. While physically *threatened* people are left with *some* degree of choice as to whether or not to yield to the threat, those physically *forced* have no choice at all. And that makes a crucial difference. For Powell and Zwolsinki's thin account of voluntary choice leaves them in a position to condemn only the latter (where the possibility of preference-evincing is blocked) but not the former (where the possibility of preference-evincing is *not* blocked). As a result, they offer a defence of sweatshops the logic of which could also be used to defend 'gunpoint slavery'.

Regarding the second allegedly uncontroversial position – that 'no partici- pant in the current debate holds that typical workers are coerced into taking sweatshop jobs' – I shall argue that sweatshop workers often *are* coerced, and by Powell's own admission. There is something honest about Powell's recog- nition of what he then goes on to discount: he explicitly recognizes – but fails to think through – the existence of *systematic* and *unjust* coercion under what he calls 'unjust background conditions' (*OP*, 102). Once the existence of such coercion is granted, however, one is no longer in a position to argue that people voluntarily choose to work in sweatshops in the material world, rather than in a fantasy world conjured by one's imagination. All one can do at this point is stipulate that making use of labour on the back of *non-physical* unjust coer- cion is morally defensible, while making use of labour on the back of *physical* unjust coercion is morally wrong. But to do so would be to invoke a binary that is misconstrued and thus cannot do the relevant moral work that the sweatshop defender needs it to do. For it simply assumes, mistakenly, that non-physical unjust coercion leaves room for preference-evincing, whereas physical unjust coercion – including coercion that merely *threatens* violence – does not.

I begin, in the first section, with a brief account of the moral foundation on which Powell and Zwolinski's defence of sweatshops rests: voluntary choice. In the second section, I argue that this foundation collapses under the weight of closer scrutiny, since many workers are – in Powell's terminology, and by his own admission – unjustly coerced into working in sweatshops. In the third section, I demonstrate that Powell and Zwolinski are in no position to invoke a strictly binary distinction between two unjust forms of coercion – physical and non-physical – to escape the conclusion that their argument about volun- tariness has failed. In their attempt to draw a clear analytic wedge between sweatshop labour and slavery, they have mislocated the relevant wrong- making feature of sweatshop labour, which is not the complete *absence* of choice in a situation of physical coercion, but rather the *terms* of choice that make it rational for prospective sweatshop labourers to subject themselves to atrocious conditions in the workplace. The *conceptual* distinction Powell and Zwolinski draw between *being physically coerced and thus not having a choice* and *not being physically coerced and hence having a choice* turns out to be a false binary; it cannot support the *substantive* distinction between slavery, which particularly Powell rules out explicitly, and sweatshop labour, which both authors think may justly be taken advantage of.

Powell and Zwolinski's inability to rule out transactions based on volun- tary choice covers both cases in which people have been unjustly coerced and cases in which they have not. For regardless of whether or not people have been subjected to the reality of an injustice or, say, that of a natural disaster, they might be begging to be given the choice to be slaves, just as they might be begging to be given the choice to work in sweatshops. The upshot of all this is that a moral defence of sweatshops based on the idea of voluntary choice demonstrates far too much to be able to demonstrate anything at all. The only meaningful moral argument one *can* make about sweatshops, I briefly conclude in the fourth section, is to interrogate and challenge the extremely hierarchical and coercive social structures that currently characterize our interconnected world; to be attentive, in other words, to material realities.

## ARGUING FOR SWEATSHOPS

Powell's and Zwolinski's defences of sweatshops are not some bizarre outliers. Rather, the view that sweatshop 'Jobs [are] Worth the Sweat'[11] abounds among today's economists. David R. Henderson, from the Hoover Institution at Stanford University, makes 'The Case for Sweatshops';[12] Nobel Prize winner Paul Krugman once wrote 'In Praise of Cheap Labor' in *Slate* magazine (before recently putting his praise into perspective);[13] and Nicholas Kristoff argues in *The New York Times* not only that there are places in the world 'where sweatshops are a dream'[14] but also that '[w]e need to build a constituency of humanitarians who view low-wage manufacturing as a solution'.[15] Such defences are also articulated in the academic literature.[16] Nearly four dozen researchers signed an open letter to the *Observer* in December 2016, titled 'When work is right for children'.[17]

Many of these defences are based on a single core assumption that economic laws and moral conduct are reconcilable as long as the former are allowed to determine the latter. As Powell writes, 'Economics . . . dictates what is attainable and what is not'.[18] Sweatshop defenders, much like their war and torture counterparts, provide the most vivid and horrifying pictures of the only attainable alternatives to what they endorse. 'In Cambodia', Powell writes, 'hundreds of people scavenge for plastic bags, metal cans, and bits of food in trash dumps' (*OP*, 2). Kristoff, whom Powell quotes in support, similarly offers a dramatic description of a teenager's life in Bangladesh: 'Neuo Chanthou . . . earns a bit less than $1 a day scavenging in the dump. She's wearing a "Playboy" shirt and hat that she found amid the filth, and she worries about her sister, who lost part of her hand when a garbage track ran over her. "It's dirty, hot and smelly here," she said wistfully. "A factory is better" '.[19] And *because* a factory is better, 'the central challenge in the poorest countries is not that sweatshops exploit too many people, but that they do not exploit enough'.[20]

In a similar vein, Powell does not deny that sweatshop labour is exploitative; he merely insists that it is not '*wrongfully* exploitative' (*OP*, 98, emphasis added). Exploitation can be *rightful* 'on consequentialist grounds' (*OP*, 5). Importantly, however, consequences are not a *sufficient* condition of rightful exploitation, according to Powell; rather, a necessary condition of rightful exploitation is that the sweatshop worker must 'voluntarily choose to work' (*OP*, 3). Should we not conclude, nonetheless, that people who work under 'atrocious conditions' (*OP*, 3) have '"bad" jobs'? Not according to Powell, who thinks that 'nothing could be further from the truth' (*OP*, 53). After all, 'sweatshops are still in the best interest of the workers who choose to work in them' (*OP*, 3). One can make a case against sweatshops, then, only by denying sweatshop workers the capacity to make rational choices in their lives. And Powell 'know[s] of no systematic reason why their rationality should be questioned' (*OP*, 40). The sweatshop critic, in this configuration, would be guilty of a particularly harmful sort of paternalistic racism.[21]

That people choose to work in sweatshops voluntarily is seen to be morally transformative in two ways. It is either the case that people exercise their autonomy when working in sweatshops, which is to be respected, or that they – at the very least – express their preference in so doing. Both 'autonomy-exercising' and '[p]reference-evincing' choices give the observer reason *not* to interfere.[22] This is crucial: Powell and Zwolinski's pro-sweatshop case is centrally a case for non-interference. It is a case *against* import bans, boycotts and '[ameliorating] working conditions in sweatshops by regulating the use of and pay for overtime, minimum wage laws, or workplace safety'.[23] Because 'all economic decisions are made on the margin' (*OP*, 27), one should not even attempt to eliminate sexual harassment through legal regulation: 'The analysis of sexual harassment on the job is *much the same* as the analysis of other working conditions. Laws that effectively eliminate sexual harassment would lower wages. If employees desired this, then market forces would remix the compensation package to minimize harassment and lower wages' (*OP*, 69, emphasis added). In other words, it would be wrong to introduce such laws because they would restrict the workers' choice set. Some women might prefer to run a high risk of being sexually harassed and receive higher compensation; others might prefer to go to work with a reasonable degree of certainty that they will not be sexually harassed and accept lower wages in order to enjoy such security. This is a matter of voluntary choice. It would be wrong for anyone to demand laws that would *force* workers to decline the sexual harassment bonus which they might reasonably consider the better option. This does not mean that Powell and Zwolinski would, as Zwolinski puts it, consider such an 'employment relationship a morally praiseworthy one'; it means only that 'a worker's autonomous choice to accept conditions of employment establishes a strong claim to freedom from certain sorts of interference by others'.[24] Note the argumentative position in which Powell and Zwolinski aim to place sweatshop critics, who must either be arguing for the sort of interference that prohibits the immediate transaction or cease to be critics.[25]

It is also important to note that this argument about voluntary choice, which rules out interference, applies not only to those who sell their labour in sweatshops but also, for instance, to Bangladeshi citizens who, as Monir Moniruzzaman points out, 'sell their body parts to try to get out of poverty', thus voluntarily allowing their bodies to be treated as 'raw materials in their own right'.[26] It must also apply to a poor woman who 'reluctantly carries and delivers a child for a wealthy infertile couple, but at the expense of her own health'.[27] And it must apply to Third World children who choose to engage in brutal fights with other children as they prefer to earn a living for their family by way of entertaining a blood-thirsty audience over prostituting themselves.[28] And so on. In Powell and Zwolinski's view of the world, all these people – whether they opt for being sexually harassed in sweatshops, selling parts of their body, being financially rewarded for granting access to their body for the purposes of gestation, or hitting and being hit by other children – would be configured as voluntary choosers (and so would those taking advantage of the services offered). We need to be clear about the fact that a defence of sweatshops based on voluntary choice is not *merely* about sweatshops. Neither is my critique.

Why can sweatshop defenders not simply dispense with voluntary choice? The answer is that an unqualified commitment to defending sweatshop jobs on the grounds that alternatives are (even) worse might not rule out the possibility that enslaving people is sometimes the right thing to do. And this is a bullet that sweatshop defenders are not willing to bite. In fact, Powell's awareness of this matter is sufficiently acute for him to make his objections to slavery explicit. Having established the voluntariness of sweatshop labour as a necessary condition of its rightness, Powell contrasts it with slave labour, which is not voluntary: 'Sweatshops that coerce their workers with the threat of violence or use the local government to do it for them are the one type of sweatshop I condemn and will not defend. That is slave labor and has no place in a moral society' (*OP*, 3).

Sweatshop workers' voluntary choice is thus the moral foundation of Powell and Zwolinski's defence – Zwolinski even thinks it is morally 'magic'[29] – seeing that '[f]orced labor is inconsistent with both the autonomy-based and welfarist justifications of sweatshop labor. . . . Obviously, a worker who is physically compelled to work in a sweatshop cannot be said to autonomously choose sweatshop employment. Nor can it be inferred that sweatshop labor is his or her most preferred alternative (and hence likely his or her most welfare-enhancing alternative) if his or her employment is forced, and not chosen'.[30] And, as Zwolinski categorically insists, 'Physical coercion is too rare and too uncontroversially bad to be an issue for any real moral debate'.[31] Indeed, Powell rules out not only slavery itself but also the potential *making use of it* from some comfortable distance: 'It is morally wrong and unethical to buy products made with coerced slave labor' (*OP*, 109). I take this to imply that it is also morally wrong and unethical to *sell* such products. By contrast, it is *not* 'morally wrong and unethical' to buy and sell products made with voluntary sweatshop labour. In fact, it is to be commended. Sweatshop critics, on this view, fail to recognize not only the material realities of people's lives but also the harmful consequences of banning or boycotting sweatshop products; namely, that sweatshop workers will be pushed into conditions that are even worse. But sweatshops critics need not be committed to bans and boycotts. Rather, they can and must be committed to opposing – intellectually and politically – the constant reproduction of what Powell and Zwolinski refer to as 'unjust background conditions',[32] the conditions that result in sweatshop workers being system-atically coerced into their jobs.

## CHOOSING TO SWEAT

In this section, I will show how Powell and Zwolinski's argument about voluntariness implodes under the weight of analysis. '*True* coercion', according to Powell, is the sort of coercion that 'takes away options by restricting the worker's choice set' (*OP*, 40, emphasis added). Similarly, Zwolinski invokes the notion of '*genuinely* forced labor', and makes it clear that labour into which workers are coerced through poverty does not qualify as such.[33] So, while many sweatshop labourers might be working under atrocious conditions, these are not *truly* coercive. For they are simply an added option – an option that sweatshop workers can make the voluntary choice to refuse to take advantage of. Their choice to make their way *into* a sweatshop, and to stay in taxing times, is seen here to testify to the non-existence of coercion *in* sweatshops. The mystic moment of contractual exchange has always already settled the matter conclusively.[34] Even women who enter a sweatshop despite the fact that they know they are going to be sexually assaulted in it are not truly coerced or genuinely forced. As Zwolinski writes, after feeling the need to point out that '[r]ape is likely to be condemned as a rights violation by any plausible moral theory',[35] we have 'reason to think that sweatshop workers *prefer* and *voluntarily choose* the package of "employment plus rights-violation" to the package of "no employment plus no rights violation" '.[36]

Indeed, on this view, it may not even be the case that a rights *violation* is actually taking place if a worker has knowingly chosen to work in a sweatshop where she will have to allow herself to be sexually assaulted in order to be able to keep the job and then does so. In their joint article, Powell and Zwolinski ask, 'What if workers are required to perform sexual acts as a condition of employment?', only to answer with a second, rhetorical question: 'If workers' autonomy was a central value, then why would we not allow them to waive certain of their rights when they themselves judged that the benefits they could gain by doing so are worth the "cost" '?[37] It is not always clear, then, where the line between rights being *waived* and rights being *violated* should be drawn. It is also irrelevant, however, since the argument about non-interference remains unaffected. As Powell and Zwolinski write, 'The ways in which sweatshops treat their employees might be morally repugnant and absolutely impermissible. But this is not enough to establish that it is morally permissible for third parties to interfere'.[38] Similarly, one should not stop a person stranded in the desert from accepting someone else's offer to rescue them in exchange for '[consenting] to an act of sodomy'.[39] Zwolinski admits that the rescuer in this scenario 'is acting in a way that is repugnant, exploitative, and morally wrong'.[40] But he cannot, as he knows, consistently make a case for a transaction-preventing intervention if the stranded person evinces the *preference* to be treated in a morally impermissible way. The sodomizer is acting wrongly, but he is not – in Powell and Zwolinski's moral analysis – a *true* or *genuine* coercer. For he merely *adds* an option, rather than taking one away. He does not employ physical force. He is *not*, on this disturbing view, a rapist.

We will get back to this point when scrutinizing Powell and Zwolinski's attempt to demarcate sweatshop labour from slavery. For now, let us simply note that the terms of choice might be such that prospective sweatshop workers have to allow themselves to be subjected to treatments such as sexual assault as part of their choice to take the job. This being the case, it is difficult to imagine that anyone who claims that their 'ethical standard' is '[t]he welfare of poor workers and potential workers in the Third World' (*OP*, 3) would deny that what is urgently required is a critical interrogation of the social structures which make it the case that allowing oneself to be sexually assaulted might appear a rational thing for a sweatshop worker to do. *Why* it is that people choose to allow themselves to be treated in such ways? It is in their perfunctory attempt to answer *this* question – a question that really *is* of supreme importance when subjecting the phenomenon of sweatshop labour to a critical moral and political analysis – that Powell and Zwolinski's failure is at its most spectacular.

Their failure takes the form of blindly celebrating, as morally virtuous, the deeds of economically rational agents who – however inadvertently – stop people from perishing in the slums. Powell even suggests that 'sweatshops look . . . like cases of professional rescuers who acquire the skills and machinery to rescue people only because they expect to get paid. Absent the expected pay, there would be no rescue at all' (*OP*, 101).[41] Western consumers are able to play a virtuous role in this scenario too; in fact, Powell recommends that they should get themselves printed a T-shirt which 'would have a sweatshop worker on the front with a caption that says: "She fed and clothed her family" and the back of the shirt would read, "and all I got is this lousy T-shirt"' (*OP*, 100). What underlies this celebration of virtue is the idea of a civilizational divide; on one side, we see the poor, semi-rational other, with little agency, helplessly toiling and scavenging; on the other, we see the enlightened, corporate, professional rescuer who has found a way of combining the pursuit of self-interest with doing good in the world. Working in sweatshops, in this configuration, is the first step that the uncivilized person has to take on their long journey towards *becoming* civilized. The corporations whose exploitation they subject themselves to might not give them *much*, but they enable *some* of them – the more industrious, rational and deserving ones among them – to survive in exchange for profit and thereby to build a better future for themselves, their families and perhaps even their countries. While it is their selfish desire for profit within a competitive marketplace that makes our corporations plunge into the slums of an otherwise disconnected world, this is to 'tremendous' – and much celebrated – moral effect.[42] As Zwolinski writes, with impeccable logic, 'If the empirical data we have surveyed about sweatshop wages are correct, sweatshops are providing significant benefits to their workers, while firms that do not outsource are (as far as we know) doing *nothing* to benefit them. How, then, can it be permissible to *neglect* workers in the developing world, but impermissible to *exploit* them, when exploitation is better for both parties (including workers who are in desperate need of betterment)?'[43] Again, firms that outsource *add* a choice, rather than taking one away.

What strikes one as odd about this celebration, however, is that Zwolinski is happy to engage in it despite – in the very same article – expressing a general awareness of the inevitable limitations of his moral defence of sweatshops. He does so in a passage worth quoting at length:

> I sincerely hope that readers will not take away from this paper the message that structural injustice does not matter, or is of small importance. The unjust seizure of land and other natural resources by governments and plutocratic interests, the suppression of alternative opportunities for workers through restrictive

intellectual property laws and trade barriers, the failure to uphold the right of workers to freely organize into labor unions, and so on are all significant injustices that affect the lives of workers in the developing world for the worse. And they may, indeed, be injustices without which sweatshops as we know them would cease to exist. To the extent that it is in our power to do so, we should work to stop and rectify them.

My concern in this essay has been to explore the moral responsibility of sweatshops, not of humanity in general. And to explore in particular their responsibility for one specific kind of wrongdoing – exploitation. There is a danger, however, in the analytic philosopher's tendency to brush aside as irrelevant those issues that do not fit neatly within the concept he is exploring. Structural injustice may not have much to do with transactional exploitation, but it has a tremendous amount to do with people's ability to live peaceful and fulfilling lives. It is thus an issue of the utmost concern for us not only as philosophers (in other papers, at other times), but as human beings.[44]

The problem is, however, that almost everything else Zwolinski writes about sweatshops falls prey to the danger to which he pays lip service in this passage. He has reduced the field of analysis to such an extent that the title of the piece from which the paragraphs are taken – 'Structural Exploitation' – no longer adequately reflects its narrow moral concern. The aim instead is to investigate responsibility *specifically* of sweatshops *specifically* for wrongful exploitation, and to defend sweatshops against the charge of wrongful exploitation. This mirrors the strategy pursued by Zwolinski in his previous major article on the matter, where he refers to 'the choice-diminishing activities of sweatshops or their multinational partners' as 'a done deal'.[45] It is a done deal not just for the workers but also for analytic truth seekers who keep their moral judgements clinically separate from the wider context in which the deal is made:

Many philosophers, myself included, find this severely constrained set of options objectionable. For the purposes of this paper, however, I am treating sweatshops as a somewhat isolated moral phenomenon. That is, I am asking what we should do about sweatshops, while holding most of the other conditions of the world (large inequalities of wealth among nations, severe poverty in the developing world, and a growing system of global capitalism) constant. I hold them constant not because I think they are good things, nor because I think that we ought to do nothing about them, but because this seems to me the only way to make any progress on an issue that is pressing and cannot wait for the resolution of these other problems. Poverty, inequality, and economic development all need to be addressed. My paper seeks to tell us what we should do about sweatshops in the meantime.[46]

Essentially, what is being suggested here is that because we must be realists in the sense that we cannot (for now) tackle the big questions of structural injustice, the only way for us to be moral is to do little things that relieve the poverty of at least *some* people who would otherwise be crawling in the slums. One is reminded here of the slogan, 'Every little helps' (to keep things as they are). Not only does Zwolinski think that he can offer a meaningful moral defence of sweatshops if we treat them as a 'somewhat isolated moral phenomenon' unaffected by the conditions of the world in which they are located; he also seems to assume that whatever it is that 'we should do about sweatshops in the meantime' will, in turn, be entirely inconsequential for the resolution (or not) 'of these other problems'! As I will argue later, however, we *cannot* engage in a morally meaningful analysis of sweatshops that proceeds on the basis of 'somewhat isolating' sweatshops from the conditions under which they come into existence. For any prescription that might follow from such an analysis can serve only to perpetuate these conditions.

Zwolinski might claim in response that – as a philosopher – he does not have sufficient expertise to write papers concerned with a deeper analysis of global social structures, rather than individual transactions.[47] But his collaborator Powell, a scholar concerned with the global economy, presumably does. In the remaining part of this section, I will go on to show that *some* of Powell's knowledge – at least once thought through in its implications – ought to induce Zwolinski to withdraw his claim that 'consideration of background injustices [should] play' a 'fairly little' role 'in the correct understanding of exploitation'.[48] In fact, he has reason to position himself firmly in the camp of those who consider sweatshops morally indefensible.

Why so? In a little section on 'background injustice', Powell points to 'injustices in the global economic order, including the unjust seizure of land and natural recourses by states and other entities' (*OP*, 102). He introduces the example of Indonesia, where 'many of the available [workers'] alternatives have been unjustly destroyed by companies in cooperation with the Indonesian government' (*OP*, 103). But, given this, would we not have to conclude that the moral defence of Indonesian sweatshops collapses – and with it any other defence of sweatshops articulated on the grounds that they are better only because available alternatives have been unjustly destroyed? Is it not true, then, that workers – in Indonesia and elsewhere – are being truly coerced into their jobs? And would this not pose an insurmountable obstacle for the committed sweatshop defender who, one assumes, does not want to defend sweatshops just *hypothetically* but as they exist in the material world? Powell, however, clearly assumes that his admission of 'background injustice' does *not* deal his moral defence of sweatshops a devastating blow. The interesting question is why he makes that assumption. Three possible explanations spring to mind, but none of them work; and neither does a fourth explanation, to which the following reflections lead.

*Belittling*: First, it might be supposed that the unjust seizure of land is only a marginal phenomenon. But this is not the case. Powell himself refers the reader to Fred Pearce's 'story of many modern unjust land seizures' (*OP*, 102, footnote 6), stating unambiguously that '[t]he governments of the countries where sweatshops locate systematically violate the economic freedoms and property rights of their citizens' (*OP*, 104). The recent phenomenon of land grabbing is, according to Stefano Liberti, 'spread out on a planetary scale'.[49] It is, however, only the latest chapter of a long colonial and neo-colonial history of peasants and indigenous people being driven off their lands. While Powell has not even begun to scratch the surface of what Robin Dunford calls 'the complex range of actors and processes that generate and reproduce peasant oppression',[50] he cannot, and in fairness does not, deny that unjust dispossession is a widespread phenomenon. But if it is indeed the case that available alternatives for prospective sweatshop workers have been *systematically* and *unjustly* destroyed, then it is not clear on what grounds one could base a defence of contemporary sweatshops on the idea that workers are not being truly coerced into their jobs. After all, they have had an option taken away from them to continue living their lives as they have always done. It will not be of any help here to insist that what was taken away from people was merely the option to live in abject poverty, and that people quite possibly ended up being better off as a result of having been unjustly dispossessed. For to do so would change the argument in defence of sweatshops from one based on voluntariness to one concerned *solely* with consequences, and indeed only with *some* consequences but not with others. I will get back to this point at the end of this chapter.

*Blame-shifting*: Second, one might insist that those who are responsible for unjust dispossession and those who are exploiting opportunities that arise on the back of such dispossession are not always the same agents. A familiar strategy here would be to point the finger at local governments (see *OP*, 102). While Powell concedes that MNEs '[s]ometimes . . . bear partial responsibility for the unjust background conditions against which labor agreements are formed', he goes on immediately to shift the blame, making it appear as if the involvement of MNEs in putting these conditions in place were a relatively marginal phenomenon, or in any case an exception rather than the rule: 'More often . . . limiting background conditions are not the result of any injustice assignable to MNEs' (*OP*, 103). There are solid grounds for scepticism regarding the empirical accuracy of this claim, since even a cursory engagement with the literature reveals, as Dunford puts it, that 'transnational economic actors like corporations and investment funds *drive* processes of dispossession'.[51] But rather than enter an argument about empirical matters, I want to ask what precisely Powell could hope to gain from winning it. As far as I can see, victory could serve only to highlight a contradiction in his defence, which claims *both* that sweatshop labour can be justified only if workers have not been unjustly coerced *and* that the absence of unjust coercion is not a necessary condition of the workers' being rightfully exploited. For what has surreptitiously replaced it is the condition that the exploiters have not done the coercing themselves but merely engage in exploitation on the back of coercion that is locally attributable. Thus, if it is the case – more often than not – that land grabs are not the responsibility of the agents employing workers in sweatshops, then the moral defence of sweatshops has somehow been won. In light of Powell's insistence on voluntariness as the moral foundation of his sweatshop defence, however, it remains his secret as to why the answer to the question of whether or not people can be considered to be working in sweatshops voluntarily should depend on who is responsible for the coercion that led to it.[52] The only possible escape route for Powell would be to insist that people can be said to be working in sweatshops voluntarily *despite* the fact that it was their being unjustly coerced that created the very conditions under which they then had to choose between working in a sweatshop and perishing in the slums.

*Atomization*: This leads to the third possible explanation as to how Powell might try to preserve the integrity of his sweatshop defence in a world inundated with unjust coercion. He might insist on the strict separateness of two events: (1) the event of prospective sweatshop workers being unjustly coerced and (2) the event of prospective sweatshop workers being offered rescue. In fact, Powell *needs* to separate these two events for his argument to succeed, since he knows very well that it is sometimes the very same agents that engage in 'joint coercion' (*OP*, 103) *and* offer rescue. As he writes, 'MNEs can make their economic investment in a country contingent upon the government's willingness to use its power to secure special benefits', including the benefits of 'seizure of land, or bans on workers voluntarily bargaining collectively' (*OP*, 102). Does it not follow from this that the pro-sweatshop argument is a fraud, and rather obviously so? Powell tries to argue his way out of this conundrum by suggesting that 'the real wrong of which MNEs are guilty is a form of joint coercion with the government rather than exploitation, per se' (*OP*, 103).[53] He explains this by way of an analogy: 'This joint coercion would be equivalent to booby trapping someone's boat so that it will sink and they will need to be rescued. The booby trapping is wrong independent of any price offered for rescue' (*OP*, 103). What Powell is *actually* saying in the last sentence, however (indeed what he *must* be saying for his sweatshop defence to succeed) is that the price offered for rescue – namely '[demanding] . . . that the worker toil for long hours in dangerous and unpleasant conditions' (*OP*, 99) – is *right*, independent of the wrongness of booby trapping, provided that the drowning people voluntarily choose to pay it. It is right in the sense of demanding non-interference with people's choice. In this configuration, one's adding to a person's set of options becomes a pristine event in space and time – an event that is ontologically and morally disconnected from the immediately preceding event of one's having taken an option away from that same person. The magic of analysis enables us to keep coercion and rescue clinically separate.

The boat rescue example serves well to illustrate the full reach of Powell's analytic atomism. For *whatever* choice people have to make, we are effectively asked to erase – instantly, and always – our moral memory of the way in which it has come about. What this means, though, is that Powell's argument about the wrongness of taking people's options away has completely lost its bite; it can never reach even the next moment in time. One may bring people close to death one moment and be praised for rescuing them the next. The prescriptive advice to be taken from this by the selfish moralist may be absurd, but it follows directly: should one ever desire to receive Powell's moral praise, all one needs to do is engage in an act of joint coercion and then rescue people on the back of having done so. Powell will happily recognize the independent wrongness of one's original act, and so will Zwolinski. But their hymn of praise will eclipse the blame. Otherwise, why should they be writing *in defence* of sweatshops?

In offering this defence, Powell and Zwolinski effectively brush aside the complex realities of global social structures in an interconnected world. Whatever is morally problematic about sweatshops is not, from this view, identified as a problem caused by those who – as civilized, virtuous, self-interested profit-seekers – try to make the most of whatever opportunities present themselves (such as the opportunity to do business with a ruthless dictator at the expense of peasants who lose their land as a result). It is also not a problem caused by those democratically elected governments that play a key role in writing the legislation that allows MNEs to seize these business opportunities if and when they arise.[54] And, of course, it is not a problem caused by those who have voted these governments into office. In other words, it is not a problem caused by a multitude of agents within complex global social structures: structures in which these sorts of unjust seizure – and the exploitation undertaken on the back of them – are not just possible, but common place. The underlying strategy – to put the blame primarily on *their* governments – is to take a drastically reduced perspective at the expense of careful analysis. Such an analysis might indeed reveal that the unjust seizure of land and resources that results in peasant dispossession are but *one* feature of what Powell refers to as 'background injustice' – the tip of the iceberg.[55] I am at a loss to see what Powell and Zwolinski think justifies Powell's inadequate treatment of, and Zwolinski's deliberate brushing aside of, these matters.[56] What *explains* it, I think, is that any comprehensive defence of sweatshops must be based on a radically *incomprehensive* account of 'background injustice', the latter being portrayed as disconnected from the object of moral analysis. Indeed, using the term 'background injustice' already reflects a consequential epistemic choice: to place – or rather hide – somewhere in the background what we should insist on locating very much in the foreground, simply because there is no good reason *not* to do so. In displacing what should be at the centre of the critic's attention, however, liberal sweatshop defenders do *nothing* to help us understand the colonial roots and neo-colonial operating mechanisms of global structures of violence.[57] Their transaction-focussed moral defence can therefore produce only one effect: to detract our attention from the *unjust foreground conditions* that result in people preferring to work in sweatshops.

Let us imagine, however, that, despite having conceded the existence of systematic unjust coercion, Powell and Zwolinski continue to insist that unjustly coerced workers can *nonetheless* be said to have chosen to work in sweatshops; that the people whose boat got booby-trapped are *both* victims and choosers. This points to a fourth possible explanation as to why one might be under the impression that the moral foundation of voluntariness remains intact even in the face of unjust coercion: the *non-physicalness* explanation. According to this explanation, we can clearly distinguish between *physical* and *non-physical* forms of unjust coercion, and MNEs would be exploiting workers wrongfully if – but *only* if – those workers had been *physically* coerced. While we must categorically rule out utilizing sweatshop labour on the back of *physical* unjust coercion, we *can* allow it on the back of *non-physical* unjust coercion. Indeed, we can in the latter instance reconfigure such utilization as a deed of virtue, such that MNEs ought to be seen as 'professional rescuers' even if they bear partial responsibility for the unjust coercion that made the rescue necessary in the first place. To draw a clear-cut distinction between physical and non-physical unjust coercion in this way, and to insist that physical coercion is distinct because it leaves people *literally* with no choice, whereas dispossessed peasants still have *some* choice not to work in sweatshops, is the only remaining escape route for Powell and Zwolinski to take. They will, however, find it blocked. To see why, let us return to the supposedly clear-cut distinction between sweatshop work and slavery.

## SWEATING LIKE A SLAVE

Recall that Powell and Zwolinski are adamant that theirs is not a defence of slavery: 'Obviously, a worker who is physically compelled to work in a sweatshop cannot be said to autonomously choose sweatshop employment'.[58] But is this really that obvious? Surely it can be obvious only if it is *also* obvious what it means to be physically compelled (or physically coerced). But that does not seem very obvious at all. Powell thinks that someone *is* physically coerced when they are being coerced with the threat of violence, but *not* when their boat has just been booby-trapped, they are about to drown as a result, and one of the booby-trappers is giving them the option of rescue against payment of some extortionate price. But where precisely should the line between these two cases be drawn? If anything, the booby-trapping example serves as a *clearer* instance of physical coercion, seeing that physical violence has not just been *threatened*, but *enacted*; the physical status of those at its receiving end has been changed through forces beyond their control from being on a boat to drowning in the water. Have they not been physically coerced? Or, to relate this to the overwhelming reality of land grabbing, what is it about physical coercion understood as *coercing someone with the threat of violence* that can be said to eliminate choice, while the purportedly non-physical coercion involved in 'people having their ancestral land pulled from beneath their feet' does not?[59] And on what grounds do Powell and Zwolinski assume that threats of violence are not an integral part of such processes of peasant dispossession? How exactly, other than through the aggregation of lots of individual instances of threatening people with violence, is the unjust seizure of land supposed to play out in practice? And is Halima, the eleven-year-old girl who is being 'slapped' to make sure she does not fall behind when processing 150 pairs of underwear per hour – that is, 7,200 per week – *not* being physically coerced?

Ultimately, the pressing concern to which this set of questions points is that Powell and Zwolinski might not have an adequate grasp of what it means to be physically coerced. In a crucial paragraph on this matter they seem to equate 'threatening to physically coerce someone' with a situation where 'A forcefully moves B's body'.[60] But surely *threatening* physically to coerce B is not the same thing as *forcefully moving* B's body.[61] So which of these two things do Powell and Zwolinski mean when they say that B is being physically coerced? From what we have seen, they must mean *both*.[62] The trouble is, however, that they cannot also be committed to the view that *threatening* someone has the same effect of eliminating choice as does *forcefully moving* them. For while there is *no* choice involved in having one's body forcefully moved, there *is* an element of choice involved in yielding or not to a threat of violence; it is not *impossible* not to yield, while it *is*, as Cohen writes, 'impossible to do what one is not free to do'.[63] And here is the problem: Powell and Zwolinski are in no position to demand interference with a person's choice to yield to the threat of physical violence – it is, after all, this person's rational preference – just as they are in no position to demand interference with a person's choice to yield to the threat of starvation. They have, in other words, no way of stopping their choice-based sweatshop defence from having the inadvertent side effect of also functioning as a defence of non-interference with instances of physical coercion. If the *stranded* person in the desert can make a voluntary choice between dying and being sodomized, and if the *drowning* person can make a voluntary choice between dying and being rescued for an exorbitant price, then surely the *threatened* person can make such a choice too – between yielding to the threat of violence and bearing the consequences of refusing to do so. And, as with the stranded and the drowning person, Powell and Zwolinski are in no position to demand that the threatened person's choice be interfered with – 'even if', as Zwolinski submits – and whatever he might mean by this – 'it is not a *fully* autonomous one'.[64]

The crucial question, then, is this: does the inadvertent side effect just described – that the sweatshop defence cannot fail to function also as a defence of non-interference with threatened people's choices – extend to the coercion of people into *slavery*? What happens if slavery is *preferred*? But before I address this question, I need to show that Powell and Zwolinski are in no position not to condone voluntary slavery *when it is an added option*. That is, they must demand non-interference with people's voluntary choice to become slaves (even if this means that people, by virtue of becoming slaves, voluntarily enter a situation in in which they know they are *going to* be physically coerced). Disturbingly, this means that Powell and Zwolinski cannot help but condone the choices of those many millions of people in today's world who have voluntarily – on the back of economic hardship rather than through physical coercion – entered 'bonded labour' contracts. Having shown this, I will then be in a position to argue that Powell and Zwolinski cannot even refuse to condone slavery that is *not* an added option as long as people, when threatened, evince the preference to be slaves.[65]

I shall begin with a modification of the problematic desert case, where the party offering rescue does not demand that the stranded person consent to being sodomized in return for being rescued, but, rather, that they consent to becoming the rescuer's slave. In the same vein, we can imagine someone offering rescue to a person drowning in the sea: 'You can either become my slave, or drown. It's your choice.' What would Powell and Zwolinski make of these situations? Seeing that they must be committed to consider the *terms of choice* immutable – that is, located beyond interference – I think they would have to bite the bullet and call for non-interference. After all, as Zwolinski points out, 'Preference-evincing choices often give us reason for non-interference as well, but *only because* we think the consequences of doing so [non-interfering] will be better in some respect for the agent'.[66] Indeed, the consequence of interference in these two situations – that is, of making it impossible for people to accept the only available offer that would enable them to survive – would be for these people to *die*.[67] On what moral grounds could Zwolinski act against the person's preference to become a slave over being dead? His insistence on the morally transformative nature of voluntary choice, paired with a broad conception of such choice that incorporates autonomy-exercising and preference-evincing choices, puts him in a position where he cannot but demand non-interference with a person's choice to be enslaved in order to avoid death – much as he cannot but demand non-interference with a desert-stranded person's choice to be sodomized in order to avoid dying of thirst.

Powell and Zwolinski must thus demand non-interference with slavery in cases where it is (1) an added option and (2) the preferred option. And they must also condone the physical coercion that, as the chooser knows, is going to be the future consequence of their present choice to become a slave. For that is just a logical extension of Zwolinski's claim that 'the presence of coercion – *whatever precise form it takes* – does not license third-party interference in the conditions of sweatshop labor'.[68] And it has direct implications for how Powell and Zwolinski would have to evaluate existing forms of slavery. As Bales estimates, there are twenty-seven million slaves in the world (in 2004):

> The biggest part of that 27 million, perhaps 15 to 20 million, is represented by *bonded labor* in India, Pakistan, Bangladesh, and Nepal. Bonded labor or debt bondage happens when people give themselves into slavery as security against a loan or when they inherit a debt from a relative. . . . These slaves tend to be used in simple, nontechnological, and traditional work. The largest group work in agriculture. But slaves are used in many other kinds of labor: brickmaking, mining or quarrying, prostitution, gem working and jewelry making, cloth and carpeting, and domestic service; they clear forests, make charcoal, and work in shops. Much of the work is aimed at local sale and consumption, but slave-made goods reach into homes around the world.[69]

I am not making any claims about the accuracy of Bales's or anyone else's estimates.[70] The relevant point is that there *are* slaves in the world, and that many of them will have *chosen* to become slaves. They have not been physically forced or threatened into it but simply considered it the better alternative. And many of them will have made their choice without being under any illusions about the nature of the contract they enter. I would thus like to know from Powell and Zwolinski if they are willing to bite the bullet on this matter; that is, if they are happy to write a comprehensive defence not just of sweatshops but also of bonded labour that people enter voluntarily in situations where these people do so in knowledge of the consequences, one of which is that 'the bond is completely open-ended; the slave must work for the slaveholder until the slaveholder decides the debt is repaid'.[71] Are we, the potential consumers, morally praiseworthy for buying – rather than boycotting – products made by slaves who have *chosen* to be slaves? It seems to me that Powell and Zwolinski cannot possibly refuse to think this. Their argument in defence of sweatshops thus functions – whether or not this is intended – to justify the slavery of a great number of people in the world.

This leads to a second observation. How would Powell and Zwolinski deal with a scenario in which a person is asked at gunpoint to choose between being shot and becoming a slave? Here, an option is taken away, rather than added. But does this mean that Powell and Zwolinski would interfere by blocking the transaction, thus forcing the person at gunpoint to die? There is an irresolvable tension here between their categorical commitment to the 'moral magic of choice' and their categorical condemnation of the 'true coercion' of threatening someone with violence. It is easy enough to add some details to this scenario in order to make it relevantly analogous to the sweatshop case.[72] Imagine that the survival of a charcoal-producing slave, *S*, depends on two things. First, *S* must continue being a charcoal-producing slave, because as soon as *S* refuses to continue, the slaveholder will shoot *S* (*S* is, in a sense, continuously held at gunpoint). Second, people must continue buying the charcoal produced by *S*, for as soon as they stop doing that, the slaveholder will shoot *S* anyway (since *S* would have become useless). *S* has a preference to stay alive and continue producing charcoal, rather than be shot. Would Powell and Zwolinski nonetheless interfere by way of boycotting the clothes produced by *S*? They would of course insist on the moral wrongness of physically coercing *S* in this way – just as they would insist on the moral wrongness of making the sorts of offer mentioned earlier. But so what? The point is that, having isolated choice from the wider context within which it is made, they cannot help but condone *S*'s slavery in the relevant sense of demanding non-interference with it – unless they prioritize their moral integrity and non-complicity over *S*'s only chance to stay alive.

They also cannot help but condone the wrongful treatment of sweatshop workers. It is all very well for them to say that '[o]ur own view is that there is [*sic*] probably not wrong for sweatshops to demand long overtime hours, that it might or might not be wrong to demand that injured workers meet production quotas or be fired, depending on the circumstances, and that it is almost certainly wrong to refuse permission for a worker to seek urgently needed medical care'.[73] But why should we take the slightest notice of this view? The relevant point is that if an injured worker, or a worker denied urgently needed medical care, evinces the preference to continue working *despite* being injured and/or in urgent need of medical care, Powell and Zwolinski are in no position to demand that their voluntary choice be interfered with. It would be wrong for us to refuse to buy sweatshop products only because the worker who voluntarily produced them was, at the time of production, injured and/or in the early stages of slowly bleeding to death. For we would be acting *against* their (presumably rational) preference.[74]

It is radically unclear, then, what precisely Powell and Zwolinski are trying to convey when they call treating workers in a particular way 'almost certainly' wrong, or, indeed, when they speak out against slavery. What *is* clear is that they cannot help but condone making use of slavery by selling and buying things produced by slaves *who prefer to be slaves*. After all, depending on their circumstances, people might be *begging* to become – or continue being[75] – slaves. And if our making use of the products of their labour is a necessary condition of their begging to succeed, then surely it would be wrong for us to boycott these products. What this reveals is the foundational myth of the liberal defence of sweatshops: that we can clearly distinguish between the two scenarios of people being *physically coerced* into working and people *voluntarily choosing* to work; that we can categorically condemn the former and morally defend the latter. On reflection, this neat binary collapses, and the only clear-cut distinction we *can* draw – between people who have at least *some* choice (such as sweatshop workers and many slaves in today's world) and people who have *no choice at all* (because their bodies are being forcefully moved) – cannot be mapped onto the foundational distinction between sweatshop labour and slave labour on which the pro-sweatshop case rests. If the conditions under which a person chooses to become a charcoal-producing slave are taken as given, Powell and Zwolinski *must* demand non-interference. Indeed, much as it is morally commendable to make use of the critically injured worker's labour from a comfortable distance, it is also commendable to buy and sell products from charcoal-producing slaves *who prefer to be charcoal-producing slaves*. There is nothing in the liberal defence of sweatshop work that would render it dysfunctional as an argument in defence of the sort of slavery which to enter – or not to leave – is, at *some* level, a matter of choice. A choice-based argument for non-interference is a bottomless pit.

What are we to conclude from this? The fact that many actual and prospective slaves in the long and ongoing history of slavery will have had *some* choice – not to become or not to continue being slaves – is entirely irrelevant for any moral evaluation of slavery. It does not allow us to withdraw or qualify our condemnation of it, let alone to write a comprehensive defence. Powell and Zwolinski could of course object to this line of reasoning by relaxing their otherwise binary perception of choice somewhat, insisting that people who prefer to become slaves have no *proper* choice. Precisely: they have *not*, and that is the point.[76] Sweatshop workers do not have a *proper* choice, either, and, as Powell has already conceded – though without thinking through the implications of so doing – their lack of choice is often the direct result of social processes which have made them see an alternative option unjustly destroyed. Powell and Zwolinski might well *wish* to be able to defend sweatshops on the basis of voluntary choice, but they cannot. For, as Powell ironically recognizes, 'Economics puts limits on peoples' utopias. Wishing does not make things so' (*OP*, 4). Powell and Zwolinski's imagined world of voluntary choosers and morally virtuous exploiters is indeed a utopia – literally a non-place, a phantom; it does not exist. We need to stop making philosophically careless arguments about voluntary choice.

## SWEATING FOR ETERNITY?

The liberal defence of sweatshops defends, as we have seen, virtually anything and thus defends nothing at all. Powell and Zwolinski would doubtless point out in response that an account according to which 'coercion is everywhere in the workplace . . . seems too overinclusive [*sic*] to be much use in moral theorizing'.[77] But this would be a valid argument against such an account *only* if the foreground conditions which made it appear over-inclusive – conditions of radical inequality – were accepted as the starting point of moral theorizing, rather than the conditions that such theorizing ought to be directed against. I wonder why the strict economism that underpins the pro-sweatshop case – essentially, a view of the world that accepts morality only insofar as it is reconcilable with purported economic laws – has not led Powell and Zwolinski to embrace the obvious conclusion that morality has in fact no bearing on economic matters. Alternatively, following the wild beast Thrasymachus in Plato's *Republic*, they could have argued that morality is reducible to what is in the interest of the economically, politically or otherwise powerful – those who impose the conditions under which the powerless are then left to choose between appalling options.[78] But they did not.

How could they try to rescue their case? I think the only way would be to stop telling the tale of voluntary choice and, instead, rest their case *exclusively* on the observation that workers' – and indeed slaves' – alternatives are often worse. This argument could either take the form of a crude consequentialist calculus according to which Halima's being a child slave is *right* if it serves the minimization of human suffering (and perhaps of Halima's own suffering too) or a *dirty hands* case according to which Halima's being a child slave is an instance of her being *rightly wronged* for the sake of the greater good. This may of course be a greater good opaquely located somewhere in the future, seeing that '[s]weatshops themselves are part of the very process of economic development that will lead to their own elimination' (*OP*, 129). The point is that Powell and Zwolinski would need to step out of their current intellectual framework – which is based on the illusion of voluntariness – to be able to offer what they intend to offer: a *moral* defence. A case reconfigured in this way would assure buyers and sellers of clothes that they had no reason to worry *even if* the clothes they buy and sell had been produced by slaves. On the contrary, if they *did* start to worry and allow their worries to get in the way of selling and buying such products, they would be withdrawing from the process of economic development to which every decent liberal can reasonably be expected to contribute.

Would sophisticated consequentialists make such a case though? It seems to me that they might *not*. Instead of blindly incorporating whatever material realities present themselves in a moral argument that holds other conditions constant, they might, for instance, question the way in which these realities have been, and are being, politically constructed. They might also consider such realities to be transformable through moral agency. They might demand a recognition and careful analysis of the history and contemporary politics of global social structures, which are characterized, as Maeve McKeown puts it, by 'gendered, racialized and class-based socio-economic hierarchies'.[79] In other words, sophisticated consequentialists concerned with sweatshops might do all sorts of things. What they would be extremely unlikely to do, however, would be to swallow, without significant scrutiny, Powell's simplistic narrative about 'the process of economic development' (*OP*, 127–37) and the status-quo-affirming realism that this narrative supports. For the idea that '[t]he *same* process of development that occurred everywhere else can still occur in' countries that 'are the last to develop' (*OP*, 136, emphasis added) is patently absurd. Or is it the case, to put it bluntly, that last-developing countries are in a position to ship over slaves and engage in colonial plunder as part of their process of development? And where will the sweatshops go, seeing that 'we are likely to witness [them] moving again' (*OP*, 136)? To African countries, where peasants are currently being dispossessed at an unprecedented scale? What will happen when that sweatshop-moving business finishes? Or is it circular? Simply to speculate that, at some future 'stage of world economic development, *perhaps* textile manufacturing in the former Third World will look like it does in the United States today, *perhaps* better' (*OP*, 137, emphases added) is intellectually irresponsible.[80] For, as Mike Davis has demonstrated in *Planet of Slums*, the slums of this world are there to grow, and 'there is no official scenario' for their barely surviving inhabitants to be reincorporated 'into the mainstream of the world economy'.[81]

The work that needs doing – urgently – does not finish with the argument presented in this chapter; it only commences with it. Here, I have begun only superficially to put into political context the claims made by liberal sweatshop defenders – an enterprise which I hope I have prompted readers to pursue further.[82] What is already clear from the present analysis, however, is that Powell and Zwolinski categorically refuse to think beyond the narrow parameters of the immediate transaction. Their work reflects a paradigmatic failure to question the historical and political conditions which *make it so* that people allow themselves to be sexually assaulted, slapped or denied access to a toilet during their twelve-hour shift, having previously been forced to leave their lands and enter a slum. In offering such a limited analysis, they give us no vision of a world where the richness of the have-mores no longer depends on there being have-lessers; where suffering could be reduced *universally* and *in the long run*; and where Halima will no longer have to be beaten for the sake of humanity's moving ever closer to the promised land of future prosperity for all. It is clear that such a world can be constructed only *politically*, on the basis of sound moral analysis, and not by leaving the market to itself. As Monique Deveaux and Vida Panitch have recently suggested, 'The solutions will of necessity lie in remedying the inequalities that render some social groups vulnerable to exploitation at the hands of others'.[83] The grim alternative is clear, and captured well by Jeff Noonan: 'Left to operate according to its own value system, capitalist economic growth is indifferent to the life conditions of people beyond supplying what is necessary to ensure that they can contribute to further economic expansion'.[84] But it is an alternative that we ought to resist, and that we can resist *only* through collective action.[85] To think that there is no need for such action, but that we can display our lack of indifference to people desperately trying to survive simply by going shopping, might be one of the most deluded, deluding and harmful ideas of our times.

## Chapter 4

# Torture

Readers might be familiar with the foundational myth of the liberal defence of interrogational torture: the 'ticking bomb scenario'.[1] Imagine that a 'terrorist' has planted a bomb in a metropolis, which is going to detonate in the near future and kill thousands of innocent people (or make it millions if you think the stakes need to be higher than that). Further imagine that 'we' manage to capture the terrorist, that they refuse to reveal the location of the bomb, and that it is too late to evacuate. Would it be morally right to torture the terrorist to elicit the relevant information that would enable us to find and defuse the bomb? According to countless pro-torture arguments drafted by a whole army of contemporary liberal philosophers and lawyers, it would indeed be.[2]

In this chapter, I call into question the adequacy of this defence of interrogational torture as a form of just liberal violence, for it is based on an unexamined liberalism that engages in various reductions.[3] It reduces, first, the violence of interrogational torture to the singular act of torture itself, rather than seeing this act as necessarily embedded within the wider social structure of a 'torturous society', 'a society in which breaking people by torture were institutionalized, normalized and recognized as a valuable service'.[4] Second, it reduces moral agency to mere reactiveness. It shrinks our moral horizon to the question of how to react to a situation of forced choice, instead of asking a set of very different questions about human agency, such as how to transform the ideological landscape that has made it possible for the ticking bomb myth to gain as much traction as it has, and how to prevent this myth from being constantly reimagined and reproduced. Third, it reduces perspective by fabricating a world where evil others are seen to keep turning up, seemingly out of nowhere, instead of engaging in a critical, structural and historically informed analysis of the phenomenon of 'terrorism' in an interconnected world. As with defences of sweatshops and war, these reductions point towards the foundational problem of analytic atomism. Not only does the defence of interrogational torture rely on the myth of the ticking bomb scenario to get off the ground; it also configures this scenario as an *isolatable* event in space and time: as if calling for torture *then*, on that particular and exceptional occasion, were otherwise inconsequential. In the end, the apolitical myopia of the interrogational torture defence provides fertile grounds for its moralistic realism: a moral prescription directed – inadvertently or otherwise – to the production and reproduction of a torturous world.

To argue that the case for interrogational torture fails is a delicate operation, since it carries the risk that one ends up lending credibility to what one argues against by virtue simply of engaging with it, and of doing so publicly. Fritz Allhoff's work on interrogational torture places one in such a compromised position. In purely quantitative terms, Allhoff is prolific; yet, the defence of interrogational torture he presents is of such a power-subservient kind that any attempt to argue against it raises the problem of 'intellectual dirty hands'.[5] For to suggest that Allhoff's case warrants an argument in response is to impute to it a seriousness it does not deserve. I cannot resolve this dilemma, but will try, in the first section, not so much to *argue* as simply to allow Allhoff to speak for himself by quoting – and briefly commenting on – some of his lines.

In the second section, I turn to a liberal defence of interrogational torture that does *not* take the form of a political apologia – Uwe Steinhoff's.[6] I first present the reader with what would appear to be good reasons for thinking that Allhoff's defence *must*, after all, be an aberration within the body of liberal defences of interrogational torture, for some of Steinhoff's pages offer an explicit and cutting critique of this sort of power-subservient philosophy. But then, in the third section, I expose three significant errors in Steinhoff's argument – errors which locate him in the same liberal camp as Allhoff, albeit in a different corner. First, Steinhoff puts forward the view that he can argue for the legalization of interrogational torture without arguing also for its institutionalization.[7] Second, he assumes both that he can keep his *moral* defence of interrogational torture clinically separate from the "political" context of his time and that the legalization of interrogational torture will be unproblematic in a liberal-democratic context.[8] And third, he develops a moral argument that justifies far too much to be able to justify anything at all. I briefly conclude, in the fourth section, by offering some reflections on intellectual complicity in torture.

## ALLHOFF: 'OR AT LEAST SO GO MY INTUITIONS'[9]

The purpose of this section is *not* to give an extensive critique of Allhoff's moral defence of interrogational torture but to show that his argument takes the form of a parochial and power-subservient apologia. This apologia fails to recognize the violence of the 'virtuous', who are seen to be merely reacting to the violence of the world in which they find themselves. Not only is Allhoff's defence based on a radically reduced perspective on the politics of our time; it also gives *carte blanche* for political (ab)use by granting unlimited epistemic superiority to political and military leaders when it comes to making empirical judgements about the justifiability of allegedly reactive violence, including the violence of interrogational torture. This is a mistake Steinhoff would never make.

Allhoff begins *Terrorism, Ticking Time-Bombs, and Torture* by reflecting on *9/11* and what followed it, wondering if President Bush's 'legacy could possibly be repaired, whether the ensuing protection against further terrorist attacks or the liberation of future generations of Iraqis could redeem him under American or international judgment' (*TTT*, vii). While he suggests, cautiously, that Bush 'perhaps overzealously responded to the 9/11 attacks' (*TTT*, viii), he also wonders what 'exactly . . . Bush was supposed to have gotten so wrong'. After all, 'the unassailable fact is that the Bush administration kept us safe from terrorism since 9/11; this is probably even more striking if we consider the ill will that his military operations surely generated' (*TTT*, viii).

In this same vein, Allhoff asserts that '[Bush's] strategies worked . . . in some relevant sense' (*TTT*, ix) – though without offering any argument or evidence for this claim;[10] without problematizing the difference between correlation and causation; without questioning the sole criterion he appears to be invoking for making this judgement, namely whether or not there has been 'another successful "terrorist" attack' in the United States (*TTT*, viii); and without interrogating for whom these strategies worked and for whom they did *not* work. They patently did not work for all those people who have lost their lives, limbs or loved ones to U.S. bombs since 2001. These people are located not only *outside* Allhoff's narrow spatial horizon of moral concern but also presumably – since he fails to suggest otherwise – *inside* a category he refers to as 'just instances of collateral damage' (*TTT*, 8). According to the Iraq Body Count, the '[n]umber of documented civilian deaths from violence' in Iraq since 2003 is between 174,505 and 194,979.[11] In the first two years of the Iraq war alone, '24,865 civilians were reported killed', and 37 per cent of these civilians (9,200) were killed by 'US-led forces'.[12] Note that these are only the *documented* deaths, and they are not documented by the U.S. leadership. As General Tommy Franks once clarified, 'We don't do body counts'. Note also that these numbers refer only to direct physical killing and do not take into account the wider destructive and deadly ramifications of the Iraq war.

At this point, Allhoff, who appears to be interested only in 'what counter-terrorism costs *us*' (*TTT*, 30, emphasis added), might insist that

> the foregoing discussion fails to appreciate other critical costs of terrorism: its symbolic costs. A few thousand people died on 9/11, and the economic impact of that day was catastrophic. Lives and dollars aside, however, that day cost us much more than those numbers could express. The terrorists destroyed the World Trade Center, a central icon of our economic strength. They crashed into the Pentagon, a building that represents our military strength. And, were it not for the brave passengers who helped crash United 93 in rural Pennsylvania, a plane probably would have hit either the White House or the Capitol, buildings that embody the strength of our government. These symbolic attacks against our economy, military, and government were chosen precisely because of that symbolism; as many or more lives – and, perhaps, similar economic damages – could have as easily been exacted through other targets. (*TTT*, 32)

What Allhoff fails to appreciate, however, is that U.S. bombs *also* 'destroy much more than . . . numbers could express'. It is just that the devastation and despair they bring fail to be visible in his reduced horizon of justice and vulnerability. We are confronted here with an American philosopher addressing himself to an American audience: 'Without being too cynical', he stipulates, 'we should admit that it is hardly irrational for American citizens to care more about protecting themselves from terrorism than they do about providing for those at risk outside our borders' (*TTT*, 32). And that protection may require interrogational torture. Right at the start of his book, Allhoff insists that '[i]f there were no terrorist attacks, there would be no (good) reason to torture' and that 'it is critical to approach the morality of torture within the context of terrorism' (*TTT*, ix). In fact, Allhoff complains that '[m]uch of the literature . . . treats the issue in precisely the vacuum' that he 'wish[es] to avoid' (*TTT*, ix). Not only does he 'consider fighting terrorism (whether domestic or international) as the prototypical application of torture'; he also insists that 'the choice to discuss terrorism should not be viewed as evidencing any ideological bent; I choose it merely for convenience and simplicity'.[13]

But perhaps there is more to it than mere 'convenience and simplicity'. The following section in Allhoff's book would certainly suggest as much: 'Vice President Cheney . . . has been adamant that "enhanced interrogation techniques were absolutely essential in saving thousands of American lives and preventing further attacks against the United States." Critics take this to be hubris, but I am not cynical enough to issue wholesale indictments against our political or military leadership' (*TTT*, 164). And Allhoff continues a bit further on:

> [W]e . . . should not be too greedy in our demand for actual and clear-cut ticking-time-bomb cases. First, some scepticism is warranted insofar as to whether

the present and future will resemble the past: the changing face of terrorism makes ticking-time-bomb-like scenarios more likely. It therefore follows that the lack of historical cases has limited implications for their ensuing prospects. Second, even if there has been historical precedent, there are all sorts of reasons to doubt that we would know about it. To wit, there are political and security factors that straightforwardly make it unlikely that actual cases would enter public consciousness. . . . Surely . . . it takes immense cynicism to allege that those enhanced techniques would be continued over several years if they were patently worthless. (*TTT*, 164–65)

We are called upon here to trust Allhoff's intuitions, to stop being quite so cynical, and to attribute significance to Vice President Cheney's being 'adamant'. In the world constructed by and for Allhoff, it cannot be the case – necessarily cannot, it appears – that a reasonably trustworthy and rational U.S. administration, in its endeavour to save lives and prevent future terrorism, would use unproductive or counterproductive means over a protracted period of time.[14] Just like their stated goals, American leaders' rationality must not be questioned. Nor should we make too much of their hiding information from the rest of us; rather, we can safely assume that they would not do so other than with the aim of protecting our lives and national symbols. Because of his apparently unshakable trust in those who lead America, Allhoff is happy to resign himself to offering 'some sort of theoretical framework' for them to use in the process of leading the country:[15]

As a moral philosopher, the question of real-world justifiability is really not one on which I have much to say; I am more interested in the theoretical argu- ments that can be rendered on either side of this debate. This is not, of course, to say that I do not care whether unjustifiable torture takes place in the world. To the contrary, I care very much, but I do not find myself equipped to make a contribution to that debate apart from being able to offer some sort of theoretical framework which would then require empirical inputs.[16]

Allhoff's epistemically privileged leaders may then do the job of inputting the facts and decide whether or not torture is justified. If it is, it should be carried out at one of 'ten U.S. torture sites throughout the world' that Allhoff suggests 'we might countenance' – three domestic (e.g., 'on each coast plus one around St. Louis'), another seven 'strategically placed around the world in ways sensitive to security needs (e.g., a couple in the Middle East, none in Oceania)' (*TTT*, 150). Crucially, however, Allhoff would have retired from the discussion at this point. After all, he is only a moral philosopher, who does not have sufficient knowledge about matters of real-world justifiability. He thus cannot be expected to have much to say on whether or not the input- ting was done correctly.

One wonders, though, why Allhoff finds it so difficult to equip himself to make a contribution to such a debate. For example, he could simply conduct a basic Internet search on the term 'torture dossier' and a whole world would unfold in front of him.[17] Or he could read some relevant academic literature on the matter.[18] He could do some research and find out thereby that his axiomatic belief in the virtue of 'the most enlightened societies' in which 'interrogational torture was . . . widely decried before 9/11' (*TTT*, 3) does not hold up even to the most basic reality check. Decried it might sometimes have been, but it was regularly used by the United States, Britain and France long before *9/11* (assuming that these societies belong to the ones Allhoff considers 'most enlightened'). In *Torture and Democracy* – a book which Allhoff himself recognizes to be 'painstaking and magisterial' (*TTT*, 135) – Darius Rejali reveals the 'long, unbroken, though largely forgotten history of torture in democracies' and the fact that 'police and military in the main democratic states were leaders in adapting and innovating clean techniques of torture'.[19] Indeed, he shows how 'clean techniques' of modern torture, defined as 'painful physical techniques of interrogation or control that leave few marks', originated in precisely the United States, Britain and France.[20] Specifically in relation to the United States, Jennifer Harbury has demonstrated the use of torture for decades before *9/11*, arguing that 'the CIA and related U.S. intelligence agencies have since their inception engaged in the widespread practice of torture, either directly or through well paid proxies'.[21] The trouble is that the U.S. history of torture with Bush's torture regime as its latest dramatic episode might continue being literally imperceptible for Allhoff *even if* he conducted this research, as he appears to be virtually blinded to this history's very possibility.[22] His belief in the virtues of liberal-democratic America is as solid as it is unexamined. This makes it possible for him to write that '[t]he scandal at Abu Ghraib, for example, was just that, and those involved should be punished' (*TTT*, 156). It would not occur to Allhoff, as Rebecca Gordon writes, that the scandal was not 'an aberrant action' but rather 'a glimpse of a larger, systemic practice'.[23]

So what we are confronted with here is an academic who has never questioned his intuitions, and who has not only analytically detached his philosophical case for interrogational torture from the real world of politics but is also fully invested in offering his government and military a moral framework to guide their decisions to torture. In addition, he has given them *carte blanche* to apply his framework at their discretion. These leaders might be the sorts of people who, like Franks, do not count any non-American bodies; who, like Madeleine Albright, consider the killing of half a million Iraqi children through economic sanctions against Iraq a 'price . . . worth it'[24]; or who, like George W. Bush, have a legacy of torture attached to their name.

But the point remains that they are operating in a different epistemic league, way beyond the humble philosopher's reach. It is hard to imagine a better – or worse – example of parochial, power-subservient and politically irresponsible Ivory Tower philosophy. There is nothing in it that could warn us against the rise of the sort of tyranny that was Bush's torture regime, let alone recognize it when it was towering right in front of us. One wonders whether there is *any* imaginable action Bush and his consorts could have taken during what U.S. major general Antonio Taguba, years before Allhoff published his book, referred to as a 'systematic regime of torture'[25] that would have triggered something like a critical intervention by Allhoff. But then again, critique – like reality – is not what he does.

## STEINHOFF'S RATIONALE AND DEFENCE

On the face of it, Steinhoff's defence of interrogational torture has little to do with Allhoff's apologia. Already in his earlier book on *The Ethics of War and Terrorism*, Steinhoff makes it clear that ' "terrorism" is preferably used for the acts of the *others*, not for one's own actions'.[26] Moreover, he points out that 'most "serious" commentators tend to excuse the violence committed by the stronger party. . . . This is not only immoral and hypocritical, it defies all logic'.[27] Steinhoff is unambiguous and devastatingly to the point in his analysis of the war against terrorism:

> Terrorism is not at all the instrument of the weak, as is often claimed, but rather the routinely employed instrument of the strong, and usually only the final resort for the weak. . . . This 'war against terrorism', waged by state terrorists and with terrorist means, does not have as its object universal values, but rather the attainment of undisputed power.
>
> If strong states really want to fight subnational terrorism, there are only three legitimate and recommendable means at their disposal: the rejection of a double standard; the focused persecution of crime (insofar as the commission of a punishable crime – and not of an act of justifiable resistance – may be demonstrated); and, finally, the inclusion of the excluded.[28]

In a similar vein, Steinhoff is entirely explicit in *On the Ethics of Torture* that 'this is certainly not a "*pro*-torture" book' (*ET*, ix); that it 'is not in the least intended to support "the war on terrorism" and the silly and often racist "us-versus-them" ideology that accompanies it' (*ET*, x); that 'strategic bombing may amount to torture' (*ET*, footnote 1, 161); that 'waterboarding *is* torture' (*ET*, footnote 2, 161); that 'punitive torture . . . is, incidentally, still practiced today' (*ET*, 7); that 'it is safe to assume that all the torture that happened or happens in Abu Ghraib, Afghanistan, and Guantanamo simply has nothing to do with ticking bombs or hostages who are about to die' (*ET*, 64); and that '[t]orturing so-called terrorists to find out more about their networks, that is, torturing in the course of "fishing expeditions," is not a case where . . . justifications can be validly applied' (*ET*, 158). He is also 'adamantly against the institutionalization of torture' (*ET*, 48). Furthermore, Steinhoff not only endorses 'a moral system that takes rights seriously', indeed that treats them as 'trumps' (*ET*, 43), but also 'completely agree[s] that *nearly all* torture currently being undertaken on our planet is *immoral*' (*ET*, 157) and thus constitutes a violation of 'human rights and human dignity' (*ET*, 35). It is clear from these remarks that Steinhoff's moral defence of torture is, at one important level, nothing like Allhoff's:

> I simply do not belong to that camp. Thus, I would like to make clear that if, let's say, torturing an Islamic terrorist is justified to avert the explosion of a ticking bomb that would kill thousands of innocent Americans or Israelis, it then is obviously also justified to torture a Christian or Jewish state terrorist if by doing so one can avert a more or less indiscriminate bombing campaign by the American or Israeli air force that would (once again) kill thousands of innocent Palestinians, Iraqis, or Afghans. Thus, I prefer moral universalism to double standards. (*ET*, x)

And yet, the fact remains that Steinhoff has written a book-length *defence* of torture, including *interrogational* torture. What motivated him to write this book was *not* 'annoyance' (*ET*, ix) about what he concedes to be the wrongness of '*nearly all* torture currently being undertaken on our planet'. Nor was his book triggered by the writings of Allhoff and/or countless other torture and counterterrorism apologists. Rather, it was the fact that Bob Brecher, in his critique of Dershowitz's call for institutionalizing interrogational torture,[29] had claimed that philosophizing about imaginary ticking-bomb scenarios was inadvertently careless.[30]

We know Steinhoff's motivational trigger then; but how about his moral rationale? What were his *reasons* for writing this book? What *impact*, if any, is he trying to achieve? We get some clue at the end: 'If I somehow contribute to the spread of self-defensive torture that helps to save innocent children from culpable kidnappers, then that would be a good thing. If absolutist torture opponents with their arguments or pseudo-arguments contribute to more children suffocating in the hands of kidnappers, then that would be a bad thing' (*ET*, 156). In his entire book, however, Steinhoff depicts only two historical cases in which the following three conditions were met:[31] (1) a child had been kidnapped, (2) someone had managed to capture the kidnapper, *and* (3) the kidnapper refused to reveal the child's location. (He does not list any historical case in which torturing led to the defusing of a ticking bomb.[32]) Can one reasonably not just defend torture, but express one's hope for its 'spread' – *in a context where what one concedes to be immoral instances of torture are all but epidemic* – on the basis of one's awareness of *two* historical incidents where such conditions were met? Steinhoff is prepared to enter the realm of speculation here, '[suggesting] that there are many more cases like these, but for obvious reasons police officers have an interest in denying that they used torture' (*ET*, 14). His argument at this point is reminiscent of the conjectures offered by Allhoff in relation to the war against terrorism.

It is quite difficult, then, to make sense of the reasons why Steinhoff has written a defence of torture when what would have been urgently required at the time of its production was a *critique*. He understands the political context in which he is writing;[33] he knows about the dangers of institutionalizing torture (*ET*, 61–68); he thinks that nearly all torture (as currently undertaken on our planet) is immoral; and he is apparently not in a position to offer a single example of the only situation to which his book is designed to speak as an action-guiding philosophical intervention. This is a situation with the following three features: (1) torture could have been justifiably undertaken; (2) torture was *not* undertaken, with the right of an innocent being violated as a result; *and* (3) the reason why torture was not undertaken was because those who could have undertaken it believed, mistakenly, that torturing was unjustifiable (or because they were stopped from torturing because of its being illegal). But despite all that, Steinhoff wrote *this* book on torture.

What is torture? Steinhoff defines it as 'the knowing infliction of continuous or repeated extreme physical suffering for other than medical purposes' (*ET*, 7) – and when he writes *physical* suffering, he explicitly excludes *psychological* suffering (*ET*, 9). What it means for physical suffering to be extreme 'is contentious' in his view, 'but one kind of physical suffering that clearly is extreme is the . . . pain produced by drilling on the unprotected nerve of a tooth. . . . This in no way implies that I think that lesser pains or certain other forms of pain and suffering are not also extreme' (*ET*, 9). Whatever the nature of extreme physical suffering, Steinhoff does not think a torturer needs to have any expertise in order to be able to inflict it. Even beating someone can constitute torture in his view, which, in the one real-world example of actually practised and effective 'torture' depicted in his book, he is entirely explicit about:[34]

[T]he eight-year-old Denis Mook was kidnapped in Bremen, Germany, in 1988. After the ransom payment, the kidnapper was arrested. He refused to reveal the location of the child. The police then beat him until, finally, he did reveal the child's location . . . . [F]or self-defensive torture to be effective, you do not need torture *experts*. (*ET*, 58)

This example serves to demonstrate, according to Steinhoff, that 'it is simply not true that in order to torture someone in a way that will actually retrieve the vital information, the torturer has to be skilled and experienced' (*ET*, 58).[35] Crucially, he assumes that his view according to which torture requires no expertise applies equally to interrogational torture and to other forms of torture, such as sadistic torture. I will get back to this.

There is another crucial aspect of Steinhoff's definition. He thinks that torture is only potentially, but not necessarily or even ordinarily, 'done by state agents' (*ET*, 8). It would 'of course [be] absurd' (*ET*, 10) to suggest otherwise: 'In any ordinary use of the term, torture can be practiced by private agents (for example the Mafia or a sadist)' (*ET*, 8). Torture is thus not necessarily a *political* practice. When it *is*, the conditions of its justifiability are exactly the same as they are for the private practice of torture. Whether or not the torturing is political does not matter regarding the question of justification; it does not have *any* bearing on torture's analytic defence.

While there is no need to go through this defence in technical detail, here is the gist. Steinhoff's primary justification, from self-defence, 'applies to both the . . . child-kidnapping case, and the ticking-bomb case' (*ET*, 35). The argument here is that '[h]uman beings have a right to self-defensive torture against culpable aggressors', provided such torture 'is a proportionate and necessary means of self-defence against an imminent threat'. For Steinhoff, 'this is hardly surprising . . . . [P]eople even have a right to *kill* a culpable aggressor if under the circumstances this is a proportionate and necessary means of self-defence against an imminent threat, and . . . most forms of torture are not as bad as killing' (*ET*, 53).[36] In fact, he insists that '[s]elf-defensive torture is not only justified; it is *just*' (*ET*, 35). Steinhoff then adds to this an 'argument from necessity' (*ET*, 39), making the case that 'the torture of innocents' is, under certain circumstances, '*clearly* justified' (*ET*, 44):[37] 'Of course, the idea of torturing an innocent person, in particular an innocent child, surely *is* repugnant, but we should not let our moral judgment be clouded by emotional reactions' (*ET*, 41).[38] And while Steinhoff clarifies that this argument does *not* apply to torturing innocents in the ticking-bomb scenario – where torturing innocents can be justified only 'in theory, *but not in practice*'[39] – one of the 'quite realistic' (*ET*, 44) examples he introduces to back up his insistence on the clear justifiability of torturing innocents goes as follows:

> The sadistic but honest sergeant gives a father of a twelve-year-old boy the option to either waterboard his son for 30 minutes or to have him executed by the sergeant.
>
> In this case, in my view, the father's waterboarding and thus torturing of his son for 30 minutes is *clearly* justified, precisely in light of the proportionality considerations already discussed above. The father saves his son's life here. If

indeed in this situation he did not choose the first alternative but instead the second (perhaps because he is an absolutist antitorture opponent who would rather sacrifice his son than his dubious principles), then *that* would be repugnant. (*ET*, 42)[40]

Steinhoff offers a multitude of such thought experiments – and also a great number of references to German, U.K. and U.S. law – to support his case. He argues that 'self-defensive torture is the morally preferable and more humane alternative to self-defensive killing' and – the ultimate killer argument in defence of torture – that 'torturing a culpable aggressor in order to save his innocent victim from being further tortured by him can still be justified, for torture is not worse than torture'. Steinhoff thus believes himself to have demonstrated, objectively, that '[a]ntitorture absolutism is immoral, irrational, and inhumane' (*ET*, 2).

What are we to make of this? If and insofar as Steinhoff's moral case for self-defensive (and other-defensive) torture succeeds analytically, it is philosophically trivial. That human beings should have a right to such 'torture' is indeed 'hardly surprising' if we accept Steinhoff's ostensibly innocent definition of torture. Steinhoff does not just stack the argument in his favour here; he makes his case by stipulation. No rudimentarily rational being who accepts both the premise that it can sometimes be justified to *kill* in self-defence[41] *and* Steinhoff's broad definition of torture would claim that it can never be justified to torture. For Steinhoff's insistence that torturing requires no expertise renders any sort of self-defence during the course of which one inflicts such suffering an instance of torture; and his loose understanding of what is meant by 'extreme' in 'extreme physical suffering' not only allows for many hypothetically conceivable acts of self-defence to be redescribed as torture but *of course* renders some forms of torture less bad than killing. This is not a difficult argument to make; a simple deduction will do. In the end, Steinhoff's is not so much a substantive argument in defence of torture as a conceptual point about his notion of torture; an overheated plea for understanding it in such a way that extreme physical suffering need not really be that extreme, and that any given amateur can inflict it. Let us not dwell on his analytic success. Let us rather reflect on the ways in which Steinhoff's defence of torture *fails* to succeed.

## THREE ERRORS

I argue in this section that Steinhoff makes three errors. First, he thinks that interrogational torture can be legalized without being institutionalized. Second, he assumes that he can make his moral case for such torture in a political vacuum. Third, he fails to realize that his case for torture – insofar as it is not simply erroneous when calling for the legalization of *interrogational* torture – is morally meaningless. For, much the like defences of sweatshops and war, which we encounter in the previous and subsequent chapters, respectively, it justifies virtually everything and thus nothing at all.

## Error 1

To Steinhoff's mind, legalizing torture is not a big deal, let alone a frightening prospect, for 'there is as little need to introduce a special paragraph allowing self-defensive torture into the penal codes as there is a need to introduce a special paragraph allowing throat-cutting. Both forms of self-defense and "emergency action" can be easily covered by the normal self-defense and necessity regulations, provided that whatever absolute prohibition of torture might exist is abolished' (*ET*, 159). He thus thinks it is entirely unproblematic for him to call for the scrapping of absolute torture prohibitions *and* be 'adamantly against the institutionalization of torture' (*ET*, 48). Is Steinhoff right in thinking this?

As we remember, Steinhoff's moral argument in defence of torture applies, equally, to all. This means, of course, that under his new legal regime, whatever absolute prohibition of interrogational torture might have existed previously has also been abolished for people who have a duty of care. Police officers, for example, would now be legally permitted to torture under extreme circumstances: to protect the innocent. But the trouble is that they would not just be *permitted*. As Brecher writes, 'It is not just that interrogational torture in ticking bomb scenarios would become morally permissible, or come to be seen as such, as the result of its legalization; it would become, or come to be seen as, a moral duty'.[42] While Steinhoff does not explicitly argue in his book that interrogational torture can sometimes be a *duty*, he cannot plausibly deny this. For if he did, he would shift the argument from the paramount moral importance of protecting innocents to that of making sure people would be at liberty either to engage or not to engage in justified interrogational torture *and not be charged with having acted wrongly either way.* Be that as it may, Steinhoff is at least explicit about the fact that it would be morally 'repugnant' (*ET*, 42) for a father *not* to waterboard his son for thirty minutes if he could not otherwise save his life.

Are we to infer from this that it would be morally repugnant not just for parents but also for public officials who have a duty of care to refuse to engage in *interrogational* torture once it had been legalized? The answer must surely be 'yes', since it is difficult to see why it should be legally permissible for someone with a duty of care to refrain from engaging in interrogational torture in a situation where they can do so without breaking the law. Indeed, Steinhoff would surely have to insist that it ought then to be *legally impermissible* for people acting in official innocent-protecting capacity not to engage in interrogational torture under the extreme circumstances he has specified. After all, it is not *optional*, but *required*, for a police officer to interfere with someone being beaten or sexually assaulted. It is clear what follows. Public protectors of innocents who might end up in a justified interrogational torture situation would have a *right* to be trained in the practice of torture to avoid a situation in which they could not help but break the law. If Steinhoff denied this, he would impose an impossible obligation; he would be arguing that police officers – and anyone else whose public role is at least partially about protecting the innocent – might be facing situations in which they are *legally required* to do what they *lack the ability* to do.

Steinhoff's mistake here is to take for granted that people could, without relevant training, engage in interrogational torture; that doing this 'is simply not that difficult' (*ET*, 58).[43] Is it really not? *Inflicting physical suffering* is not difficult, technically, for some of us. Some are even capable of inflicting *continuous or repeated* extreme physical suffering. But to inflict continuous or repeated extreme physical suffering *so as to get information* is quite simply something a torture novice *cannot* do. One needs to know *how* to do it: how to administer the right amount of pain, and the right sort, so as to elicit the right information. As Henry Shue writes, 'Torture is not for amateurs – successful torturers need to be real "pros", and no one becomes a "pro" overnight'.[44] Hence, as Brecher explains, the ticking-bomb scenario 'requires us not to imagine what *we* would do, but to imagine what we would require *someone else* – a professional torturer – to do on our behalf; and not, furthermore, as an act of supererogation or altruism, but as the practice of their profession'.[45] Interrogational torture is something one needs to be taught.

Steinhoff denies this. But his denial comes in the form of two cases in which nobody appears to have been tortured at all: First, 'In the famous Daschner case, the mere *threat* of torture (and some think that threatening *is* torture) sufficed to make the child kidnapper, Markus Gäfgen, disclose the location of the child'; and second, as already mentioned, the police 'beat' Denis Mook's kidnapper in 1988 'until, finally, he did reveal the child's location' (*ET*, 58). Steinhoff's definition of torture becomes *so* loose here that his defence of torture seems to have turned into a defence of sometimes threatening and beating people. The trouble is, however, that *even if* Steinhoff could identify a historical case where someone without any torture experience managed not only to engage in the practice of torture but also to elicit life-saving information as a result of so doing, this would not help his case at all. For he could hardly infer from *someone*'s ability to do this that *everyone else* would be in a position to do so too. And at this point – notably the only point of prescriptive relevance of Steinhoff's work[46] – torture inevitably becomes what Steinhoff fervently denies it to be: a *necessarily political* practice. This is the sort of practice that Steinhoff's target Brecher was concerned with in his book. Duty-bound police officers would have a *right* to be trained. Indeed, they would have no right *not* to be trained: if interrogational torturing would in some conceivable scenarios be their professional duty, then acquiring the skills to torture effectively (to fulfil one's professional duties) would *also* be such a duty. And *because* they have such a right and duty to be trained in how to become effective interrogational torturers, Steinhoff's attempt to draw a clear-cut analytic distinction between legalization and institutionalization by way of offering the following analogy does not even get off the ground:

> A police officer can [stab a pencil in a person's eye] legally in the United States, the UK, and Germany if it is a necessary and proportionate defense against an attack – as it might well be under the circumstances, including in circumstances where the police officer acts in official capacity (for example, when he tries to arrest a criminal, but the criminal surprisingly and viciously attacks). Yet . . . it would be ridiculous to say that in the United States, the UK, or Germany 'state eye stabbing' is an institutionalized practice. (*ET*, 48)

Well, it would indeed be 'ridiculous' *literally* to say that '"state eye stabbing" is an institutionalized practice'. But that is irrelevant, because self-defence training for police officers, the overall category under which Steinhoff's example of stabbing pencils in people's eyes falls, *is* an institutionalized practice. And there are good reasons for institutionalizing self-defence training for police. If police officers have an obligation to put themselves in harm's way, if and when required in the course of acting in official capacity, then they also have a right to receive the sort of training that enables them to defend themselves and others against such harm. If *this* is the case, however, and if it is also the case that engaging in legitimate self- and/or other-defence may require the practice of interrogational torture, then there simply are no grounds on which Steinhoff could plausibly deny police officers the right *also* to learn how to *inflict continuous or repeated extreme physical suffering so as to elicit information*. One would then, of course, need experts to teach them how to do that. And one would need experts to train the experts. And so on. Steinhoff is thus unquestionably off the mark when he uses the pencil-stabbing example to argue that '*[i]n the same vein, torture is not institutionalized merely by virtue of being legal or tolerated* in the extremely rare cases of self-defensive torture' (*ET*, 48, emphasis added). And perhaps he is already inadvertently acknowledging as much when he writes that inflicting the sort of pain that constitutes torture 'does not require *long* training and experience' (*ET*, 58, emphasis added).[47] Are we to infer that a *brief* torture workshop – conducted in the safe space of liberal democracy – will do?

Steinhoff might reject the earlier line of argument by pointing out that justified interrogational torture situations are unlikely to occur very often. As he writes when arguing against the institutionalization of torture,

> Situations . . . in which it is justified for the police to torture someone *are enormously rare*. Institutionalizing torture in order to be equipped for such a rare occasion is like stationing a police officer at a lake somewhere in the wilderness because a parachutist might land in it and drown otherwise. And while there is nothing worrying or particularly off-putting about police officers on lakesides, there is something worrying and off-putting about torture specialists and a torture bureaucracy in police departments. Thus, given the rarity of the relevant circumstances, the exceedingly hypothetical benefits of a rudimentary institutionalization of torture are not worth the risks. They are, in fact, not even worth the bitter aftertaste. (*ET*, 67)

But this is irrelevant, since the enormous rarity of what he considers justified interrogational torture situations would not trump the right of tax-paying innocents to be protected by people with a duty of care who are efficient at what they are doing. Nor would it trump the right of the latter to be trained such that they do not have to break the law – for reasons of incompetence – when these situations do occur. After all, Steinhoff is a true believer in the possibility of the ticking-bomb scenario (*ET*, 138–47). He *must* therefore take into consideration the very real possibility that, one day, the lives of thousands of people will depend on someone being efficient at the practice of interrogational torture. Indeed, he openly envisages such a scenario when he writes that 'it is clearly . . . a myth that the harms of thousands or millions of people being blown up by a nuclear bomb are suffered by those thousands or millions of people alone. Not only ticking-bomb terrorists have friends and relatives. You do the maths' (*ET*, 52). Seeing that Steinhoff explicitly anticipates the possibility of such a disaster, he will – if and when it does occur – need to explain himself to these friends and relatives. He will need to explain why the new legal regime that was adopted on the back of his philosophical intervention made it *legal* to torture ticking nuclear bomb planters while keeping it *illegal* for anyone to acquire the requisite skills to be able to do it. Has he done the maths?

It is also worth making three further observations about Steinhoff's insistence on the enormous rarity of justified interrogational torture situations. First, these situations appear to be sufficiently likely for him to have deemed it necessary to write his book in the first place. But if he has a right to write such a book, is it then not also the case that those who might be duty-bound to implement its prescriptions have a right to be trained in how to do so? Second, Steinhoff's reliance on rarity makes his argument against institutionalization hostage to contingencies – and radically so. What if, one day, such situations had become much *less* rare? Is Steinhoff going to happily plod along with whatever likelihood the world was going to present us with, without ever asking *why* it is that such situations occur? Third, even in the present world the likelihood might not be as low as Steinhoff makes it out to be. Indeed, it might not be as low by his own inadvertent admission. If terrorism is what he thinks it is – a 'routinely employed instrument of the strong, and usually only the final resort for the weak' – then those who defend themselves against it might in fact routinely be in a position where they can engage in justified torture. Remember Steinhoff's insistence on the rightness of '[torturing] a Christian or Jewish state terrorist if by doing so one can avert a more or less indiscriminate bombing campaign by the American or Israeli air force that would (once again) kill thousands of innocent Palestinians, Iraqis, or Afghans'.[48] Should not those with a duty to protect these innocents against the actions of state terrorists have a *right* to be trained in the practice of interrogational torture? Or do they, paradoxically, lack this right despite engaging in legitimate self-defence? Do they lack it simply because they are not in a position to offer protection from within the sort of liberal political framework that, to Steinhoff's mind, proves the only fertile ground for torture's legalization?

It is clear by now that any attempt to distinguish a call for the legalization of interrogational torture from a call for its institutionalization is destined to fail; it would defy all logic to legalize interrogational torture without offering relevant training to those who might end up facing a situation where they have a duty to engage in it. Steinhoff's error is a dangerous one to make; he opens – however unintentionally – the floodgates for the institutionalization of interrogational torture in contemporary liberal democracies; the sort of thing that, by his own judgement, is 'serious overkill' and 'too dangerous' (*ET*, 3 and 64). Steinhoff argues against Alan Dershowitz here, who, in the immediate aftermath of *9/11*, made the case for institutionalizing torture and introducing 'torture warrants'[49] – the very argument which triggered Brecher's intervention that ended up annoying Steinhoff so much. As opposed to Steinhoff, however, Dershowitz was – in that respect – at least consistent in being wrong. And Brecher knew – as did many others – that a philosophically careful intervention was needed in response.

## Error 2

Does this mean that Steinhoff is politically irresponsible? He anticipates this charge, formulating it as follows: 'Even if you [Steinhoff] were right about self-defensive torture, by publicly justifying torture in some cases you contribute to a slippery slope, you contribute to there being more cases of illegitimate torture too'. While he admits that one's right to speak one's opinion can sometimes be 'overridden', he also insists that, 'if it were to be overridden, this would have to happen on grounds of *credible and substantial evidence* that my speaking my opinion indeed does cause harm on a scale large enough to override my right to free expression' (*ET*, 157).[50] Unless it can be proven that he has made a *causal* contribution to the sort of torture he· is *not* defending, no one can reasonably blame him, he thinks, for such torture being practised. And *even if* it could be proven that he has inadvertently made a causal contribution to the practice of illegitimate interrogational torture – for example, the torture practiced in Guantanamo – he could simply point to the fact that he has explicitly condemned it (*ET*, 157). Steinhoff *cannot*, it appears, lose the argument.

The reason why he cannot lose, however, is that he makes the error appear to be located where it is not. Why should making a *causal* contribution to illegitimate practices be a necessary condition of one's being intellectually irresponsible? Steinhoff's contributions on torture may indeed have no causal impact whatsoever on the *actual* practice of interrogational torture in the world. But this is irrelevant for our assessment of whether or not he is act- ing politically irresponsibly by pronouncing himself in the way he does. He *very clearly* is. As Brecher writes, 'Some actions, practices, or events issue not only in direct consequences for specific individuals or groups, but also affect the moral attitudes of people, the moral climate within which direct consequences are characterized and assessed'. This means that 'morality- affecting harm may wreak its damage in ways other than straightforwardly causal ones'.[51] One of the troubles with Steinhoff's book is that it functions as a contribution to *framing* perceptions of, and moral discussions about, interrogational torture. In so doing, it may also function as incitement – just like a philosopher's defence for the right of self-defensive killing could, contrary to what Steinhoff assumes, *of course* '[contribute] to an atmosphere in which murder thrives' (*ET*, 158). As I will suggest in the next chapter on war, liberal defences of violence can indeed contribute to an atmosphere in which *war* thrives.

The broader point here is that philosophers need to be wary of the historical and political context in which they articulate moral arguments. They cannot absolve themselves from this responsibility simply by postulating that their arguments are to be regarded as detached from their political context and independently philosophically valid. Those who take it upon themselves to pronounce publicly on as important a topic as interrogational torture ought to think very carefully about their responsibilities *here and now*, and about the ways in which their pronounced views might frame and influence the way in which interrogational torture is being thought of and talked about. Brecher and many other contemporary critics of liberal defences of torture have attempted to do precisely that when looking at interrogational torture as a *politically embedded* and *currently rampant* practice. Steinhoff, on the contrary, had nothing better to do – in the very midst of this 'time in the shadows'[52] – than to launch a condemnatory, bitter, one-size-fits-all philosophical counter-attack. In trying his hardest to make the torture critics look like fools, however, he failed to realize that, in Brecher's words, 'Whatever we do . . . *is done in a particular social context*. . . . That is why discussions of moral practices, acts, problems, or dilemmas which seek to isolate their subject from the social setting in which it takes places are peculiarly sterile – which is hardly surprising, since our moral relations are after all relations with real people'.[53]

There is no need, then, to engage with the question of whether or not Steinhoff's theoretical defence of interrogational torture has made a causal contribution to its actual practice. The point is that context matters, and that moral philosophers – particularly if they are sufficiently equipped to do otherwise – ought not to be steamrolling abstract analytic moral defences of violence across a political landscape inhabited by an audience obsessed with, and/or indifferent to, practicing such violence as they see fit.

Perhaps there is a need to alert Steinhoff to his own very accurate description of the particular political contingencies which characterize the war against terrorism of our times. After all he does not seem to have any reservations about legalizing interrogational torture in *any* existing liberal democracy with the exception of Israel, which Steinhoff considers 'a colonialist and militarist state' where 'things can get out of control' (*ET*, 72). He then goes on to claim, however, that the case of Israel 'teaches us very little about what will happen in *completely different situations*' (*ET*, 72). And since he fails to suggest otherwise and indeed frequently draws on U.S. law for support of his moral case, he is clearly of the view that the case of the United States *does* present us with a completely different situation. Steinhoff is thus defending the legalization of interrogational torture in a country that not only has Bush's torture regime attached to its recent historical record but was capable of electing, only several years later, a presidential candidate who had announced that he would 'bring back a *hell* of a *lot worse than waterboarding*' if he became the president.[54] Does Steinhoff want to see interrogational torture legalized in a country run in a manner that he knows to be beyond any, let alone his, rational control? How about the United Kingdom? Has Steinhoff read Ian Cobain on *Cruel Britannia*?[55] At the crucial moment in the development of his argument at which Steinhoff offers at least *some* reflections on the political context to which his prescriptions are meant to speak, he defends himself against the charge of not recognizing associated dangers by drawing on the case of *Liechtenstein* (*ET*, 71).

Steinhoff's own political reflections on the immoralities of 'the stronger party', as previously cited, thus turn out to highlight the dramatic extent of his irresponsibility. He embraces a form of analytic atomism that enables him to make astute and critical comments about existing liberal democracies while at the same time mythologizing lawfulness in such democracies for the purpose of his moral defence. This allows him to treat law and morality as something pure and sacrosanct, and as disconnectable from political practice. It is precisely because Steinhoff thinks it is possible to produce a philosophical book in defence of torture in a political vacuum – detached from, and irrespective of, the historical, political and discursive context in which the production occurs – that he cannot help but enter an unholy moral alliance with the likes of Allhoff. And any expectation that Steinhoff might, at the very least, strongly object to being perceived as Allhoff's intellectual ally is disappointed when he refers to him, without appearing to be troubled at all, as if the two of them *did* belong to the same camp (*ET*, 88–89). In fact, he is happy to put Allhoff and himself on the very same list of torture defenders, a list including 'Winfried Brugger, Stephen Kershnar, Fritz Allhoff, Seumas Miller, Francesco Belvisi, Mirko Bargaric, Julie Clarke, Jeff McMahan, and me' (*ET*, 55).

## Error 3

I have thus far talked about the impossibility of legalizing interrogational torture without institutionalizing it. I have also highlighted Steinhoff's inability to separate his moral defence of interrogational torture from the political context of its production. His third error, which applies to non-interrogational torture as well, is to assume that he is asking the right question about torture; that he is even in a position to demonstrate anything at all. And because Steinhoff would at no point drop this assumption, his second argument in defence of torture, the 'argument from necessity', has no in-built limitation in terms of what it must be committed to justifying in light of imagined catastrophic alternatives. Indeed, this argument turns out on closer inspection to collapse into a moralistic realism, because the boundaries of what is morally right are, on this view, dictated by *whatever* disastrous choice the evil world happens to force one to make. This is the sort of action-guiding philosophy that would, in all seriousness, morally call on us to waterboard a child *once* in order to prevent it from being waterboarded *10 times*, and to waterboard it *10 times* in order to prevent it from being waterboarded *100 times*. It somehow manages to frame the waterboarding of a child as *the morally right thing to do*.

Steinhoff begins his very inquiry by asking the question of whether torture is sometimes justified (*ET*, 1). He seems to take for granted not only that this is the right question to ask but that *every* conceivable situation that the world might present us with is subsumable under a binary moral structure of right (i.e., just or justified) and wrong. *Whatever* situation we face, *regardless* of how grim things get, it *must* be possible for moral agents to do what is *right*. This would even be the case – to modify one of Steinhoff's own examples – if a sadist gave you the choice between drilling into the unprotected nerve of your child's tooth for one hour and watching the sadist herself doing it not just for one hour but until your child has died a painful death. You would be *justified* in torturing your child. It would be *right* for you to do so, and *wrong* – indeed repugnant – not to.

Steinhoff's method, then, is to fabricate scenarios so immeasurably awful that one would appear to be a philosophical monster to let it happen out of some sort of unworldly, quasi-sectarian commitment to 'dubious principles' (*ET*, 42).[56] I can only call on readers to join me in being entirely unimpressed by the moral argument which derives from employing this philosophical method. Why? Because, much like the defences of sweatshops and war encountered in the previous and subsequent chapters, it has no built-in limitation in terms of what it is capable of justifying. As Luban writes, 'The worse the world is, the worse the behavior that morality countenances to combat it, with no limit to how low we can sink'.[57] Reality and/or conjectures of the philosopher's inventive mind can *always* expand the realm of the morally justifiable yet one step further into (im)moral infinitude. Steinhoff's 'argument from necessity' surely demands not only that it would be right for us to torture *one* child in order to prevent it from being executed but also to torture *ten thousand* children if some sadistic dictator had given us the choice between doing that and seeing the children executed? And no doubt we would be right to torture these children again the next day if the dictator fancied one more round? What is the value of a moral argument that knows no limits to what it is prepared to call *right*?

Steinhoff's argument not only justifies virtually anything and thus nothing at all, however; it is also presses human action into a binary straightjacket of right and wrong. In so doing, it simply denies that there are situations where morality has run out of anything meaningful to say.[58] It is nonsense to say that we are '*clearly* justified' (*ET*, 42 and 44) – let alone to attribute any significance to the possibility that 'we might well *feel* justified' (*ET*, 53, emphasis added) – in drilling into the unprotected nerve of a child's tooth. A philosopher – particularly one claiming to be of a rights-respecting disposition – should have nothing to say on these matters other than that there can be situations where morality is silent; where no right can be done; where in fact one has been deprived of one's moral agency in a situation of forced choice. What one *would* do in such a situation – insofar as one can be said to be in a position to 'do' anything at all – is no longer a moral question; for it is entirely independent of the question of rightness, to which a meaningful answer can no longer be given. To force these sorts of situation into a binary philosophical straightjacket of right versus wrong is to fail to recognize that the very possibility of moral agency can sometimes be eliminated. As Luban puts it, 'Ordinary practices of moral rationality fail in cases where all courses of action are monstrous'.[59] There comes a point when action-prescribing philosophers should, quite simply, shut up: for *anything* they could argue would be a case of 'cover[ing] over the monstrousness with a veneer of rationality'.[60]

Or can we say, in all rational seriousness, that Sophie, in the novel *Sophie's Choice* (see *ET*, 44), was exercising her moral agency when the Nazis forced her to choose one of her two children to be sent to the gas chambers, her only alternative being to *not* choose and see them *both* go?[61] Would it be appropriate for the moral philosopher to give her expert advice? Can we seriously characterize her situation as one in which she ought to engage in moral deliberation to make sure she gets it right? Can we say that she *chooses*? The distinction between justified and unjustified conduct sometimes fails to get any grip at all, and moral philosophers are well advised not to pretend otherwise. Imagine a human world even more awful than the world in which we currently live; a world whose badness transcends even Steinhoff's admittedly vivid imagination; a world where sadists are omnipresent and constantly force one to make horrible choices; a world of fear, despair and agony, where children are kidnapped, tortured and killed on a regular basis. And now imagine being a moral philosopher trying to say something intelligent about morally justified conduct in *that* world. What *could* you say?

Instead of theorizing about rightness and wrongness in such cases, we should conclude, with Luban, that 'there are some abominations that, as a society, we do not have moral debates about because they fall so far below the threshold of the acceptable that we do not need to argue about them'.[62] Drilling the unprotected nerve of a child's tooth *is* such an abomination, and there is no way in which a rights-based moral theory can justify it without collapsing into something quite obviously incoherent. It is indeed the case that we do not need to argue about this. All we can try to do is adopt policies (for instance education policies, foreign policies, economic policies) that make it unlikely for such situations of forced choice ever to occur – policies that increase the chance of people not turning into monsters.

Do we need to argue, though, about situations in which some villain is '*liable* to torture'?[63] Is *that* sort of torture not right? Let me just point out two problems with this view – one about consequences, the other about the way in which Steinhoff's argument is politically distorting. First, as we have already seen earlier, we cannot make an argument about *liability* without also making an argument about *consequences*. Any liability-based defence of interrogational torture that fails to recognize this very straightforward implication quite simply obscures its '*consequentialist* dangers'.[64] If the material reality of liberal democracies is anything to go by, one of these dangers is that a great many non-liable parties are going to end up being tortured. They are going to be tortured by people who have been trained in a process that 'produces dispositions closely linked to crimes of obedience because it produces individuals who are very likely to obey illegal and immoral orders'.[65] So the paradox of liability-based liberal arguments in defence of torture is that they may function to produce the very thing they purportedly set out to avert: rights violations on a large scale. People who buy into arguments in defence of torture in Jamie Mayerfeld's analysis,

> [O]ften deaf to repeated demonstrations that torture produces bad information, that the information sought from torture can usually be obtained by other and better means, that torture spins out of control, that it hinders more effective counter-terrorist strategies, that it enrages existing enemies and recruits new ones, that it wrecks the lives of those ordered to torture. It's as though people stop listening after they've learned that the captive person is a terrorist. I believe these habits of thought may be encouraged by stark formulations such as the claim that a ticking-bomb terrorist makes himself 'liable to be tortured' or that 'torturing him would not wrong him'.[66]

Not only does torture do damage by enraging existing enemies and encouraging new ones; it can also lead to incorrect information obtained through torture *being acted upon*. Indeed, incorrect information obtained through torture was used by Colin Powell in justifying the Iraq war in 2003, a war that killed hundreds of thousands of people and has stimulated international terrorism.[67] As Mayerfeld points out, this 'is the cataclysmic ticking bomb scenario in reverse. And it is an *actual* case unlike the fictional cases that dominate public discussions of the morality of torture'.[68]

Ultimately, arguments about liability contribute to a moral climate in which 'the liability view has become a thin disguise for uncontrolled anger'.[69] The assumption of the liability of the 'other', if made in a political context characterized by fear, anger and perhaps widespread racism, has the effects of muting analysis and silencing critique.[70] Not only is it the case that anger 'finds an outlet in the liability'; it also 'undermines the ostensible rationale of the liability view. Whereas fear makes us exaggerate the dangers posed by ticking-bomb terrorists, anger makes us *overlook* the dangers caused by our own retaliatory actions, including torture'.[71] So the problem with any liability-based defence of interrogational torture is revealed as soon as we see it – as we must do – in the political context of its production.

The second problem with Steinhoff's argument about liability to torture – whether interrogational or otherwise – is that it is politically distorting. The story he tells is alluringly simple: villains keep turning up, out of the blue, and we are *justified* in defending ourselves and/or other innocent victims against them. In fact we may do so *justly* (as long as we do not harm any non-liable parties). But is it not peculiar that Steinhoff complains, on the one hand, about the war against terrorism and its 'silly and often racist "us-versus-them" ideology' (*ET*, 10) while assuming at least *some* version of us (innocents) versus them (villains) in many of the hypotheticals used in his book? The issue with Steinhoff's hypotheticals is not so much that they are unrealistic but that they are *political* despite appearing not to be. They are predicated on an 'idealised' and distorting representation of the world as one which can neatly be divided into us and them while, at the same time, speaking to a world in which moral agents are for the most part *not* simply good or evil; in which structures shape and constrain human conduct; and in which, quite simply, politics matters.

The reductionist story of just liberal violence, however, is all about individual agency and responsibility, exercised on some imagined level-playing field. It is not part of this story to ask why it is that these villains keep cropping up and why they have become the people they are. Rather, what is assumed, in good liberal and inadvertently realist tradition, is that this is simply what villains do, and that one must be in a position to *react* to their doing so in a way that is *just*: without being – let alone *feeling* – morally compromised. As a moral philosopher who speaks in a particular political context, however, one has a responsibility to ask *why* it is that situations keep arising (if indeed they do). To be able to do that, however, one cannot simply detach one's moral philosophy – let alone the moral calamities that are said to justify torture – from the structures and politics of violence that permeate one's times. This is where Steinhoff's error lies, and it is actually quite similar to Allhoff's. For both fail to recognize, in Luban's words, 'the ease with which arguments that pretend that torture can exist in liberal society, but only as an exception, quickly lead to erecting a torture culture, a network of institutions and practices that regularize the exception and make it a standard operating procedure'.[72]

## INTELLECTUAL COMPLICITY IN TORTURE

The liberal defence of interrogational torture fails. Not only does it offer an inadequate moral analysis that is inattentive to consequences; it is also severely epistemically limited in that it artificially isolates the terrible calamities that are said to justify torture – specifically the phantasy of the ticking bomb – from the social structures and political context of their production. It is this analytic atomism which makes it possible for Allhoff to write that 'the spread of more (justified) torture . . . has to be a good thing' (*TTT*, 155). In this analysis, moral agency is reduced to *reactive* agency – an agency that deals with moral calamities *when it is too late*. This is not the sort of agency that could hope to address the underlying causes of these real or, as is often the case, fabricated calamities in a structurally violent and interconnected world. Once agency has been reduced in this way, it can of course no longer fulfil the purpose of preventing all those evil, child-kidnapping and bomb-setting villains from rapidly jumping onto the stage, placing the virtuous in a position where they are, it is claimed, *morally forced* to torture. What torture defenders also fail to realize is that a liberal society in which interrogational torture were widely regarded as sometimes morally right, let alone a society in which it were legalized,[73] would be profoundly *violent*; that it would be, in Brecher's words, a 'torturous society'. The violence of such a society could not, however, be captured within the intellectual framework governing liberal defences of interrogational torture. For within this framework, violence cannot be structural; rather, it is taken to be attributable – *always* attributable – to individual perpetrators.

The added assumption here is that there is a clear-cut divide between two sorts of perpetrators of violence: the vicious and the virtuous. It is the latter to whom the defences of interrogational torture are addressed because their violence is considered to be of a particular kind within this binary configuration. It is burdened, laudable and civilized. As Luban puts it, 'Torture to gather intelligence and save lives seems almost heroic. For the first time, we can think of kindly torturers rather than tyrants'.[74] Virtuous liberals would never torture unless they were *forced* to do so by some evil villain.[75] They would not do so because they are taken to be essentially immune to the danger warned against by Galtung that '[a] violent structure leaves marks not only on the human body but also on the mind and the spirit'.[76] Their immunity stems from being located on the brighter side of the civilizational divide, and from being addressable in moral language and controllable through liberal law. The point about just torturers, then, is that they do not *intend* to intend to torture. They are simply forced, by powers beyond their control, to do so; to suspend their virtue or, rather, to exhibit it through a heroic willingness to carry the moral burden of having to torture. Paradoxically, the more drastic and brutal their violence, the more assured we can be of their virtue.

What we have here, on the one hand, is a reduction of agency to reactiveness to the challenges posed by evil, irrational others. These are – in a radically reduced and distorting perspective that assumes a disconnected world of good and evil – seen to be located on the other side of the civilizational divide (a divide to be found not only *between* societies but *within* 'civilized' societies too, cutting right through them). On the other hand, however, we have a relentless celebration of moral agency thus reduced. The very classifying of an act of interrogational torture as *just* or *justified* already signifies such celebration. Those located on the brighter side have a *right* to be just – a right which includes a right to engage in brutal violence against evil, liable others. In ascribing such a right, however, liberal defenders of interrogational torture can serve only to contribute to a moral climate in which torture finds an ideal habitat. In the end, they share with defenders of other forms of just liberal violence a complete lack of vision as to how to transcend our violent world. They are, on the contrary, complicit in maintaining it.

# Chapter 5

# War

Contemporary liberal just war theorists are at least partially concerned with defending the view that it can be *just* to use the means of war to defend human rights and/or to minimize human suffering.[1] The task of this chapter is to show that the justifications they offer for this view are inadequate. While I focus on two thinkers, Michael Walzer and Jeff McMahan, my critique applies to *whomever* is happy to be identified as a liberal just war theorist and has contributed to the literature in obedience to the basic parameters set by this signifier.[2] It applies even to those who – like Walzer and McMahan – have used just war theory as a critical tool.

I argue that liberal just war theorists, just like defenders of sweatshops and interrogational torture, engage in three reductions. First, they reduce the violence of war both epistemically (by capturing its horrors almost exclusively in terms of *killing*) and morally (by being nonchalant about killing with foresight, provided that the killing is unintentional). Second, they reduce agency to *reactive* agency, limiting the object of inquiry to the question of when, and whom, one may justly kill in response to some unjust aggression. And third, they reduce the perspective taken on the world to one where evil villains are assumed to keep turning up out of nowhere, leaving the virtuous innocent in the deplorable position of needing to be prepared – morally and militarily – to *fight back*.

In presenting their arguments for violence, just war theorists treat the human world as one that consists of analytically disconnectable units that can, moreover, be neatly separated into unjust attackers and just defenders. This is the analytic atomism of liberal just war theory, and the latter's recent move towards discovering moral truth by way of engaging in abstract thought experiments can be seen as the zenith of this epistemic reduction at the level of methodology. In these thought experiments, the question of moral justifiability is decontextualized and treated in a historical and political vacuum. It is simply not recognized that individuals and political entities in the contemporary world are interconnected in extremely hierarchical global social structures. Despite this disconnection from the world, however, just war theorists aim to provide prescriptive advice to political actors determining whether or not to engage in warfare. In so doing, they fail to challenge a structurally violent world. Theirs is a world in which one can rest assured that yet another war-mongering villain will pop up in the not-too-distant future; and also a world in which those to whom just war theory is addressed, the virtuous innocent – 'we' – are unlikely to begin to reflect on their own positionality and privilege vis-à-vis the 'uncivilized other'. Instead of encouraging a sober political and structural analysis, just war theory is designed to enable the virtuous innocent to react to singular instances of physical aggression in a way that is morally just. This is another feature of its realism: that what is judged to be right is always amenable to whatever scenario the world presents one with. The intellectual epitome of this distinct lack of an in-built limitation to what just war theory is prepared to call morally *right* is Walzer's account of *supreme emergencies*.

This chapter is divided into four sections. In the first section, I will show – in the interest of fairness – that Walzer and McMahan are putting forward just war theory not only for the purpose of justification but also as a critical tool, and that they themselves have used it as such a tool when criticizing recent wars waged by the United States and other liberal democracies. In the second section, I will give a brief account of Walzer's and McMahan's understanding of what constitutes a just war, and why they think that war can be just even if it involves the killing and maiming of innocent people. I will then, in the third section, reveal the crucial points at which Walzer and McMahan struggle to account for their own just war thinking, arguing that it is hardly surprising that they should find themselves so puzzled.[3] For what they are trying to solve is nothing less than the essential – and, I argue, *irresolvable* – problem of any allegedly just war, namely, that too much is putatively justified for theorists to be able actually to justify anything at all.

Both Walzer and McMahan are trying their hardest to force the politically complex, morally calamitous and radically unpredictable world of war into a binary moral structure of right and wrong. To do so successfully, however, their moral defences of war cannot help but collapse into a crude calculation of consequences under conditions of radical uncertainty – a calculation, moreover, that knows no limits in terms of the horrors it is capable of justifying. Morally speaking, just war theorists are thus trying to square the circle.[4] In the fourth and final section, however, I go on to suggest that a meaningful demonstration of the inadequacies of just war theory must go beyond the immanent moral critique that I offer. It must be *political* and attend to some of the assumptions that just war theorists must make in order to get their moral case off the ground. In fact, these assumptions are antecedently built into the very structure of the just war inquiry, setting the very rules for how a moral discussion about war is to be conducted. Theorists seem genuinely to believe that they are rational avant-gardists who reveal some deep, objective and universal moral truth about war – in the conviction that liberal political communities are already beginning to become receptive to that truth, and in the hope that, one day, we will all have turned into virtuous liberals who will act fully in accordance with it. But rather than being such avant-gardists, just war theorists are in fact exponents of an unexamined liberalism that is obsessed with the conduct of rights-holding and duty-bearing moral agents – whether collective or individual – on some imagined level-playing field, at the expense of being attentive to the way in which these agents are radically interconnected in hierarchical global social structures. In short, just war theorists are disconnected from their material object of analysis. They have invented war for themselves.[5]

## JUST WAR THEORY AS A CRITICAL TOOL

Walzer is explicit about the horrors of war: 'We hate war: It is a coercively collectivizing enterprise; a tyrannical enterprise; it overrides individuality, and it makes the kind of attention that we would like to pay to each person's moral standing impossible; it is universally oppressive'.[6] To his mind, just war theory has no normative predisposition to *justify* such tyranny, but only to make 'actions and operations that are morally problematic *possible* by constraining their occasions and regulating their conduct'.[7] Hence, when we talk about 'just wars', we must be clear that we are using 'a term of art here' (*AW*, x):

> [I]t means justifiable, defensible, even morally necessary (given the alterna-
> tives) – and that is all it means. All of us who argue about the rights and wrongs
> of war agree that justice in the strong sense, the sense that it has in domestic
> society and everyday life, is lost as soon as fighting begins. War is a zone of
> radical coercion, in which justice is always under a cloud. Still, sometimes we
> are right to enter the zone. (*AW*, x–xi)

At other times, however, we are wrong, and it is precisely the task of just war theory to tell us when.[8] Walzer explicitly acknowledges the dangers of 'imperial ambition and the global struggle for resources and power', but then goes on to ask: 'How can imperial warfare be criticized if not in just war terms? What other language, what other theory, is available for such a critique? Aggressive wars, wars of conquest, wars to extend spheres of influence and establish satellite states, wars for economic aggrandizement – all these are unjust wars' (*AW*, xi). But not *all* wars involving the United States and/or the West are like that, according to Walzer. Rather, he offers a case-by-case approach, giving whatever war is waged by the 'supposedly decent people on this planet' (*AW*, 81) a fair chance, as it were:[9] 'Even if we (in the West) have fought just wars in the Gulf, in Kosovo, and in Afghanistan, that is no guarantee, not even a useful indication, that our next war will be just' (*AW*, 15).[10] Are we to infer from this that, even if we have fought *unjust* wars in the past, this is no useful indication that our next war will be unjust too? In any case, the assumption here is that some of our wars will be just, others unjust; so whenever we fight another war, it ought to be subjected to critical scrutiny. Walzer himself was opposed, for example, to the war against Libya in 2011.[11] He was also opposed to the 2003 war against Iraq, judging at the time that it 'is neither just nor necessary' (*AW*, 151). What is a more crucial observation, though, is that he did not regard the question of whether the Iraq war was just as located beyond reasonable debate, arguing that 'the threat that Iraq posed could have been met with something less than the war we are now fighting. And a war fought *before its time* is not a just war' (*AW*, 161, emphasis added). Walzer's problem with the Iraq war here seems to be not so much that it was *waged*, but that it was waged *too early*. Or indeed that it was *too big*. On 7 March 2003, shortly before the invasion of Iraq, Walzer published a piece in *The New York Times*, calling for a '*little* war'.[12]

There are a number of similarities in McMahan's 'critical' moral thinking about war. First, he shares Walzer's general normative disposition *against* war, or at least against *unjust* wars.[13] For example, he is entirely explicit in the preface of *Killing in War* that he has 'written this book in the hope of promoting a reconsideration of certain beliefs that have hardened into unquestioned orthodoxies yet encourage complacency about killing in war and thus make it easier for governments to lead their countries into unjust wars'.[14] Second, McMahan does not think that qualifying wars as 'just' is problematic, as it is not meant, he insists, to disguise the horrors of war – horrors which, however, he tends to capture in a language rather more clinical and desolate than Walzer's:

> I think . . . we should, so far as possible, speak the same language as our predecessors in the just war tradition. Writers in this tradition have always known that it is virtually impossible to fight a war without physically harming people who are innocent in the sense of not being morally liable to be physically harmed. Yet despite this knowledge, they have consistently referred to certain wars as just wars. Just war theorists have thus always applied the term 'just war' to wars they knew involved the infliction of unjust harms . . . [I]t seems that we have always understood what they meant; hence their way of using the word 'just' must be intelligible.[15]

Third, McMahan follows Walzer's epistemic footsteps in approaching the question of (our) wars' justifiability on a case-by-case basis: 'The idea that the Iraq and Afghanistan wars are 'fronts' in a larger 'War on Terror,' or that the Korean and Vietnam wars were phases of a protracted war against communism, is incompatible with accepted criteria for the individuation of wars, including the criteria found in international law'.[16] McMahan reasons that '[a] war is necessarily [fought] against specific adversaries, who must, if the war is just, have made themselves liable to be warred against'.[17] We can, indeed we *must*, thus always analyse – and justify and/or criticize – *one war at a time*.[18] Very much in line with this insistence on keeping wars analytically separate, McMahan also seems to follow Walzer's pattern of allowing individual wars as waged by the United States a reasonable chance to be just: 'Apart from the initial strikes against al Qaeda bases in Afghanistan in 2001, the major uses of military force by the United States that *might* be considered just have been instances of collective defense (for example, the Korean War) and humanitarian intervention (for example, Kosovo)'.[19] The latter instances seem to be particularly likely candidates for just wars.[20] For example, McMahan seems to judge that the harms imposed in the 'humanitarian' North Atlantic Treaty Organization (NATO) war against Serbia in 1999 – which killed at least 1,500 civilians through high-altitude bombing – was 'neither disproportionate nor otherwise wrong';[21] that the war against Libya in 2011 – which left the country in an ongoing state of civil war – is 'an *apparent* exception' to the rule that 'there are better ways of supporting the spread of democracy and respect for human rights than the use of military force'[22]; and that '*if* [limited strikes against Syria] could be expected to be both effective and proportionate, the Obama administration has a strong case for conducting them'.[23] While McMahan tends to hide behind hypotheticals and avoid definitive judgements when leaving his philosophical pedestal to comment on real wars that he thinks *might* be just, the subtext is important: it is, *in principle*, eminently possible for advanced, civilized, liberal, democracy-spreading, rights-respecting powers to wage just wars.

Fourth, however, and again mirroring Walzer, McMahan insists that we must be wary. For '[e]xperience has repeatedly shown that in a matter as serious as war, it is unwarranted to trust in the wisdom and honesty of *even* a democratically elected government and therefore unreasonable simply to defer to its judgment'.[24] McMahan 'doubt[s] that in most cases democratic political institutions offer even a presumption of epistemic reliability in decisions about the resort to war, much less a decisive reason to defer to the judgements of a democratic government' (*KW*, 70). On the contrary, he points out – without trying to hide his epistemic parochialism – that '[o]ur own societies are . . . perpetually in danger of fighting unjust wars' (*KW*, 3). Indeed, McMahan displays a considerable degree of political cynicism in his writings – arguably more so than Walzer.[25] While he seems to think that liberal democracies have entered a post-barbarian phase in their development in that they have become *addressable* in moral language and *might* be receptive to it, he is also aware – much to his frustration – that they often are not. For instance, contrary to Walzer, McMahan considered the war against Iraq in 1991 unjust, arguing that 'an unnecessary war that is deliberately pursued in preference to nonviolent means in part in order to serve aims that unjustly advance the national interest is not a mere mistake; it is a crime'.[26] And as regards the Iraq war in 2003, he points out, scathingly, that many people (in Iraq) 'preferred to continue to live under domestic despotism than to risk dying in a war fought by an untrusted and, as it turns out, untrustworthy foreign power – one that had helped to maintain Saddam Hussein in power as long as it was in its interest to do so, that had bombed their capital just over a decade earlier, and that had a manifest interest in ensuring the availability of their oil reserves'.[27] This reflects McMahan's general awareness of the United States's propensity to wage unjust wars: 'There are a great many states that have been victims of unjust American intervention (Cuba, Chile, Guatemala), American military aggression (Vietnam, Laos, Cambodia), American terrorism (Libya) and American-sponsored terrorism (Nicaragua, El Salvador) in recent decades'.[28] Importantly, however, this awareness does not lead McMahan to question the United States's *general ability* to wage just wars. Nor does it stop him from evaluating every single new war *afresh*, on the basis of a *prima vista* epistemic disposition. For despite the discouraging historical record, there is always a chance, as it were, that the *next* U.S. war might be just, provided the adversary faced *then* is 'liable to be warred against'. Indeed, this might have well been the case in Iraq 2003, had Iraq *in fact* possessed the weapons of mass destruction that the Bush administration falsely claimed it possessed.[29]

Before I argue that Walzer's and McMahan's analytic atomism should be rejected, we need to take a look at why they think that wars can be morally just. After all, it may not strike readers as immediately 'intuitive' – a term we will have reason to revisit – that actions which lead to mass killing, mass mutilation, mass displacement and mass sexual violence should be straightforwardly associable with the adjective 'just'. This is true even if – as one suspects at least some of the more enthusiastic participants in military parades may be at risk of failing to realize – it is meant to be used merely as a term of art and to keep in line with the language spoken by our predecessors.

## JUSTIFYING WAR

Walzer's thinking about war is profoundly shaped by the horrors of Nazism: 'Nazism was an ultimate threat to everything decent in our lives, an ideology and a practice of domination so murderous, so degrading even to those who might survive, that the consequences of its final victory were literally beyond calculation, immeasurably awful. We see it – and I don't use the phrase lightly – as evil objectified in the world, and in a form so potent and apparent that there could never have been anything to do but fight against it'.[30] He actually cannot fathom how anyone can possibly *reject* just war theory: 'There are acts of aggression and acts of cruelty that we ought to resist, by force if necessary. I would have thought that our experience with Nazism ended this particular argument' (*AW*, xi).

While the threat posed by Nazism serves as just war theory's historical cornerstone, the structure of the just war argument *always* requires that someone commit the crime of aggression (*JUW*, 21–32): '*Nothing but aggression can justify war*' (*JUW*, 62), and the defence of rights is 'the only reason [for fighting]' (*JUW*, 72). The unjust aggressors threaten not only people's rights to life and liberty, however, but also their right not to be challenged 'in the sum of things they value most, including the political association they have made' (*JUW*, 53).[31] Indeed, Walzer postulates that 'the survival and freedom of political communities – whose members share a way of life, developed by their ancestors, to be passed on to their children – are the highest values of international society' (*JUW*, 254). And whenever these highest values cannot be protected other than by means of war – a war waged by virtuous innocents against villainous aggressors – war can be *just*.

McMahan's *revisionist* account of just war preserves this binary normative structure, but radically individualizes it:[32]

> First imagine a case in which a person uses violence in self-defense; then imagine a case in which two people engage in self-defense against a threat they jointly face. Continue to imagine further cases in which increasing numbers of people act with increasing coordination to defend both themselves and each other against a common threat, or a range of threats they face together. What you are imagining is a spectrum of cases that begins with acts of individual self-defense and, as the threats become more complex and extensive, the threatened individuals more numerous, and their defensive action more integrated, eventually reaches cases involving a scale of violence that is constitutive of war. But if war, at least in some instances, lies on a continuum with individual self- and other-defense, and if acts of individual self- and other-defense can sometimes be morally justified, then war can in principle be morally justified as well.[33]

How does McMahan justify war and the killing and maiming that comes with it? One of two justifications he offers is based on the notion that some people are 'liable to be warred upon' (the other is a lesser-evil justification, as we shall see later).[34] What does it mean for someone to be *liable* to attack? It means, at least partly, that this person 'would not be *wronged* by being attacked, and would have no justified complaint about being attacked' (*KW*, 8).

And how are we supposed to determine what wrongs are serious enough to make people liable to be killed and maimed?

> We can . . . consult our beliefs – which are quite robust and stable – about which kinds of wrong are sufficiently serious that the killing or maiming of the perpetrator could be justified if it were necessary to prevent or correct the wrong. Most people agree, for example, that one person may permissibly kill another if that is necessary to prevent the other person from wrongfully killing, torturing, mutilating, raping, kidnapping, enslaving or, perhaps, imprisoning her. Many people would also accept that it can be permissible to kill in defense against unjust and permanent expulsion from one's home or homeland, and even, perhaps, in defense against theft – though here questions of scale are obviously relevant to proportionality.[35]

So it is in accordance with our purportedly 'quite robust and stable' beliefs that we may wage war against someone who is 'liable to be warred upon'. Crucially, however, it also forms part of our 'quite robust and stable' beliefs that *innocent* people – or *non-liable* parties in McMahan's preferred language – may rightly be killed and maimed in the wars we wage. The fact is that both Walzer and McMahan think that it is possible for a war to be just *despite* its involving such killing and maiming. How so?

Walzer relies on what he considers a stringent version of the doctrine of double effect to justify such killing.[36] According to the standard version of this doctrine, one may kill innocents in war *with foresight* only as long as: (1) the military action serves a just moral goal (i.e., the destruction of a munitions factory); (2) the just moral goal is intentionally pursued, while the killing of innocents is an unintended side effect; (3) the killing is not a means to achieve the direct, good effect that is actually intended by the otherwise legitimate action; and (4) the killing is proportionate, or at least not disproportionate, to the goodness achieved by that action.

But there might be a problem. For the doctrine of double effect, so understood, 'invites an angry or cynical response: what difference does it make whether civilian deaths are a direct or an indirect effect of my actions? It can hardly matter to the dead civilians, and if I know in advance that I am likely to kill so many innocent people and go ahead anyway, how can I be blameless?' (*JUW*, 153). This is why Walzer thinks that 'the two outcomes' must be 'the product of a double intention: first, that the "good" be achieved; second, that the foreseeable evil be reduced as far as possible' (*JUW*, 155). He thinks that 'civilians have a right that "due care" be taken' "even if 'this means risking soldiers' lives"' (*JUW*, 156). And yet he immediately puts this additional demand into perspective, arguing that 'there is a limit to the risks that we require. These are, after all, unintended deaths and legitimate military operations, and the absolute rule against attacking civilians does not apply. War necessarily places civilians in danger; that is another aspect of its hellishness. We can only ask soldiers to minimize the dangers they impose' (*JUW*, 156). On his view, there is *nothing* wrong with killing the innocent with foresight, as long as the killing is an unintended, proportionate, non-instrumental side effect of an agent's pursuing a just moral goal, with *some* due care being taken.[37] Walzer is entirely explicit about this by writing that '[a] legitimate act of war is one that does not violate the rights of the people against whom it is directed' (*JUW*, 135) – *even if* it includes the killing and maiming of these very people. They have a right that due care be taken, but they have no right not to be killed if due care *has been* taken. Innocent people who have the bad luck to be bombed in accordance with Walzer's doctrine of double effect do not belong to the category of people whose rights are being violated.

McMahan, too, refuses to place these people in that category. And yet his approach to the question of killing and maiming non-liable parties collaterally appears at first sight to differ from Walzer's since he does not deny that such parties are *wronged*.[38] Let us see how the argument goes. McMahan invokes the notion of the 'justified tactical bomber': 'His action is . . . objectively mor-ally justified but will have as a side effect the killing of people who have done nothing to lose their right not to be killed. Like the person who intentionally kills an innocent person to save a much greater number of other innocent peo-ple, the tactical bomber justifiably threatens people who have done nothing to make themselves liable to be threatened' (*KW*, 173–74). The objectively justified tactical bomber does not *violate* the rights of non-liable parties but only *infringes* them (which makes a crucial difference to McMahan):

> One . . . way in which an attacker might be unconstrained by the victim's right not to be attacked is that the right may be *overridden* by other morally signifi-cant considerations. For example, assuming that rights are not absolute, it may be permissible to attack someone who has a right not to be attacked if, for exam-ple, that is necessary to avoid violating other, stronger rights, or if it is a neces-sary means of preventing some terrible calamity that would involve significantly greater harm to others. In such a case, one may permissibly do to another what she has a right that one not do. When one thus permissibly acts against a right, I will say that one *infringes* that right, whereas when one impermissibly does what another has a right that one not do, one *violates* that right. Even though an agent acts permissibly in infringing a right, the victim is nonetheless wronged and may thus be owed compensation. (*KW*, 9–10)

On this conception, infringements are justified, while violations are *not*. But infringements are not *just*. This is not some peripheral viewpoint which McMa-han may consider renouncing, but rather a fundamental touchstone of his moral philosophy. He explicitly denies 'that one wrongs innocent bystanders only if one attacks them intentionally', insisting 'there is nothing . . . anywhere . . . in my writings, that says or implies that'.[39] For McMahan, a person can be liable only if '*his own* action has made it the case that to harm him . . . would not wrong him' (*KW*, 11, emphasis added). Toddlers *cannot* be liable to be killed on this view. And yet, despite insisting – contrary to Walzer – that those who are killed collaterally in war are *being wronged*, McMahan thinks that it *is not wrong* for toddlers to be killed in war. Such killing can be *right* because it might be necessary 'to avoid violating other, stronger rights' or to prevent 'some terrible calamity'. Bizarrely, however, McMahan has written a whole book titled *Killing in War* – the culmination of his moral thinking on war – without offering in it any elucidation as to why such bombing should be *right*. He seems to assume its rightness axiomatically, writing in a response to an earlier critique of mine, that

> [a] just war . . . is one in which the harms that must be intended as a means are justified on the ground that the victims are liable to suffer those harms, while the harms that are expected to be caused to those who are not liable to suffer them are unintended effects that are justified on the ground that they are the lesser evil. This is the way the term 'just war' has always been used within the just war tradition. What is new, perhaps, is the explicit recognition that all just wars require two distinct forms of justification: a liability justification for the intended harms and a lesser evil justification for the unintended harms caused to those who are not liable to suffer them.[40]

The reasoning here seems to *begin* with the assumption that it must be possible for wars to be just, and, *hence*, that it must be possible for the harming or killing of innocents with foresight to be morally permissible (see *KW*, 38). So how do we establish what *counts* as a lesser evil? Once again, we cannot help but take recourse to intuition.[41] And intuition – McMahan's intuition, or what he diagnoses as 'common sense intuition' (*KW*, 29) – suggests that it may be permissible to kill innocents 'as a foreseeable side effect . . . if it is intended to achieve good effects that exceed the bad by a *certain* margin' (*KW*, 29, emphasis added). Indeed, intuition suggests that it might even 'be permissible to cause the same amount of harm to the innocent as an *intended* means of achieving the same good effect' if doing so 'could be the means of achieving *much greater* good effects' (*KW*, 29, emphases added). In any case, the assumption is that there *is* a right answer to any moral question that might arise in the context of war; that the binary moral structure of just war theory is *sacrosanct*; and that it *must* be possible – at whatever cost – to press the material reality of war into the conceptual apparatus and binary moral structure that the just war mind has invented for it.

## MORAL CONUNDRUMS

In their attempts to justify killing the innocent, both Walzer and McMahan have, however, encountered moral conundrums that have left them puzzled.

While Walzer agonizes over the question of how it can be right to kill innocents *intentionally* in situations of supreme emergency, McMahan is at pains to reason his way through a fictitious scenario in which objectively justified (and thus non-liable) tactical bombers meet non-liable targets who are in a position to *fight back*. Once we have understood the nature of these puzzles, we will see that just war theory, as a theory grounded in individual rights and/or individual liability, fails to give us satisfactory moral answers even on its own terms; we will see that it is, in Cheyney Ryan's words, 'essentially morally incoherent'.[42]

So what is Walzer's conundrum? He thinks that political communities engaged in war may, under exceptional circumstances, decide to kill innocent civilians *intentionally*, rather than merely *with foresight*, namely when their 'deepest values and . . . collective survival are in imminent danger' (*AW*, 33). This is the supreme emergency exemption, an exemption from the moral and legal rule that the intentional killing of innocents in war – and elsewhere – is impermissible. Supreme emergency situations are unlike any other situation in the moral world, for they make it impossible for a moral agent *not* to commit a severe moral crime. The decision here is not just right *or* wrong; it is both.

Why is it sometimes right to kill innocents intentionally? Walzer's answer remains radically unclear. On the one hand, he states that something may be 'the right thing to do in utilitarian terms'.[43] A 'utilitarianism of extremity' imposes itself in these situations, as opposed to what he considers a 'rights normality' (*AW*, 40). In supreme emergencies, 'political leaders can hardly help but choose the *utilitarian* side of the dilemma' (*JUW*, 326). It is then 'morally defensible' (*AW*, 35) for them to break the rules and violate individual rights for utilitarian reasons. On the other hand, however, Walzer writes that '[s]upreme emergency is a *communitarian* doctrine' (*AW*, 45, emphasis added), and that the intentional killing of innocents in self-defence can be justified only because 'it is possible to live in a world where individuals are sometimes murdered, but a world where entire peoples are enslaved or massacred is literally unbearable' (*JUW*, 254). Indeed, at least in the context of supreme emergencies, it is not even clear if Walzer considers the overriding force to be a *moral* one at all. There are some challenges in politics, he suggests, which 'bring us under the rule of necessity (and necessity knows no rules)' (*JUW*, 254). This is from a thinker whose first chapter in his *Just and Unjust Wars* is explicitly directed 'Against Realism' (*JUW*, 3–20).

Supreme emergencies are, then, an existentially perplexing feature of the moral-political world. And they are deeply troubling for any moral theorist of war committed to the defence of rights: 'We find ourselves in that world less often than we think, certainly less often than we say; but whenever we are there, we experience the ultimate tyranny of war – and also, it might be argued, the ultimate incoherence of the theory of war' (*JUW*, 325). Walzer openly admits that he does not really know how to make sense of the rightness of killing innocents intentionally. As he writes,

> [I]t is not usually said of individuals in domestic society that they necessarily will or that they morally can strike out at innocent people, even in the supreme emergency of self-defense. They can only attack their attackers. But communities, in emergencies, seem to have different and larger prerogatives. I am not sure I can account for the difference, without ascribing to communal life a kind of transcendence that I don't believe it to have. (*JUW*, 254)

In other words, Walzer is *certain* that the 'deliberate murder' (*AW*, 46) of innocent people in war can be *right* in supreme emergencies – while also being wrong – but *uncertain* as to whether or not he can account for making this claim. For, as he knows very well, he cannot coherently do so within his allegedly non-utilitarian, rights-based framework. Rather, he *has to* rely on a 'utilitarianism of extremity' that he otherwise eschews.

Crucially, however, this 'ultimate incoherence' is not one of the moral theories of *war*, according to Walzer, but only of the moral theory of *supreme emergency war*.[44] 'In most wars', he claims, 'there are no supreme emergencies; the normal defense of rights holds unquestioned sway . . . (I leave aside questions about the side effects of legitimate military actions)' (*AW*, 46). But the trouble is that what is put in brackets here is precisely what renders his *entire* moral theory of war incoherent. Walzer relies on his revised version of the doctrine of double effect – with its added moral magic of double intention – to transform an innocent person's fully intact right not to be killed into a thing of the past. This is now a right that has come to be not just *overridden* – as it would be in supreme emergencies when the killing is done intentionally – but *eliminated*.[45] But Walzer never explains exactly how a killer's moral virtue and double intention can have this eliminative effect on rights. He simply assumes it. This is peculiar for a thinker who insists that '[i]ndividual rights (to life and liberty) underlie the most important judgments that we make about war' (*JUW*, 54); that '[a]t every point, the judgments we make (the lies we tell) are best accounted for if we regard life and liberty as something like absolute values' (*JUW*, xxiv); and that 'no one can be threatened with war or warred against, unless through some act of his own he has surrendered or lost his rights' (*JUW*, 135). According to Walzer, killing people in accordance with his version of the doctrine of double effect, while sad, repulsive and to be prevented even at very high cost, is *not* a moral crime, *not* a violation of rights. It is such a violation *only* when we have to rely on a 'utilitarianism of extremity' to make our moral case.

What Walzer fails to realize here is that his moral defence of killing innocents merely with foresight *already* relies on such a utilitarianism. He simply
refuses to accept this, insisting that the justification of ordinary warfare is not
utilitarian at all, as if judging the proportionality of negative effects that are
brought about with foresight, rather than intentionally, were somehow *not*
a utilitarian philosophical pursuit. On the one hand, Walzer writes that 'the
deliberate slaughter of innocent men and women cannot be justified simply
because it saves the lives of other men and women. . . . To kill 278,966 civilians (the number is made up) in order to avoid the deaths of an unknown but
probably larger number of civilians and soldiers is surely a fantastic, godlike,
frightening, and horrendous act' (*JUW*, 262). On the other hand, however,
he leaves no doubt that the kind of non-emergency warfare which results in
people being killed merely as a foreseeable side effect is not quite 'fantastic,
godlike, frightening and horrendous'; it is either just or not. But this is an illusion, because a moral defence of *double intention killing* could not even get
off the ground were it not accompanied by an insistence on the killing's being
proportionate. Walzer *cannot* justify the violence of war simply by insisting
that it serves to protect rights. For if he did that, then any innocent victim of
war could confront him with a very simple question: 'How about *my* rights?'
Walzer has no answer to this; in the end, he needs to do the maths.

While Walzer recognizes incoherence only in relation to supreme emergency situations, McMahan, at one point, seems to come close to realizing
that there might be an incoherence at the very heart of the theory of just war.
Here is the case that troubles him: 'Intuitively, it seems that innocent civilians threatened by the action of just combatants are not morally required to
submit passively to being killed but are permitted to engage in self-defense'
(*KW*, 46). And yet, McMahan finds it 'difficult to explain how the innocent
potential victims of morally justified action could be permitted to engage
in harmful defensive action against those whose moral justification both
exempts them from liability and guarantees that their action is the lesser evil,
impartially considered' (*KW*, 46). He is in quite some predicament: according to one intuition he has, the civilians *must* be in a position legitimately to
defend themselves; according to another, it *cannot* be the case that they are.
After all, their death is necessary for the bringing about of what is *objectively*
the lesser evil. But before we take a closer look at how McMahan tries to
resolve this conflict, let us examine the perplexing scenario in more detail –
partly because it might give readers unfamiliar with contemporary just war
theory a better sense of the nature of the beast, as it were, since the example
is helpfully emblematic:

> A tactical bomber fighting in a just war has been ordered to bomb a military
> facility located on the border of the enemy country. He knows that if he bombs
> the factory, the explosion will kill innocent civilians living just across the border

in a neutral country. But this would be a side effect of his action and would be proportionate to the contribution that the destruction of the facility would make to the achievement of the just cause. As he approaches, the civilians learn of his mission. They cannot flee in time but they have access to an anti-aircraft gun.[46]

When McMahan first introduced this example, he immediately pointed out that '[b]ecause the tactical bomber acts with justification, he will *merely infringe* the civilians' rights' – he will not *violate* them.[47] Despite this, however, he found it 'hard to believe' that 'the civilians may not kill [the tactical bomber] in self-defense', though he also expressed the caveat that the bomber's mission might be 'so important that [the civilians] are morally required to sacrifice themselves for the sake of its success'.[48] McMahan identified a 'symmetry' at the time: 'Intuitively it seems that, just as it is permissible for the civilians to kill the tactical bomber in self-defense, it is also permissible for the tactical bomber preemptively to kill the civilians in self-defense'.[49] And thus he thought he had come up with an 'intuitively satisfactory way' of dealing with this problem by '[establishing] the intuitive moral parity between the tactical bomber and the civilians. Neither party to the conflict is liable to be killed by the other, but each is justified in killing the other in self-defense'.[50] Restating his case 'in the language of rights', he wrote that '[the tactical bomber] is justified in dropping his bomb, though that would infringe the rights of the civilians; they are justified in killing him to prevent him from infringing their rights; but their killing him would infringe his rights; hence he is also justified in killing them to prevent them from infringing his right not to be killed'. Finally, he added to this that 'disinterested third parties may not intervene on behalf of either party to the conflict'.[51]

This was McMahan's first attempt at reconciling, at the level of theory, his conflicting intuitions on the matter.[52] He restated it in *Killing in War* (*KW*, 45–46) but seems to have become rather less certain about the matter. Not only had the earlier intuitive moral parity now turned into a '*rough* moral parity', but McMahan also admitted that his response to 'various objections' to the moral symmetry view was only '*probably* adequate' (*KW*, 48, emphases added). While he still thought that 'justice is silent with respect to their conflict' (*KW*, 49), he now wrote, more cautiously, that '*it is not implausible to suppose* that third parties must not intervene' (*KW*, 49, emphasis added). Indeed, 'To the extent that there are impartial considerations that favour intervention, they support intervention on behalf of the just combatants rather than on behalf of the civilians. For the action of the just combatants contributes to the achievement of a just cause, whereas the action of the civilians is *merely* self-preservative' (*KW*, 49, emphasis added).

A more recent essay – which appeared in a volume titled *How We Fight* – then saw a more decisive intellectual shift in favour of the tactical bomber.[53] McMahan now considers 'not obviously implausible' the view that that 'five innocent villagers could rationally consent to be killed as a side effect of saving the much greater number of civilians' – the number being 100 – whereas 'the 100 civilians could not rationally consent to be allowed to be killed in order that the five not be killed'.[54] Again, we are given an exposé of his conflicting intuitions on the matter:

> I am sympathetic to this intuition [that the villagers are permitted to shoot down the bombers' plane, killing the crew and thwarting the mission] and once sought to defend it. . . . But the more I have thought about the case, the more I have come to mistrust my intuitions about it. I now think that the balance of reasons favors the conclusion that the villagers are *not* morally permitted to kill the bombers in self-defense.[55]

One of the reasons McMahan offers is that – in his newly invented scenario, where the tactical bomber is accompanied by four crew members – '[s]elf-defense by the villagers would intentionally kill the same number of people it would save and would also prevent an additional 100 people from being saved'.[56] And he backs this up with yet another appeal to intuition: 'What is counterintuitive is the claim that, while the five villagers are permitted to kill the five bombers in self-defense, the bombers are not permitted to kill the villagers in self-defense'.[57] After all, what the bombers do is 'morally admirable, for they are exposing themselves to risk in order to do what they have most moral reason to do. Self-defense by the villagers, by contrast, would be based entirely on reasons of self-interest and would produce a significantly worse outcome, impartially considered'.[58] The formerly identified moral parity has simply evaporated; it has been replaced by a clear moral asymmetry between the two parties involved (much to the delight, one can imagine, of military strategists). While McMahan still believes that there are 'symmetrical defense cases', at least 'in principle', he 'no longer think[s]' that 'the conflict between the bombers and the villagers is such a case'.[59]

That innocent villagers are *not* permitted to use an anti-aircraft gun to shoot down a justified tactical bomber who is about to kill them seems to be the leading just war theorist's final verdict after all those years of conflicting intuitions and moral reflection. This verdict is based upon a rough calculation of how many people are going to die. And McMahan *has to* draw this conclusion, because his binary understanding of the morality of war cannot, ultimately, live with the fact that the problem is not resolved. In the end, impartial reason quite simply demands that those unfortunate innocents have to allow themselves to be killed. For if they *were* permitted to fight back, then we would have to conclude that the very notion of a just war in the world as we know it is ultimately incoherent. We would also have to conclude that, even on McMahan's own terms, there is a moral parity – importantly not just in terms of the odd individual case but, *writ large*, between the many non-liable victims of war and their many justified killers – that can neither be denied nor resolved. We would have to conclude that considerations of justice must, after all, remain silent. But this, of course, is not a possible conclusion for a committed analytic just war theorist to draw, as *it must never be the case that justice is silent in matters of war*.

Where does this analysis leave us? I think it leaves us in position similar to the one we were already in at the end of chapter 3. There, we noticed that it is impossible to defend sweatshops on grounds of voluntary choice, and that the pro-sweatshop case, in the end, collapses into a crude calculation of consequences (though one that is *inattentive* to consequences). Here, we now come to see that a moral defence of war grounded in rights and/or liability *also* collapses into a crude, intuitive calculation of consequences (though one that is similarly inattentive to consequences, as I will suggest in the following section). Even with the most inventive of philosophical and linguistic conjectures – whether the introduction of double intention as a necessary condition of justifying the negative side effects of war or the semantic displacement of rights *violations* through rights *infringements* – Walzer and McMahan cannot get around the fact that their rights-based case in defence of war is ultimately incoherent. This is so because, in the final analysis, both of them *must* ultimately rely upon a calculation of consequences, regardless of the extent to which they think the killer's good intentions are said to have a bearing on the precise way in which such measuring is to be done. The calculation of numbers is what does the ultimate work.

I say 'precise', but of course there is not a precise way of setting about this. Proportionality judgements in just war theory are *always* and *necessarily* crude; in fact, they never amount to more than a report of the respective theorist's intuitions about the matter. Here are some examples. McMahan thinks that '[p]roportionality requires, *roughly*, that the relevant bad effects attributable to the war must not be excessive in relation to the relevant good effects'.[60] What does 'roughly' mean, and what would it mean for bad effects to be 'excessive'? We surely deserve more clarity here, seeing that what is justified – ostensibly justified *with certainty* – is the killing and maiming of innocent people. But no clarification ever comes. Instead, we keep getting mere redescriptions of what has already been said: '*In general*, it is impermissible to kill morally innocent people as a means of saving other innocent people, unless the ratio of those saved to those killed is *very high*' (*KW*, 50, emphases added). For example, in the context of denying the innocent a right to fight back against the tactical bombers, McMahan articulates the view that when 'the ratio of innocent people saved to innocent people killed will be 20 to one', it *'seems* proportionate'.[61] Or take McMahan's *'crude* illustration . . . that an act of war that would prevent ten of one's own combatants from being killed but would kill one innocent civilian as a side effect would be proportionate, while an act that would kill ten civilians as a side effect but save only one combatant would not be' (*KW*, 31, emphasis added). A crude illustration it indeed is, and I challenge McMahan to offer one that is not. In response, he might of course point to a situation where what is needed to 'prevent the killing of several thousand noncombatants' is the killing of *'only a couple* of noncombatants as a side effect'.[62] But what is so negligible about killing 'a couple of' people, and what is so obvious about its being the right thing to do?[63] In the final analysis, what justifies the killing of non-liable parties in war is a proportionality calculation that *seems* to make sense to McMahan. It is a calculation that he finds *intuitively* plausible, on the explicitly stated assumption that, whenever we compare the killing of innocent people with the killing of (other) innocent people, 'the values compared are *obviously commensurable*: lives are weighed against lives and harms against harms' (*KW*, 31, emphasis added).

I am not at all sure that this is quite so obvious, but I am not concerned with demonstrating it one way or another. Nor do I wish to show that consequentialism is generally mistaken as a moral outlook. Rather, the crucial point here is that a defence of war based on rights and/or liability cannot do without considerations of proportionality, and that these considerations cannot work out in war's favour unless the theorist is prepared to accept the paradox that justified wars *violate* rights in order to *protect* rights,[64] and that they kill and maim *some* non-liable parties in order to stop or prevent the killing and maiming of some *other* non-liable parties. The theory of just war cannot get around this; it can only ever redescribe the incoherence. In the words of Ryan, 'attempts to make just war theory coherent . . . only solve one problem to create another, or rely on ever more arcane distinctions that have less and less relation to the reality of war they are describing'.[65] Just war theorists are condemned to go around in circles in their analytically desperate attempt to justify the violation of rights. They can, of course, present us with fictitious scenarios so drastic that the unyielding critic of just war – much like the unyielding critic of just torture we encountered in the previous chapter – must appear to be an absolutist monster. *Surely* it would be proportionate to kill one innocent person to save a million? I think we need to start thinking about what is wrong with asking this very question, instead of trying to answer it in a way that is 'surely right'. But my point *here* is that considerations of proportionality are, in the final analysis, necessarily insensitive to the very liberal idea that just war theory utilizes to get off the ground: that individuals have rights, and/or that they are not liable to be killed and maimed unless they *have made themselves* liable to be killed and maimed.

What I have described, then, is the ultimate incoherence of a theory of just war that pretends to be something other than a crude utilitarian moral calculus. Just war theorists cannot plausibly come to judge that a rights-defending war and/or a war waged against parties liable to be warred upon is *just* – at least not in the world as we know it – unless they can demonstrate that the war is *proportionate*. They will thus need to import a moral principle that is not about protecting *rights*, but about protecting *more* rights. They will need to *calculate*, and they will need to so do in a way that reduces violence, makes it measurable and runs roughshod over the very thing that theorists set out to protect – the rights and/or non-liabilities of individuals. And note that such calculations have no built-in limitation to what they are capable of justifying. Rather, those who engage in them seem to be prepared to plod along with *whatever* scenario they are presented with – or they present themselves with – as long as the ratio seems right. One simply cannot imagine that there might ever come a point at which just war theorists would put down their moral arms and say: 'To *this* I can no longer speak'. Rather, it seems more likely that they will *always* have something to say; they will *always* aim to construct unbreakable chains of analytic reasoning aimed at pressing the complex moral and political world into a rigid moral structure of right and wrong; and that the real-world versions of this sort of binary moral reasoning will *always* continue serving the purpose of justifying unspeakable horror. To my mind, this is an intellectually irresponsible approach to thinking normatively about matters of war, or indeed to thinking normatively, *period*. That this tradition of thought has been going for some two millennia is absolutely no reason to continue with it.

## THE UNEXAMINED LIBERALISM OF JUST WAR

In the previous sections, I have scratched only the surface of what is wrong with the theory of just war. While there *is* a place for immanent critique – not least to get through to those who might not pay attention to critical thinking that is articulated outside their conceptual comfort zone – we need to move beyond it. In this final section, I want to draw attention to some of the assumptions that defenders of just war make; assumptions that, once made explicit, reveal their unexamined liberalism. In so doing, I am not calling for anything unreasonable at all, only a paradigm shift that sees the disappearance of the idea of just war.

Just war theorists simply assume that it is methodologically unproblematic to individuate war.[66] They thus give moral prescriptions that, essentially, are aimed at ensuring the lesser evil with regard to particular wars and with regard to specific operations within particular wars. They reduce the world of war to a non-place that can be grasped, neatly, with just war theory's binary moral structure and tight conceptual apparatus. Whatever falls outside these narrow parameters – whether extreme power hierarchies, radical inequalities, economic interdependencies or ongoing histories of colonialism and coloniality – turns out to be unobservable if we look at it through the lens of a discourse obsessed with making binary moral judgements based on individual rights and/or liabilities. Indeed, it is wars themselves that fall outside the narrow epistemic parameters of contemporary analytic just war theory. The virtual obsession with killing sterilizes and renders invisible the horrors of war, whether endemic rape, mass displacement – including the displacement of single mothers who are so common in warzones – or long-term ramifications for development.

What is also rendered invisible is the fact that war is not some neutral instrument, but rather the sort of means that *creates its own ends*. Just war theorists give little (if any) thought to the fact that, as Laurie Calhoun writes, 'Powerful economic forces conspire to perpetuate the reigning state security model and foster the conditions for the incessant expansion of military institutions'; that '[t]wenty-first century war profiteers generate not only weapons, but also structures and supplies needed to rebuild lands devastated by bombing'; that '[e]ven pharmaceutical companies have come to profit from war, through the liberal dispensation of drugs to active duty soldiers and veterans upon their return home'; or that 'modern war has become the most profitable enterprise in the history of human society'.[67] All these things are of no concern to the analytic just war mind that is, rather, preoccupied with offering an abstract moral analysis of when killing and going to war is just. Would these not be crucial facts to consider, though, for moral thinkers who intend to make a valuable intellectual contribution to a world in which there is *less*, or *no*, war?

If it is the case that just war theorists are genuinely concerned with eliminating wars, or at least with reducing the number of wars in the world, then they would have to broaden their epistemic and moral horizons; it simply will not do to keep painting the same old picture – a picture that always captures that one dramatic scene where the unjust aggressors turn up, from nowhere, to launch their vicious attack. It will not do because it cannot help us to understand the material object of analysis. Take, for instance, McMahan's framing of the 'just combatant': 'The probability that a just combatant will kill an innocent bystander is in general considerably lower than the probability that an unjust combatant will kill a just combatant or other innocent person, in part because . . . just combatants generally strive *not* to kill innocent bystand- ers, just as drivers take constant care to avoid harming pedestrians and other drivers' (*KW*, 40).

Are we to infer from this that dropping a bomb is like driving a car? That, as long as you are being conscientious, and even if you end up 'infringing' people's rights, there is nothing wrong with it? War is framed as an *innocent* activity here, as something perfectly well integrated and integratable into our civilized everyday life; a thing that more or less every adult does do and/or is capable of doing but needs to learn how to do *properly* – like driving. And if our liberal politicians *were* to learn to do war properly, perhaps this could address the problem that '[t]he retention rate for young officers [in the United States] is . . . alarmingly low' (*KW*, 76). It is clear that the driver analogy – much like analogies involving trolleys running towards people caught on tracks or fat men falling off cliffs on top of people equipped with vaporizers[68] – can serve only to dehistoricize, depoliticize and ultimately distort and euphemize our perception of war. But it cannot help us *understand* war.

Reading contemporary just war theory – with its plethora of outlandish thought experiments – one might get the impression that its proponents take little interest in the material object of their analysis. Or, worse, that real wars sometimes serve as some sort of imperfect heuristic device to elucidate one's theoretical interests. Mostly, however, real wars are an inconvenience to the rigid just war framework. With all their historical and political complexity, let alone their radical uncertainties, they can only get into the way of the theorist's attempt to unearth some deep, universal moral truth. For just war theory to work, wars consequently need to be replaced with something else, something fabricated in the theorist's mind. Indeed, this method of eliminat- ing the object of inquiry from one's moral analysis is sometimes even explic- itly justified. Helen Frowe's account is a beautiful example:

> [U]sing fictional examples helps us identify principles that can be obscured by the complexities of historical cases. For example, many people have firm views about the morality of the United States. Using a historical example that concerns the actions of the United States might thus throw up more questions than it solves if we are tempted to evaluate those actions on the basis of what we already know or believe about a particular case. When we're trying to identify general rules or principles, we want to abstract from features that might exert an illicit influence on our judgements. Fictional cases help us to do this.[69]

Frowe thinks that '[b]y abstracting away from real life examples, we are able to focus on what strike us as salient or interesting features of a moral prob- lem for the purposes of answering a specific question, and this will allow us to produce more informed and lucid responses to new occurrences of war, or to new calls to go to war'.[70] What does *not* occur to her, however – nor would this be noticed by McMahan or any other just war theorist following this procedure – is that the attempt to delete history and politics from the moral picture is *itself* a deeply political manoeuvre. It is political because it frames war in a particular way, as a social practice that can – indeed *must* – be analysed on a case-by-case basis, in a historical and political vacuum and in clinical isolation from the broader context and power relations within which it occurs. To assume that we can neatly divide the world into unjust aggressors and just defenders *of course* reflects a prior political commitment, namely the assumption that it is possible – empirically and normatively – to abstract from the way in which individual and collective agents are interconnected in complex and hierarchical global structures.

The liberalism that underlies this move – which presupposes morally responsible but otherwise disconnected agents that are operating on some level-playing field – is taken to be an axiomatic political truth. Indeed, just war theory's post-Walzerian move towards using fictional scenarios represents the zenith of this unexamined political commitment at the level of methodology. It is a commitment that reduces and distorts the material world to whatever can be captured by the conceptual just war apparatus, pressed into its binary moral structure and grasped by theorists at the level of what they call 'intuition'. This problem of 'false erasure'[71] is located at two levels. First, it is a mistake to think that we can understand wars unless we understand their histories, politics and structural contexts. Second, it is a mistake to think that we can think morally about war in a way that is depoliticized. A related mistake, of course, is thinking that the prescriptions that just war theorists derive from their flawed methodology can speak to the world of liberal-democratic politics in a way which satisfies just war theory's purported critical ambitions of reducing the number of wars in the world. This is just war theory's inadvertent political realism – that it can serve only to perpetuate war, rather than to challenge it by way of offering a critical analysis of the very conditions under which war keeps thriving.[72]

A final note on thought experiments. The assumption that they are politically neutral simply because they do not mention politics might well be one of the crassest and most vexing illusions entertained by many contemporary moral and political philosophers. I am not sure what makes it possible for people who dedicate their lives to reading books and exchanging ideas to make such an assumption. Perhaps it has to do with the epistemic closure that might come with being part of an academic circle in which everyone reads the same texts, makes the same assumptions and asks the same questions. Perhaps there comes a point at which one genuinely believes that thought experiments that do not mention politics are apolitical; they can help us find out some otherwise inaccessible objective moral truth that can *then* be used to speak to what was erased – falsely – from the moral picture. But however that may be, in the end, this approach results in nothing more than the mass production of rather complicated crossword puzzles, designed to find out, in strictly binary fashion, who is liable to be killed, or who can be killed collaterally or even intentionally because killing them would be a lesser evil. In producing these crossword puzzles, just war theorists not only keep whizzing around in circles but also help to make sure that, as Judith Butler writes, 'wars become permissible forms of criminality'.[73] They are intellectually irresponsible.

*Chapter 6*

# Complicity

Kazuo Ishiguro's novel, *Never Let Me Go*, is set in England in the late 1990s. It is narrated by Kathy, a thirty-one-year-old woman who – she tells us – has been a carer for eleven years and is going to continue being a carer for eight more months (this is what they have told her). As the reader finds out later, Kathy is a clone who has been created so that her organs can be harvested, and so are the people she has grown up with. The script of their lives is quickly told: they first go to a school, Hailsham, a place where they are taught by the guardians and where they spend every single minute of their childhood and teens; then they live in the Cottages for a year or two, waiting for what will happen next; then they work as the carers of people who are donating; and then they become donors themselves. Finally, they complete. This usually happens after their fourth donation, at the latest.

One of the things that is most striking about Ishiguro's violent dystopia is that it does not require any *physical* violence to keep itself going. There are no beatings, no handcuffs, no prisons, no police, no deportations. Indeed, there is an acute sense in which the students who go on to be carers and donors subject themselves to whatever happens to them *voluntarily*. At no point are they threatened or coerced. And yet there is not a single moment where Kathy and her friends entertain the very possibility of *resistance*; it simply would not occur to them to reject the bloody script and break out. They can move about freely; they can enter friendships and have sex; they can read *Daniel Deronda* and *War and Peace*; they can write and produce art; they even have money to spend. But they literally *cannot* choose simply to *go*. They cannot run away, hide or kill themselves. Rather, they simply follow the prescribed motions: sheep-like, mechanically, one step at a time. The clones' lives are but one road to death, and the suffering they endure on the final stretch is immense. While they might be only clones, they can feel pain just like the rest of us.

One of the things that struck me most about *Never Let Me Go* was a passage near the end, when Kathy is caring for her friend Tommy, who is nearing the point of completion. Kathy and Tommy find themselves in the house of Miss Emily, their former head teacher at Hailsham. They ask her why Miss Lucy, another teacher of theirs at the time, had suddenly disappeared from Hailsham (which no longer exists). Miss Emily explains:

> Why? She meant well, I'm sure of that. I can see you were fond of her. She had the makings of an excellent guardian. But what she was wanting to do, it was too *theoretical*. We had run Hailsham for many years, we had a sense of what could work, what was best for the students in the long run, beyond Hailsham. Lucy Wainright was idealistic, nothing wrong with that. But she had no grasp of practicalities. You see, we were able to give you something, something which even now no one will ever take from you, and we were able to do that principally by *sheltering* you. Hailsham would not have been Hailsham if we hadn't. Very well, sometimes that meant that we kept things from you, lied to you. Yes, in many ways we *fooled* you. But we sheltered you during those years, and we gave you your childhoods. Lucy was well-meaning enough. But if she'd had it her way, your happiness at Hailsham would have been shattered. Look at you both now! I'm so proud to see you both. You built your lives on what we gave you. You wouldn't be who you are today if we'd not protected you. You wouldn't have become absorbed in your lessons, you wouldn't have lost yourselves in your art and your writing. Why should you have done, knowing what lay in store for each of you? You would have told us it was all pointless, and how could we have argued with you? So she had to go.[1]

Hailsham was justified by Miss Emily as an alternative to a more obviously inhumane and brutalizing way of 'growing' the clones. For her, it was a humane intervention: she saved Kathy and Tommy (and many other clones) from what would otherwise have been – in her terms, at least – a far worse fate. It is clear that Miss Emily's defence in many ways *fails* to be analogous to defences of just liberal violence. Unlike defenders of war and torture, for example, she is not justifying *physical* violence. And unlike sweatshop defenders, who are against regulating sweatshops, she is trying to introduce reforms to make things more 'humane'.[2] And yet there are parallels. For much *like* defenders of just liberal violence, Miss Emily is *reducing* violence. Not only does she fail to see the violence of Hailsham; she is also blinded to the violence that is unfolding right in front of her. She is speaking *the language of moral justification* and to two people on their road to death: Tommy, who is already in the process of being slowly executed, and Kathy, who will be killed soon. These two might just be tortured, exploited bodies, but, to Miss Emily's mind, their lives are eminently locatable within a moral framework that allows us to make clear and meaningful distinctions between right and wrong. There is a violence in her very attempt to moralize; a violence in the words she speaks.

Miss Emily also reduces agency to *reactive* agency. She puts forward an argument according to which what matters is that one *acts rightly regardless* of how awful things get. The social structure within one is forced to 'act' is axiomatically accepted as immutable, beyond the reach of agency. Just as it would not occur to Kathy and Tommy that they might at least *try* to resist, it would not occur to Miss Emily either. There is, however, a crucial difference. Kathy and Tommy *cannot* resist; it is not part of their being. They are *programmed* to not be able to resist. Miss Emily, on the contrary, has *chosen* not to resist. One might of course be tempted to think that resistance is not possible for Miss Emily *either*, since she too – like the clones – operates in a world where the justness or at least inevitability of the clones' exploitation is beyond question; where the possibility of a clone refusing their purpose – or someone else doing so on their behalf – falls outside the spectrum of the thinkable. If they cannot resist, how could she? And yet there seems to be a difference, a sense in which Miss Emily's ignorance is – perhaps – *culpable*. For Kathy and Tommy have been brought up in (necessary) ignorance of their purpose, she has not. They have been raised to resign themselves to their fate once they knew what it was, she has not. I think the novel also suggests that the clones are a relatively recent phenomenon, so Miss Emily grew up and was educated in a world without this form of exploitation and then saw it introduced; whereas Kathy, Tommy and Ruth grew up in a world where clone exploitation was, to use a term we encountered in the defence of sweatshops, a 'done deal'. So perhaps it is indeed the case that Miss Emily has *chosen* not to resist and not to 'ask about [her] social and cultural order what it needs [her] and others not to know'.[3] What makes her response to Kathy and Tommy so unbearable is not just her failing to resist and ask pressing questions though; it is her being self-righteous in so doing. She is a moral missionary who somehow manages to celebrate not only her own moral 'agency' but Kathy's and Tommy's too – the agency they have not got. Seeing them in front of her makes her *proud*.

Miss Emily reduces perspective then. She looks at the world exclusively through the lens of her own virtue, mythologizing Hailsham and disconnecting it from its broader social structure. By reconstructing Hailsham as a shelter, and its guardians as agonized heroes, she casts a veil of ignorance over the essential function performed by this 'school': to manufacture ignorant, obedient, exploitable bodies. Indeed, it is almost as if the protection once offered to Kathy and Tommy on the back of Miss Emily's virtue *justifies* what is happening to them now. She effectively tells them – referring to them as 'poor creatures' at one point – that they are collateral damage: mutilated and terminated, yes, but fortunate enough to be treated with respect and good intentions along the way. It is an agonizing read.

These reductions point to Miss Emily's acute and inevitable failure to sustain a moral argument that does not collapse into nothingness. They also point to the inadvertent function she performs within a broader structure of complicity, as a reluctant, regretful guardian of a shameful world. She might have the best of intentions, but she ends up supporting 'them', the invisible, brutal powers that be; the irremovable ones; the slaughterers. What this means, of course, is that nothing will ever change in a world populated by well-intentioned, complicit reformers; people who occupy responsible positions in a society whose 'unjust background conditions' are axiomatically accepted as immutable. The maiming and killing will simply go on; critique will be choked; resistance shattered. To challenge the smooth workings of tyranny would require not only overcoming one's obsession with making arguments about individual responsibility but also comprehending, confronting and resisting the hierarchical and oppressive social structures within which these individuals are placed; to be *defiant*, in theory and practice. Perhaps, then, defenders of just liberal violence seem rather like Miss Emily in *Never Let Me Go*. They find it easier to moralize in the face of horror than to look horror in the face.

If my analysis is broadly right, their justifications of violence are wholly inadequate. The liberal framework from which it derives is obsessed with individuals, blind to social hierarchies and interconnectedness, and fanatically fixated on pressing the complex material world into a binary moral structure of right and wrong. In failing to take a step back and reflect critically on the defects of their framework of analysis, however, defenders of just liberal violence contribute to a moral climate characterized by a pervasive amnesia about the histories, structures and politics of violence. They are indeed Miss Emily's. It is our common task to resist this way of thinking; to be *anti*-complicit.

# Notes

## ACKNOWLEDGEMENTS

1  I do not need to tell you how particularly special you are. Thank you for everything you – including, of course, the legendary Stefan Platte – have done for me. Thank you also for the lovely present some of you once 'organized' for me. I will take it with me wherever I go.

## CHAPTER 1

1  For the sake of readability, I will – throughout this book – refrain from putting certain words such as 'just', 'unjust', 'justified', 'unjustified', 'just war theorist', 'innocent', 'non-liable', 'collateral' and 'choose'/'choice' in scare quotes (other than in exceptional circumstances, or when I introduce specific terms such as 'justified interrogational torture situation'). The reader may – rightly – find this extremely alienating at times. See also note 6 in my third chapter on this matter.

2  For an excellent exploration of complicity, including the complicity of the academic, see Thomas Docherty, *Complicity: Critique between Collaboration and Commitment* (London: Rowman and Littlefield, 2016).

3  I am taking this formulation from Todd May, *Nonviolent Resistance: A Philosophical Introduction* (Cambridge: Polity Press, 2015), viii.

4  I am grateful to an anonymous reviewer of my proposal for this suggestion.

5  This formulation is another reviewer's.

6  I will mention some of them in the notes.

7  I am not making this up for rhetorical effect. For relevant citations, see chapter 3.

8  For the purpose of my argument – which is concerned with violence purportedly committed in defence of human rights and/or in order to minimize human

suffering – there is no need to distinguish between 'liberal' and 'libertarian' defences of sweatshops. Also see chapter 3, note 3.

9  See Bob Brecher, *Torture and the Ticking Bomb* (Oxford: Wiley-Blackwell, 2007). Also see Bob Brecher and Michael Neu, 'Intellectual Complicity in Torture', in *Exploring Complicity: Concept, Cases and Critique*, ed. Afxentis Afxentiou, Robin Dunford and Michael Neu (London: Rowman & Littlefield International, 2017), 143–60.

10  Steinhoff also defends other forms of what he considers 'self-defensive torture', but I am concerned here primarily with interrogational torture. See Uwe Steinhoff, *On the Ethics of Torture* (Albany, NY: Suny Press, 2013).

11  Michael Walzer, *Just and Unjust Wars: A Moral Argument with Historical Illustrations*, 4th ed. (New York: Basic Books, 2006).

12  See, for example, Jeff McMahan, 'The Morality of Occupation', *Loyola of Los Angeles International and Comparative Law Review* 31, 7 (2009): 15–19; and Michael Walzer, *Arguing about War* (New Haven, CT, and London: Yale University Press, 2004), 161.

13  A notable exception is Walzer's treatment of 'supreme emergencies' – Walzer, *Just and Unjust Wars*, 251–68; and *Arguing about War*, 33–50. I will analyse it in chapter 5.

14  Afxentis Afxentiou, Robin Dunford and Michael Neu, 'Introducing Complicity', in *Exploring Complicity*, ed. Afxentiou, Dunford and Neu, 11.


# CHAPTER 2

1  According to Todd May, whom I follow here, 'A structure is nothing more than a particular arrangement of social, political, cultural, and economic practices', and 'a violent structure is an arrangement of practices that make it difficult for certain people to conduct their lives as though they mattered' – Todd May, *Nonviolent Resistance: A Philosophical Introduction* (Cambridge: Polity Press, 2015), 56.

2  Uwe Steinhoff, *On the Ethics of Torture* (Albany: State University of New York Press), 9.

3  For a critical analysis, see Scott Veitch, *Law and Irresponsibility: On the Legitimation of Human Suffering* (Abingdon: Routledge-Cavendish, 2007), 13–24.

4  Johan Galtung, 'Violence, Peace, and Peace Research', *Journal of Peace Research* 6, 3 (1969): 171. Galtung 'see[s] violence as avoidable insults to basic human needs, and more generally to *life*, lowering the real level of needs satisfaction below what is potentially possible' (emphasis in the original) – Johan Galtung, 'Cultural Violence', *Journal of Peace Research* 27, 3 (1990): 292. For a critique of Galtung's view of violence, see C. A. J. Coady, 'The Idea of Violence', *Journal of Applied Philosophy* 3, 1 (1986): 3–19. A defence of Galtung's work against Coady's charges if offered by Mark Vorobej, 'Structural Violence', *The Canadian Journal of Peace and Conflict Studies* 40, 2 (2008): 84–98. Also see May, *Nonviolent Resistance*, 34–59. Readers interested in further accounts that reject a reduction of violence to physical violence are pointed towards: Newton Garver, 'What Violence Is', *Nation*, 24 June (1968), reprinted in modified form in Vittorio Bufacchi, *Violence:*

*A Philosophical Anthology* (New York and Basingstoke: Palgrave MacMillan, 2009), 170–82; James Gilligan, *Violence: Reflections on a National Epidemic* (New York: Vintage Books, 1997), 191–208; John Harris, 'The Marxist Conception of Violence', *Philosophy & Public Affairs* 3, 2 (1974): 192–220; Steven Lee, 'Poverty and Violence', *Social Theory and Practice* 22, 1 (1996): 67–82; and Jamil Salmi, *Violence and Democratic Society* (London: Zed, 1993).

5 For an in-depth exploration of such implicatedness in relation to military humanitarian intervention, see Robin Dunford and Michael Neu, *Just War and the Responsibility to Protect: A Critique* (London: Zed, forthcoming). Other critical work in this field includes Garrett Wallace Brown and Alexandra Bohm, 'Introducing *Jus ad Bellum* as a Cosmopolitan Approach to Humanitarian Intervention', *European Journal of International Relations* 22, 4 (2016): 897–919; Laurie Calhoun, *War and Delusion: A Critical Examination* (Basingstoke: Palgrave MacMillan, 2013), 67–85; Hilary Charlesworth, 'International Law: A Discipline of Crisis', *Modern Law Review* 65, 3 (2002): 377–92; and Jonathan Graubart, 'R2P and Pragmatic Liberal Interventionism: Values in the Service of Interests', *Human Rights Quarterly* 35, 1 (2013): 69–90.

6 Bob Brecher, *Torture and the Ticking Bomb* (Oxford: Wiley-Blackwell, 2007), 72.

7 Galtung, 'Cultural Violence', 294.

8 Laleh Khalili, *Time in the Shadows: Confinement in Counterinsurgencies* (Stanford, CA: Stanford University Press, 2013), 66.

9 Ibid., 67.

10 I am not suggesting here that this is true only of *modern* law, of course.

11 Veitch, *Law and Irresponsibility*. Also see Antony Anghie, *Imperialism, Sovereignty and the Making of International Law* (Cambridge: Cambridge University Press, 2004). Anghie traces the 'colonial origins of international law', arguing that 'these origins create a set of structures that continually repeat themselves at various stages in the history of international law' (ibid., 3). He diagnoses 'an international law which, even when it innovates, follows the familiar pattern of the colonial encounter, the division between civilized and uncivilized, the developed and the developing, a division that international law seeks to define and maintain using extraordinarily flexible and continuously new techniques' (ibid., 244).

12 Veitch, *Law and Irresponsibility*, 19.

13 Madeleine Albright, quoted in Sheldon Richman, 'Iraqi Sanctions: Were They Worth It?' *Global Policy Forum*, January 2004, accessed 7 August 2016, https://www.globalpolicy.org/component/content/article/170/41952.html. I was alerted to this through Veitch, *Law and Irresponsibility*, 13. Albright was U.S. ambassador to the UN when she made this comment in May 1996 and was subsequently appointed Secretary of State in 1997.

14 Quoted in Veitch, *Law and Irresponsibility*, 20.

15 Mahmood Mamdani, 'Responsibility to Protect or Right to Punish', *Journal of Intervention and Statebuilding* 4, 1 (2010): 59.

16 Brian Orend, *The Morality of War*, 2nd ed. (Peterborough: Broadview Press, 2013), 86, emphasis in the original. For an argument according to which the 2003 Iraq war *was* a morally justified humanitarian intervention, see Fernando R. Tesón, 'Ending Tyranny in Iraq', *Ethics & International Affairs* 19, 2 (2005): 1–20.

17  Orend, *The Morality of War*, 101. I write 'might have acted justly' because Orend's judgement on the matter is inconclusive. While he thinks that 'Saddam's regime had no right not to be attacked', he also points out that 'one can sometimes have the right to do something which it's still not wise, or prudent, or smart, to do'. His 'overall judgement is that it's deeply questionable whether America's going to war in 2003 was the best way not merely to remove Saddam but also to create pro-rights realization for the Iraqi people' (ibid., 103).

18  Ibid., 83 and 103.

19  Iraq Body Count, *A Dossier of Civilian Casualties in Iraq 2003–2005*, 12 July 2005, accessed 29 April 2017, https://www.iraqbodycount.org/analysis/reference/press-releases/12/. While note 16 refers to a formulation in the second edition of Orend's book, which came out in 2013, exactly the same formulation is already present in Brian Orend, *The Morality of War* (Peterborough: Broadview Press, 2006), 82.

20  Judith Butler, *Frames of War* (London: Verso, 2010), ix–x, emphasis in the original.

21  Brecher, *Torture and the Ticking Bomb*, 88.

22  Perhaps it would be more accurate to say that people in such situations do not in fact 'choose'. Rather, they merely 'pick'.

23  For an altogether different approach that celebrates autonomy – in the context of peasant struggles – as engagement in transnational resistance and solidarities, see Robin Dunford, *The Politics of Transnational Peasant Struggle: Resistance, Rights and Democracy* (London: Rowman & Littlefield International, 2016). Dunford asks 'how different, small-scale spaces of resistance can connect together to form a powerful, counter-hegemonic global movement' and has written his book 'from a position of solidarity with their struggles' (ibid., 6 and 8). Dunford's book puts 'practices of resistance and agents of change at the heart of world politics' (ibid., 11).

24  Compare Richard Seymour, *The Liberal Defence of Murder* (London: Verso, 2008). Seymour tries to 'explain a current of irrational thought that supports military occupation and murder in the name of virtue and decency' (ibid., 1).

25  Fritz Allhoff, 'A Defense of Torture: Separation of Cases, Ticking Time-Bombs, and Moral Justification', *International Journal of Applied Philosophy* 19, 2 (2005): 261.

26  Helen Frowe, *The Ethics of War and Peace: An Introduction* (Abingdon: Routledge, 2011), 60. For Frowe's similarly shallow and inconclusive comment on the 2001 Afghanistan war, read the following page too, where Frowe states that 'the Afghan government *seemed* to have rendered itself liable to attack by harbouring terrorists', only to then add that 'whilst a war fought for the wrong reasons *might* not wrong the Taliban . . . it *could* still wrong the combatants who are being asked to fight against the Taliban' (ibid., 61, emphases added). Elsewhere she writes that, 'Given the rather low prospect of success . . . it *seems unlikely* that the war in Afghanistan was, all things considered just, even if pursuing those responsible for the 9/11 attacks provided a just cause' (emphasis added) – Helen Frowe, 'War and Intervention', in *Issues in Political Theory*, ed. Catriona McKinnon, 3rd ed. (Oxford: Oxford University Press, 2015), 231–32.

27  While torture defender Uwe Steinhoff *is* concered with what is going on in practice, he does not allow his political understanding to inform his philosophical defence of torture, as we shall see in chapter 4.

28  Frowe, *The Ethics of War and Peace*, 134.

29  Jeff McMahan, 'The Basis of Moral Liability to Defensive Killing', *Philosophical Issues* 15, 1 (2005): 387. McMahan has taken this example from Judith Jarvis Thomson but has modified it. For a similar scenario that – among other changes – replaces the sun umbrella with a ray gun, see Frowe, *The Ethics of War and Peace*, 15.

30  McMahan, 'The Basis of Moral Liability', 388.

31  Steinhoff, *The Ethics of Torture*, 42.

32  Benjamin Powell, *Out of Poverty: Sweatshops in the Global Economy* (Cambridge: Cambridge University Press, 2014), 68–69.

33  The cover picture can easily be found through Internet search engines.

34  But see Walzer, *Arguing about War* (New Haven, CT, and London: Yale University Press, 2004), 160, where he (very) briefly makes the case that 'Saddam's war is unjust' (before arguing that American's war is unjust too). It may be worth pointing out in this context that those who wage 'our' wars do not tend to *call* them wars. The rebranding exercises have resulted in fanciful euphemisms: 'Operation Allied Force' for the Kosovo war (1999); 'Operation Enduring Freedom' for the Afghanistan war (2001); 'Operation Iraqi Freedom' for the Iraq war (2003) and 'Operation Unified Protector' for the North Atlantic Treaty Organization (NATO) war against Libya (2011).

35  For interesting challenges to this tendency, see Fabre, who argues that 'the very deprived have a just cause for going to war against the affluent if the latter are in breach of their negative and positive duties of justice towards them' – Cécile Fabre, *Cosmopolitan War* (Oxford: Oxford University Press, 2015), 103; Kaspar Lippert-Rasmussen, 'Global Justice and Redistributive Wars', *Law, Ethics and Philosophy* 1, 1 (2013): 65–86; and Gerhard Øverland, '602 and One Dead: On Contribution to Global Poverty and Liability to Defensive Force', *European Journal of Philosophy* 21, 2 (2013): 279–99.

36  Orend, *The Morality of War*, 37.

37  For illuminating explorations, see Laurie Calhoun, *We Kill Because We Can: From Soldiering to Assassination* (London: Zed, 2015); and, particularly, Grégoire Chamayou, *Drone Theory* (London: Penguin, 2015).

38  As Graubart writes, 'Liberal Democratic systems have proven readily compatible with aggressive, self-serving military-security policies' – Graubart, 'R2P', 77. At least three of the thinkers whose works I criticize in this book – Uwe Steinhoff, Michael Walzer and Jeff McMahan – are, as we shall see, aware of this.

39  Luban makes this point powerfully: 'Now, [the torturer] is not a cruel man or a sadistic man or a coarse, insensitive, brutish man. The torturer is instead a conscientious public servant, heroic the way that New York firefighters were heroic, willing to do desperate things only because the plight is desperate and so many innocent lives are weighing on the public servant's conscience. The time bomb clinches the great divorce between torture and cruelty; it placates liberals, who put cruelty first' – David Luban, 'Liberalism, Torture, and the Ticking Bomb', in *Torture, Power, and Law* (Cambridge: Cambridge University Press, 2014), 57. On the 'suffering servant', also see Michael Walzer, 'Political Action: The Problem of Dirty Hands', *Philosophy and Public Affairs* 2, 2 (1973): 177. For a critique of Walzer's 'dirty hands' account,

see Bob Brecher and Michael Neu, 'Intellectual Complicity in Torture', in *Exploring Complicity: Concept, Cases and Critique*, ed. Afxentis Afxentiou, Robin Dunford and Michael Neu (London: Rowman & Littlefield International, 2017), 143–60.

40  Judith Butler, 'Can One Lead a Good Life in a Bad Life? Adorno Prize Lecture', *Radical Philosophy* 176 (November/December 2012): 10.

41  Domenico Losurdo, *Liberalism: A Counter-History* (London and New York: Verso, 2014), 5.

42  Butler, 'Can One Lead a Good Life in a Bad Life?' 15. This has implications for how we ought to think and write about the human condition, as MacIntyre has rightly emphasized: 'These two related sets of facts, those concerning our vulnerabilities and afflictions and those concerning the extent of our dependence on particular others are so evidently of singular importance that it might seem that no account of the human condition whose authors hoped to achieve credibility could avoid giving them a central place' – Alasdair MacIntyre, *Dependent Rational Animals: Why Human Beings Need the Virtues* (London: Gerald Duckworth, 1999), 1. MacIntyre goes on to ask the crucial question of 'what difference to moral philosophy [it would] make, if we were to treat the facts of vulnerability and affliction and the related facts of dependence as central to the human condition' (ibid., 4).

43  Ramón Grosfoguel, 'The Epistemic Decolonial Turn', *Cultural Studies* 21, 2/3 (2007): 215 and 216. I am grateful to Robin Dunford for pointing me in the direction of decolonial thinking. While I have little knowledge of the decolonial literature and thus cannot make it central to my argument, my initial impression that defenders and sympathizers of just liberal violence might be well advised to take an extensive and open-minded look at it. See, for example, Arturo Escobar, 'Beyond the Third World: Imperial Globality, Global Coloniality and Anti-Globalisation Global Movements', *Third World Quarterly* 25, 1 (2004): 207–30; Walter D. Mignolo, *The Darker Side of Western Modernity: Global Futures, Decolonial Options* (Durham, NC: Duke University Press, 2011); and Anibal Quijano, 'Coloniality and Modernity/Rationality', *Cultural Studies* 21, 2/3 (2007): 168–78.

44  Ikechi Mgbeoji, 'The Civilised Self and the Barbaric Other: Imperial Delusions of Order and the Challenges of Human Security', *Third World Quarterly* 27, 5 (2006): 855–56. Mgbeoji elaborates: 'Inspired by certain ideological fundamentalisms and unyielding certitude, the cycle and pattern of a civilised self and a barbaric other is repeatedly re-enacted by colonialism, cultural imperialism, military depredations, and an unrelenting political and economic interference in the domestic affairs of the global South . . . . [T]he history of the relations between the "civilised self" and the "barbaric other" reveals a common and persistent pattern of domination of the "barbaric" by the "civilised", who nonetheless profess liberal ideals' (ibid., 856).

45  See, for example, Garry Leech, *Capitalism: A Structural Genocide* (London: Zed, 2012). May suggests that 'in situations of structural violence there is often a lot of self-deception that prevents people from seeing clearly their contribution to violence' – May, *Nonviolent Resistance*, 57.

46  These violent responses may then play their own role in breeding further violence in the future. See Dunford and Neu, *Just War and the Responsibility to Protect*.

47   The '[U.S.] military-industrial complex has promoted an international cycle of war and poverty' – Vijay Mehta, *The Economics of Killing: How the West Fuels War and Poverty in the Developing World* (London: Pluto, 2012), 40.

48   Iris Marion Young, 'Responsibility and Global Justice: A Social Connection Model', *Social Philosophy and Policy* 21, 1 (2006): 119. An excellent philosophical exploration of the relationship of social structures to moral agency is Alasdair MacIntyre, 'Social Structures and Their Threats to Moral Agency', *Philosophy* 74, 3 (1999): 311–29.

49   Young, 'Responsibility and Global Justice', 102.

50   Ibid., 113.

51   Seymour, *The Liberal Defence of Murder*, 217.

52   Michael Walzer, *Just and Unjust Wars*, 4th ed. (New York: Basic Books, 2006), 3–20.

53   For a classic statement of political realism, see Hans Morgenthau's 'six principles': Hans J. Morgenthau, *Politics among Nations: The Struggle for Power and Peace*, 7th ed., revised by Kenneth W. Thompson and W. David Clinton (New York: McGraw-Hill, 2006), 4–16.

54   For an extensive analysis, for example, of the ways in which those who are called upon to launch military interventions to save people from being slaughtered are at the same time heavily implicated in the production of the very circumstances that are said to justify these interventions, see Dunford and Neu, *Just War and the Responsibility to Protect*.

55   Mamdani, 'Responsibility to Protect or Right to Punish?' 60–61.

56   Losurdo, *Liberalism*, 7.

57   Robin Dunford, 'Toward a Decolonial Global Ethics', *Journal of Global Ethics*, DOI: 10.1080/17449626.1373140, 2017.

58   We should follow Butler here: 'Although certain liberal principles remain crucial to this analysis, including equality and universality, it remains clear that liberal norms presupposing an ontology of discrete identity cannot yield the kinds of analytic vocabularies we need for thinking about global interdependency and the interlocking networks of power and position in contemporary life. Part of the very problem of contemporary political life is that not everyone counts as a subject' – Butler, *Frames of War*, 31.

# CHAPTER 3

1   In writing this chapter, I have benefitted from Maeve McKeown's generous advice.

2   Benjamin Powell, *Out of Poverty: Sweatshops in the Global Economy* (Cambridge: Cambridge University Press, 2014), 3. I abbreviate *Out of Poverty* as *OP* hereinafter. Unless otherwise indicated, emphases in citations from *OP* are in the original.

3   Powell, as well as Matt Zwolinski, might argue that calling their case 'liberal', rather than 'liberal', is a misnomer. The relations between liberalism and libertarianism, like those between liberalism and neoliberalism, are a matter of much disagreement. What matters, however, is not so much the label, but the substance of the

argument. Here, as in the other chapters, I am concerned with violence purportedly committed in defence of human rights and/or in order to minimize human suffering; violence, moreover, that is morally justified in abstraction from its political context. And this is something shared by liberals and libertarians alike. So I am happy for Powell and Zwolinski to read 'libertarian' where I write 'liberal'.

4 The reader may wonder whether Halima is not being physically coerced. It seems very clearly the case that she *is*.

5 I use this term and abbreviation because Powell and Zwolinski do as well.

6 For the sake of readability, I will henceforth not be putting the following terms (and close relatives) in scare quotes despite thinking that the way in which they are used by sweatshop defenders is hugely problematic: 'transactions', 'contract', 'choose', 'choice', 'voluntary', 'voluntary choice', 'rational', 'moral', 'compensation', 'preference', 'prefer', 'offer', 'services', 'option', 'added option' and 'rescue'. See also note 1 in my first chapter.

7 On histories of dispossession, see Robin Dunford, 'Peasant Activism and the Rise of Food Sovereignty: Decolonizing and Democratising Norm Diffusion', *European Journal of International Relations* 23, 1 (2017): 145–67.

8 Benjamin Powell and Matt Zwolinski, 'The Ethical and Economic Case Against Sweatshop Labor: A Critical Assessment', *The Journal of Business Ethics* 107, 4 (2012): 464. I cannot analyse the deficiencies of existing cases against sweatshop labour, but a few telling pointers might be helpful. Arnold and Bowie, for example, accept terms of the debate that should never be conceded: 'In many developing countries, people are moving to large cities from rural areas because agriculture in those areas can no longer support the population base. When people make a choice that seems highly undesirable because there are no better alternatives available, are those people coerced? On the definition of coercion employed here, having to make a choice among undesirable options is not sufficient for coercion. We therefore assume that such persons are not coerced even though they have no better alternative than working in a sweatshop' – Denis G. Arnold and Norman E. Bowie, 'Sweatshops and Respect for Persons', *Business Ethics Quarterly* 13, 2 (2003): 229. In a similar vein, rather than offering a thorough analysis and critique of global social structures, Arnold and Hartmann responsibilize MNEs, investigating how 'moral imagination can improve managerial decision-making' and concluding, optimistically, that 'the exercise of moral imagination . . . suggests a diminishing future for sweatshops' – Denis G. Arnold and Laura P. Hartman, 'Moral Imagination and the Future of Sweatshops', *Business and Society Review* 108, 4 (2003): 428 and 426. According to these authors, MNEs ought to '[embrace] voluntary codes of conduct' – Denis G. Arnold and Laura P. Hartman, 'Worker Rights and Low Wage Industrialization: How to Avoid Sweatshops', *Human Rights Quarterly* 28, 3 (2006): 678. How can MNEs embrace such codes? Because they are 'capable of voluntarily respecting the basic rights of workers while remaining economically competitive' – Denis G. Arnold and Laura P. Hartman, 'Beyond Sweatshops: Positive Deviancy and Global Labour Practices', *Business Ethics: A European Review* 14, 2 (2005): 206. Meyers insists that 'with sweatshops, what is objectionable is not the wages that are lower than U.S. standards, which may be necessary to lure multinational corporations to the Third World. It is the *excessively* low wages and the *excessively* long hours that are

objectionable' – Chris Meyers, 'Wrongful Beneficence: Exploitation and Third World Sweatshops', *Journal of Social Philosophy* 35, 3 (2004): 329, emphases added. And Mayer, who criticizes Meyers's work, thinks that '[p]ure structural exploiters confront a kind of dirty-hands dilemma in which taking unfair advantage can be the right thing to do', concluding that 'sometimes it is morally permissible to do regrettable things' – Robert Mayer, 'Sweatshops, Exploitation, and Moral Responsibility', *The Journal of Social Philosophy* 38, 4 (2007): 605 and 606. My chapter can be interpreted partly as a critique of sweatshops critiques that – whatever their individual merits – grant too much and consider too little. McKeown is entirely correct, I think, when she points out that '[t]he philosophical literature on sweatshop labour is disappointing. The libertarian defence of sweatshops emphasizes the choice of individuals to take these jobs and the benefits to the individual. The transactional rebuttals focus on why these transactions between individual workers and employers can count as exploitative even when they are freely chosen. These approaches are individual, agential, and apolitical' – Maeve McKeown, 'Sweatshop Labour as Global Structural Exploitation', in *Exploitation: From Practice to Theory*, ed. Monique Deveaux and Vida Panitch (London: Rowman & Littlefield International, 2017), 50. This is not to say that there are no thoughtful critiques. Kates, for example, offers a sophisticated argument according to which 'even if we were to grant the truth of the economic and moral assumptions made by defenders of the Choice Argument, it nevertheless does not follow that it is morally wrong to regulate sweatshop labor' – Michael Kates, 'The Ethics of Sweatshops and the Limits of Choice', *Business Ethics Quarterly* 25, 2 (2015): 205. Other thoughtful analyses are Jason Hickel, 'The 'Girl Effect': Liberalism, Empowerment, and the Contradictions of Development', *Third World Quarterly* 35, 8 (2014): 1355–73; Mirjam Müller, 'The Relationship between Exploitation and Structural Injustice: Why Structures Matter in an Account of Exploitation', *Unpublished Manuscript*; and Joshua Preiss, 'Global Labor Justice and the Limits of Economic Analysis', *Business Ethics Quarterly* 24, 1 (2014): 55–83 – though Preiss oddly (and unnecessarily) sits on the fence when insisting that his goal 'is not to defend or reject the economic case for sweatshops' (ibid., 55). Readers might, moreover, be interested in consulting the writings of two other frequently cited critics of sweatshop defences, Miller and Snyder. See, for example, John Miller, 'Why Economists Are Wrong about Sweatshops and the Antisweatshop Movement', *Challenge* 46, 1 (2003): 93–122; Jeremy Snyder, 'Needs Exploitation', *Ethical Theory and Moral Practice* 11, 4 (2008): 389–405; and Jeremy Snyder, 'Exploitation and Demeaning Choices', *Politics, Philosophy & Economics* 12, 4 (2013): 345–60. My own analysis contributes to, and differs from, this critical literature in that it combines two claims: that sweatshop workers are often coerced into their jobs, and that those who defend sweatshops morally on the basis of choice cannot help but also defend certain forms of slavery.

9 Matt Zwolinski, 'Sweatshops, Choice, and Exploitation', *Business Ethics Quarterly* 17, 4 (2007): 694.

10 Keven Bales, *Disposable People: New Slavery in the Global Economy*, revised ed. (Berkeley and Los Angeles: University of California Press, 2004), 9.

11 Benjamin Powell and David Skarbek, 'Sweatshops and Third World Living Standards: Are the Jobs Worth the Sweat?' *Journal of Labor Research* 27, 2 (2006): 263–74.

12   David Henderson, 'The Case for Sweatshops', *Hoover Daily Report*, 7 February 2000, accessed 10 May 2017, www.hoover.org/research/case-sweatshops.

13   Paul Krugman, 'In Praise of Cheap Labor: Bad Jobs at Bad Wages Are Better than No Jobs at All', *Slate*, 21 March 1997, accessed 10 May 2017, www.slate.com/articles/business/the_dismal_science/1997/03/in_praise_of_cheap_labor.html. Note that Krugman has recently somewhat modified his earlier position; his argument is now one for moderate global regulation – Paul Krugman, 'Safer Sweatshops', *The New York Times*, 8 July 2013, accessed 10 May 2017, krugman.blogs.nytimes.com/2013/07/08/safer-sweatshops/?_r=0.

14   Nicholas Kristoff, 'Where Sweatshops Are a Dream', *The New York Times*, 14 January 2009, accessed 10 May 2017, www.nytimes.com/2009/01/15/opinion/15kristof.html?_r=0.

15   Nicholas Kristoff, 'My Sweatshop Column', *The New York Times*, 14 January 2009, accessed 10 May 2017, http://kristof.blogs.nytimes.com/2009/01/14/my-sweatshop-column/comment-page-1/. There is a 'feminist' variant of Kristoff's claim, according to which sweatshops have the added virtue of solving the problem of patriarchy by empowering women. See Nicholas Kristoff and Sheryl WuDunn, *Half the Sky: Turning Oppression into Opportunity for Women Worldwide* (New York: Knopf Doubleday, 2010). For an analysis and critique of the sort of 'feminism' espoused by Kristoff and WuDunn, see Hester Eisenstein, *Feminism Seduced: How Global Elites Use Women's Labor and Ideas to Exploit the World* (London: Taylor & Francis, 2010). Eisenstein calls for 'disentangling the project of women's emancipation from its tight embrace with capitalist modernization' (ibid., 220). I am not engaging here with feminist academic literature which offers a more careful analysis of ways in which sweatshop work, while involving forms of oppression, can challenge patriarchal norms. For more, see Naila Kabeer, 'Globalization, Labor Standards, and Women's Rights: Dilemmas of Collective (In)Action in an Interdependent World', *Feminist Economics* 10, 1 (2004): 3–35; and Dina M. Siddiqi, 'Do Bangladeshi Factory Workers Need Saving? Sisterhood in the Post-Sweatshop Era', *Feminist Review* 91 (2009): 154–74.

16   Authors other than Powell and Zwolinski include Jagdish Bhagwati, *In Defense of Globalization* (New York: Oxford University Press, 2004), 170–78; Ian Maitland, 'The Great Non-Debate Over International Sweatshops', in *Ethical Theory and Business*, ed. Tom L. Beauchamp, Norman E. Bowie and Denis G. Arnold, 8th ed. (Upper Saddle River, NJ: Pearson Prentice Hall, 2008), 597–608; Jeffrey Sachs, *The End of Poverty: Economic Possibilities for Our Time* (New York and London: Penguin, 2006), 11–14; and Martin Wolf, *Why Globalization Works: The Case for the Global Market Economy* (New Haven, CT, and London: Yale Nota Bene, 2005), 230–42.

17   Jo Boyden et al., 'Letter: When Work Is Right for Children', *The Observer*, 18 December 2016, accessed 10 May 2017, https://www.theguardian.com/theobserver/2016/dec/18/tech-companies-must-take-responsibility-for-algorithms.

18   Benjamin Powell, 'In Reply to Sweatshops Sophistries', *Human Rights Quarterly* 28, 4 (2006): 1041.

19   Kristoff, 'Where Sweatshops Are a Dream'.

20 Ibid.

21 It is very interesting how a claim not to be this sort of racist can be used to defend structural economic racism.

22 Ibid., 694–95.

23 See Zwolinski, 'Sweatshops, Choice, and Exploitation', 697.

24 Ibid., 692.

25 See also Preiss, 'Global Labor Justice', 67–68.

26 Monir Moniruzzaman, ' "Living Cadavers" in Bangladesh: Bioviolence in the Human Organ Bazzar', *Medical Anthropology Quarterly* 26, 1 (2012): 70. Zwolinski explicitly writes that some of his arguments are inspired by a 'moral case for legalizing human kidney sales' – Zwolinski, 'Sweatshops, Choice, and Exploitation', 719, footnote 38.

27 Moniruzzaman, ' "Living Cadavers" in Bangladesh', 72.

28 See Steve Marantz, 'Young Fighters Exposed to Exploitation', *Entertainment and Sports Programming Network (ESPN)*, 5 November 2013, accessed 10 May 2017, http://www.espn.com/espn/e60/story/_/id/9929399/child-fighters-thailand-vulnerable-exploitation.

29 Zwolinski, 'Sweatshops, Choice, and Exploitation', 691.

30 Powell and Zwolinski, 'The Ethical and Economic Case', 462, footnote 70.

31 Zwolinski, 'Sweatshops, Choice, and Exploitation', 720, footnote 39.

32 Powell and Zwolinski, 'The Ethical and Economic Case', 467.

33 Zwolinski, 'Sweatshops, Choice, and Exploitation', 696, emphasis added.

34 I owe this sentence to Afxentis Afxentiou.

35 One wonders two things here: why is rape only 'likely' to be condemned, and how about plausible moral theories that do not recognize rights?

36 Zwolinski, 'Sweatshops, Choice, and Exploitation', 711, emphases in the original.

37 Powell and Zwolinski, 'The Ethical and Economic Case', 470. One might be tempted to cite John McEnroe at this point: 'You *cannot* be serious!'

38 Zwolinski, 'Sweatshops, Choice, and Exploitation', 717, footnote 20.

39 Matt Zwolinski, 'Structural Exploitation', *Social Philosophy and Policy* 29, 1 (2012): 169. This problematic example was introduced by Meyers in 'Wrongful Beneficence', 324. I quote it very reluctantly, as I agree with McKeown that one should not 'reproduce this kind of wilfully ignorant and insensitive discourse' – McKeown, 'Sweatshop Labour Global Structural Exploitation', 53, footnote 16.

40 Zwolinski, 'Structural Exploitation', 169.

41 Ibid.

42 Ibid., 154.

43 Ibid., 167–68, emphasis in the original.

44 Ibid., 179.

45 Zwolinski, 'Sweatshops, Choice, and Exploitation', 704.

46 Ibid., 717, footnote 18.

47 See also ibid., 696.

48 Zwolinski, 'Structural Exploitation', 155.

49 Stefano Liberti, *Land Grabbing: Journeys in the New Colonialism*, trans. Enda Flannelly (London and New York: Verso, 2013), 79.

50  Robin Dunford, *The Politics of Transnational Peasant Struggle: Resistance, Rights and Democracy* (London: Rowman & Littlefield International, 2016), 37. Davis provides an interesting example: 'In South Vietnam, forced urbanization (described with unconscious Orwellian irony as "modernization") was an integral part of the US military strategy' and achieved through 'American terror bombing'. The result of this terror bombing was that 'the urban share of South Vietnam's population soared from 15 percent to 65 percent, with five million displaced peasants turned into slum-dwellers of inhabitants or refuge camps' – Mike Davis, *Planet of Slums* (London and New York: Verso, 2006), 56–7.

51  Dunford, *The Politics of Transnational Peasant Struggle*, 25, emphasis added. See, for instance, Liberti, *Land Grabbing* and Fred Pearce, *The Land Grabbers: The New Fight Over Who Owns the Earth* (Boston, MA: Beacon Press, 2012).

52  There is another blame-shifting strategy that fails for exactly the same reason, namely, to point out that MNEs that seize business opportunities on the back of unjust coercions are not necessarily the same MNEs as those that bear partial responsibility for these coercions. But again, the question of who is responsible for the unjust coercion has no bearing on whether or not people can be considered to be working in sweatshops voluntarily. Moreover, this argumentative strategy would not even succeed in eliminating blame. As Malmqvist, for instance, has pointed out, what is wrong about '[taking] advantage of structural injustices' is that one 'become[s] implicated in their perpetuation. One becomes, in one word, *complicit*' – Erik Malmqvist, 'Taking Advantage of Injustice', *Social Theory and Practice* 39, 4 (2013): 567, emphasis in the original.

53  I take for granted that Powell does not intend to attribute moral significance to the fact that MNEs engage in *joint* coercion, assuming that the 'joint-ness' somehow sanctifies what would otherwise be a case of wrongful exploitation. For it is neither clear how this could be argued for, rather than merely stipulated, nor how such an argument could ever amount to anything other than an apologia for the continuation of ruthless, self-righteous exploitation.

54  See also Nili, who writes, in a critical engagement with the contemporary humanitarian intervention discourse, that 'our elected governments either buy or allow our corporations to buy the world's most precious resources from brutal dictators and warlords' – Shmuel Nili, 'Humanitarian Disintervention', *Journal of Global Ethics* 7, 1 (2011): 33.

55  According to Young, 'The export processing zones many governments have established . . . are consequences of a history of structural adjustment programmes that many indebted governments have been pressured to implement by international financial institutions. The background conditions of the lives of these young workers today are structural consequences of decisions and aggregated economic processes beginning more than three decades ago' – Iris Marion Young, 'Responsibility and Global Justice: A Social Connection Model', *Social Philosophy and Policy* 21, 1 (2006): 113. For Lee, the construction of such conditions involves acts of violence: 'Whether the acts causing poverty are omissive or commissive, individual or collective, there are in most cases human agents responsible for the acts, as there are in the simple case of violence where one individual assaults another. The complexity of the causes of

poverty and the fact that they involve omissions as well as commissions serve as no bar to view them as acts of violence' – Steven Lee, 'Poverty and Violence', *Social Theory and Practice* 22, 1 (1996): 71. A thorough analysis of the political *making* of sweatshops is Ellen Israel Rosen, *Making Sweatshops: The Globalization of the U.S. Apparel Industry* (Berkeley and Los Angeles: University of California Press, 2002). Also see Hickel, who diagnoses an 'architecture of wealth extraction' – Hickel, 'The "Girl Effect"', 1365. For a more general analysis, see Garry Leech, *Capitalism: A Structural Genocide* (London: Zed, 2012).

56  I thus cannot follow Preiss's assessment that the work of Powell and Zwolinski is a 'notable exception to . . . widespread ignorance' to concerns about background injustice – Preiss, 'Global Labor Justice', 62. So when Preiss concludes, rightly, that the 'economic case for sweatshops . . . remains willfully obtuse to the relevance of conditions of background or structural justice to sweatshop exploitation' (ibid., 73), he has good reason to think that this is also true for Powell and Zwolinski's case.

57  See, for example, the classic piece by Andre Gunder Frank, 'The Development of Underdevelopment', *Monthly Review* 18, 4 (1966): 17–31. Frank argues that, 'underdevelopment was and still is generated by the very same historical process which also generated economic development: the development of capitalism' (ibid., 18). See also Anibal Quijano, 'Coloniality and Modernity/Rationality', *Cultural Studies* 21, 2/3 (2007): 168–78.

58  Powell and Zwolinski, 'The Ethical and Economic Case', 462, footnote 70.

59  Pearce, *The Land Grabbers*, ix. Pearce refers to land grabbing specifically in Africa here, the sort of place that, according to Kristoff, 'desperately needs Western help in the form of schools, clinics and sweatshops' – Nicholas Kristoff, 'In Praise of the Maligned Sweatshop', *The New York Times*, 6 June 2006, accessed 10 May 2017, http://www.nytimes.com/2006/06/06/opinion/06kristof.html?mcubz=0.

60  Powell and Zwolinski, 'The Ethical and Economic Case', 465.

61  Cohen 'think[s] . . . that, if not always, then almost always, *when someone is forced to do something there is an alternative to what he is forced to do which he is free to do* . . . when a person is forced to do something there is something else which he is free to do instead. Or, if that is not always so, then the exceptions are of a special kind. One kind of exception might be where a threat so paralyses someone's will that choosing otherwise is in some strong sense impossible for him. But I am not sure that he is even then *unfree* to choose otherwise, as opposed to *incapable* of choosing otherwise' – G. A. Cohen, 'Are Disadvantaged Workers Who Take Hazardous Jobs Forced to Take Hazardous Jobs?', in *Moral Rights in the Workplace*, ed. Gertrude Ezorsky (Albany: State University of New York Press, 1987), 66–67, emphases in the original. Also see G. A. Cohen, 'The Structure of Proletarian Unfreedom', *Philosophy & Public Affairs* 12, 1 (1983): 3–33; and Serena Olsaretti, *Life, Desert and the Market: A Philosophical Study* (Cambridge: Cambridge University Press, 2004), chapter 6.

62  Compare Kates, 'The Ethics of Sweatshops and the Limits of Choice', 206, footnote 6.

63  Cohen, 'Disadvantaged Workers', 67.

64  Zwolinski, 'Sweatshops, Choice, and Exploitation', 691, emphasis in the original.

65  In making this case, I am by no means equating contemporary sweatshop labour, or indeed contemporary bonded labour, with still-existing chattel slavery. I am only highlighting the troubling and potentially far-reaching theoretical implications of Powell's and Zwolinski's case in defence of sweatshops. Thanks to Maeve McKeown for prompting me to clarify this.

66  Zwolinski, 'Sweatshops, Choice, and Exploitation', 695.

67  Now, Zwolinski might of course insist that the preference-evincing choice of the prospective slave is *not* one of those choices that often give us reason for non-interference. But he would then have to explain to us what would make it legitimate for him to jump onto the stage and prevent the transaction from occurring. He might of course follow Mill, who famously argued that 'an engagement by which a person should sell himself, or allow himself to be sold, as a slave, would be null and void; neither enforced by law nor by opinion. . . . The reason for not interfering, unless for the sake of others, with a person's voluntary acts, is consideration for his liberty. His voluntary choice is evidence that what he so chooses is desirable, or at the least endurable, to him, and his good is on the whole best provided for by allowing him to take his own means of pursuing it. But by selling himself for a slave, he abdicates his liberty; he foregoes any future use of it beyond that single act. He therefore defeats, in his own case, the very purpose which is the justification of allowing him to dispose of himself. . . . The principle of freedom cannot require that he should be free not to be free. It is not freedom, to be allowed to alienate his freedom' – John Stuart Mill, *On Liberty and Other Essays*, ed. John Gray (Oxford and New York: Oxford University Press, 1991), 113–14. But if Zwolinski *were* to follow Mill, he would have to explain himself to the person who he insists must be disallowed not to die, making a persuasive philosophical case as to why the protection of their autonomy is an overriding moral consideration that unfortunately, on this occasion, necessitates their death.

68  Zwolinski, 'Sweatshops, Choice, and Exploitation', 720, footnote 39, emphasis added.

69  Bales, *Disposable People*, 9.

70  For another estimate, see for instance the International Labour Organization, which estimates that nearly '21 million people are victims of forced labour' – International Labour Organization, *Forced Labour, Modern Slavery and Human Trafficking*, accessed 20 May 2016, http://www.ilo.org/global/topics/forced-labour/lang—en/index.htm.

71  Bales, *Disposable People*, 16.

72  I do not think that such a thought experiment can tell us anything about the real world; I use it here merely (and reluctantly) as a tool of imminent critique.

73  Powell and Zwolinski, 'The Ethical and Economic Case', 466.

74  Preiss phrases this well when he writes that Powell's and Zwolinski's 'thin notion of autonomy . . . is only able to establish what the economic case already claims: that many sweatshop workers rationally choose to accept sweatshop wages and working conditions as their best option in the status quo' – Preiss, 'Global Labor Justice', 73.

75   Slaves might prefer to continue being slaves in order to escape the fate of death through starvation. One could imagine a scenario in which they are given a one-off chance, by their sadistic owner, to cease to be slaves. See Todd Calder, 'Shared Responsibility, Global Structural Injustice, and Restitution', *Social Theory and Practice* 36, 2 (2010): 276–77.

76   See also Peter, who thinks that 'the apparent automatic legitimization of market transactions is the result of a conflation between choice and consent in economic theory' – Fabienne Peter, 'Choice, Consent, and the Legitimacy of Market Transactions', *Economics and Philosophy* 20, 1 (2004): 3. Peter 'argue[s] against a tendency in contemporary economic theory to conflate people's choices with their consent to the social structures of constraints that shape the set of feasible alternatives' (ibid., 17).

77   Powell and Zwolinski, 'The Ethical and Economic Case', 465.

78   The latter seems to be the position taken by Thrasymachus at the outset of Plato's *Republic*. Plato, *The Republic*, trans. Desmond Lee (London: Penguin Classics, 2007).

79   Such a recognition and analysis would be likely to reveal Powell's demand for viewing sweatshops 'in the *proper* historical perspective' (a demand triggered by 'calls for new labor laws and increased government regulation' *just after* more than 1,100 sweatshop workers had been crushed to death in the Rana Plaza collapse in 2013) as yet another myth – Benjamin Powell, 'Meet the Old Sweatshops: Same as the New', *The Independent Review* 19, 1 (2014): 109, emphasis added. Indeed, it took Powell only a week to respond to the crushing of the workers, suggesting that, 'Tragedies such as this naturally provoke emotional reactions. But reason and perspective, rather than emotion, are needed when deciding how to respond.

A house fire that kills a family in the United States is also tragic. But no sane person would recommend that the rest of us move to caves until all houses have been certified as fire proof' – Benjamin Powell, 'Sweatshops in Bangladesh Improve the Lives of Their Workers, and Boost Growth', *Forbes*, 2 May 2013, accessed 10 May 2017, https://www.forbes.com/sites/realspin/2013/05/02/sweatshops-in-bangladesh-improve-the-lives-of-their-workers-and-boost-growth/#31e6c79c74ce. Speaking of proper historical perspective: as Chang has demonstrated, 'With only a few exceptions, all of today's rich countries, including Britain and the US – the supposed homes of free trade and free market – have become rich through the combinations of protectionism, subsidies and other policies that today they advise the developing countries not to adopt' – Ha-Joon Chang, *23 Things They Don't Tell You about Capitalism* (London: Penguin Books, 2011), 63.

80   Such speculation also seems to neglect what textile manufacturing in the United States is *actually* like. According to Ellen Rosen, '[W]omen in today's U.S. apparel industry often work more than eight hours a day in conditions that lack elementary safety and other legally required protections, earning less than the minimum wage' – Rosen, *Making Sweatshops*, 3. Also see Robert J. S. Ross, *Slaves to Fashion: Poverty and Abuse in the New Sweatshops* (Ann Arbor: University of Michigan Press, 2004). Ross estimates that, in 2000, there were '*approximately 255,000 sweatshop*

*workers in the United States*', which 'would place the United States' victims of labor abuse as the eight largest mass of clothing workers in the world' (ibid., 35 and 36, emphasis in the original).

81  Davis, *Planet of Slums*, 199. Davis's actual formulation here is that there is no such scenario 'for the reincorporation of this vast mass of surplus labor'.

82  Indeed, such work already exists. See Rosen, *Making Sweatshops*. Rosen offers a discussion of 'the political and economic contexts in which trade policy for the textile, apparel and retail industries were made and how they led to the globalization of these industries' (ibid., 7). See particularly chapter 12.

83  Monique Deveaux and Vida Panitch, 'Introduction', in *Exploitation: From Practice to Theory*, ed. Monique Deveaux and Vida Panitch (London: Rowman & Littlefield International, 2017), 1–11.

84  Jeff Noonan, *Democratic Society and Human Needs* (Montreal: McGill-Queen's University Press, 2006), xix. According to a UN report, 'Instead of being a focus for growth and prosperity, the cities have become a dumping ground for a surplus population working in unskilled, unprotected and low-wage informal service industries and trade. The slums of the developing world swell' – United Nations Human Settlements Programme (UN-Habitat), *The Challenge of Slums: Global Report on Human Settlements 2003* (London and Sterling, VA: Earthscan Publications, 2003), 46.

85  As McKeown writes, '[E]xploitation in sweatshops is group-based, structural and political, in the sense that it requires collective action to be overcome' – McKeown, 'Sweatshop Labour as Global Structural Exploitation', 50.

## CHAPTER 4

1  I introduce it here only as an example of the sort of action-guiding philosophy that we have every reason to stop indulging in. As a retired CIA official once pointed out, 'Nobody in intelligence believes in the ticking bomb. It's just a way of framing the debate for public consumption. That is not an intelligence reality' – David Rose, 'Tortured Reasoning', *Vanity Fair*, 16 December 2008, accessed 14 May 2017, http://vanityfair.com/magazine/2008/12/torture200812. I was alerted to this citation through Philip Devine, 'Book Review: Fritz Allhoff, *Terrorism, Time-Bombs, and Torture: A Philosophical Analysis*', *Ethics* 123, 2 (2013): 347. For an early formulation of the ticking-bomb scenario, see Michael Walzer, 'Political Action: The Problem of Dirty Hands', *Philosophy & Public Affairs* 2 (1973): 166–67.

2  Beyond analysing and rejecting the works of these two torture defenders, I offer no comprehensive overview, let alone discussion, of existing defences of torture. Central, however, are the following. Walzer famously argued that torturing would be a case of doing wrong to do right and getting dirty hands – see Walzer, 'Political Action'. Dershowitz has more recently drawn on Walzer's example and argued for the legalization of interrogational torture – see Alan Dershowitz, 'The Torture Warrant: A Response to Professor Strauss', *New York Law School Legal Review* 48 (2004): 275–94. Also see his *Why Terrorism Works* (New Haven, CT, and

London: Yale University Press, 2002), chapter 4; 'Tortured Reasoning', in *Torture: A Collection*, ed. Sanford Levinson (Oxford: Oxford University Press, 2004), 257–80; and 'When Torture Is the Least Evil of Terrible Options', *Times Higher Education Supplement*, 11 June 2004, accessed 14 May 2017, https://www.timeshighereducation. com/features/when-torture-is-the-least-evil-of-terrible-options/189257.article. Another 'classic' in the pro-torture literature is Michael Levin's 'case for torture' from 1982. Levin begins his case by asking his readers to '[s]uppose a terrorist has hidden an atomic bomb on Manhattan Island which will detonate at noon on July 4', and argues that '[t]here is little danger that the Western democracies will lose their way if they choose to inflict pain as one way of preserving order' – Michael Levin, 'The Case for Torture', *Newsweek*, 7 June 1982, accessed 14 May 2017, http://people. brandeis.edu/~teuber/torture.html. For book-length defences of torture, see Mirko Bagaric and Julie Clarke, *Torture: When the Unthinkable Is Permissible* (Albany: State University of New York Press, 2007); and Stephen Kershnar, *For Torture: A Rights-Based Defence* (Lanham, MD: Lexington Books, 2011). The view that torture can be morally justified in principle, but ought not to be legalized, has been defended by Jeff McMahan, 'Torture in Principle and in Practice', *Public Affairs Quarterly* 22, 2 (2008): 111–28; and Seumas Miller, 'Is Torture Ever Morally Justified?' *International Journal of Applied Philosophy* 19, 2 (2005): 179–92. Also see Miller's monograph, *Terrorism and Counter-Terrorism: Ethics and Liberal Democracy* (Oxford: Blackwell, 2009), chapter 6.

3  A number of academic writers have subjected defences of interrogational torture to critical scrutiny before, and I mention only some of them here. For a ruthless deconstruction of the ticking-bomb scenario, see Bob Brecher, *Torture and the Ticking Bomb* (Oxford: Wiley-Blackwell, 2007). Also see Vittorio Bufacchi and Jean Mario Arrigo, 'Torture, Terrorism and the State: A Refutation of the Ticking-Bomb Argument', *Journal of Applied Philosophy* 23, 3 (2006): 355–73; David Luban, *Torture, Power, and Law* (Cambridge: Cambridge University Press, 2014), 74–107; Jamie Mayerfeld, 'In Defense of the Absolute Prohibition of Torture', *Public Affairs Quarterly* 22, 2 (2008): 109–28; Henry Shue, *Fighting Hurt: Rule and Exception in Torture and War* (Oxford: Oxford University Press, 2016), 58–66; and Jessica Wolfendale, 'Training Torturers: A Critique of the "Ticking-Bomb" Argument', *Social Theory and Practice* 32, 3 (2006). For a critique of the 'liberal ideology of torture, which assumes that torture can be neatly confined to exceptional ticking-bomb cases and surgically severed from cruelty and tyranny', and which 'represents a dangerous delusion' (73), see David Luban, *Torture, Power, and Law* (Cambridge: Cambridge University Press, 2014), 43–73. On the question of intellectual complicity in torture, see Bob Brecher and Michael Neu, 'Intellectual Complicity in Torture', in *Complicity: Concept, Cases and Critique*, ed. Afxentis Afxentiou, Robin Dunford and Michael Neu (London: Rowman & Littlefield International, 2017), 143–60. For an important legal analysis, see Jeremy Waldron, 'Torture and Positive Law', in *Torture, Terror, and Trade-Offs: Philosophy for the White House* (Oxford: Oxford University Press, 2010), 186–260. There are also many book-length critiques. I recommend Brecher, *Torture and the Ticking Bomb*; Luban, *Torture, Power, and Law*; Yuval Ginbar, *Why Not Torture Terrorists? Moral, Practical, and Legal Aspects of*

*the 'Ticking Bomb' Justification for Torture* (Oxford: Oxford University Press, 2010); and Rebecca Gordon, *Mainstreaming Torture: Ethical Approaches in the Post-9/11 United States* (New York: Oxford University Press, 2014). A recent account of why interrogational torture does not work (contrary to *all* defenders of torture, who presume that it does) from a neuroscientific point of view, is Shara O'Mane's, *Why Torture Doesn't Work: The Neuroscience of Investigation* (Cambridge, MA: Harvard University Press, 2015). I am hoping to make a contribution to this extensive critical literature by offering an analysis of the philosophical and political carelessness to be encountered in the writings specifically of two prominent torture defenders, and by placing these defences in the broader context of a discussion of just liberal violence.

4  Brecher, *Torture and the Ticking Bomb*, 72 and 85.

5  Ibid., 3.

6  His defence is not limited to interrogational torture, but this is the form of torture I am concerned with in this chapter unless I indicate otherwise.

7  Even Allhoff would not *quite* argue that, insisting instead that '[w]hat ultimately matters is that we not institutionalize torture beyond what our moral calculus supports'. He judges himself to be 'more sanguine about institutionally minimal torture than others' – Fritz Allhoff, *Terrorism, Ticking Time-Bombs, and Torture: A Philosophical Analysis* (Chicago, IL: The University of Chicago Press, 2012), 153 and 154. The most radical liberal proposal is Derwhowitz's. But again, the crucial point here is that all these views are based on an unexamined liberalism; that we can have legalization without institutionalization (Steinhoff); that we can have *institutionalization light* in liberal democracies if moral reasons dictates so (Allhoff); or that full-blown institutionalization in liberal democracies can only be a good thing (Dershowitz).

8  Allhoff does this somewhat differently, as we shall see, namely by granting unlimited epistemic superiority to his political leaders.

9  Allhoff, *Terrorism, Ticking Time-Bombs, and Torture*, 8. When I write '(*TTT*, page number)' in this chapter, I refer to this book. Unless otherwise indicated, emphases in citations from *TTT* are in the original.

10  Elsewhere in his book, Allhoff writes that '[t]he absence of terrorist attacks since the proliferation of our powerful counterterrorism campaign can hardly be a coincidence.

So let us now assume that our counterterrorism campaign is working' (*TTT*, 33). Again, this is neither an argument nor evidence; it is speculation.

11  Iraq Body Count, accessed 14 May 2017, https://www.iraqbodycount.org/.

12  Iraq Body Count, 'A Dossier of Civilian Casualties in Iraq 2003–2005', accessed 14 May 2017, https://www.iraqbodycount.org/analysis/reference/press-releases/12/.

13  Fritz Allhoff, 'Terrorism and Torture', *International Journal of Applied Philosophy* 17, 1 (2003): 117, footnote 11.

14  For a devastating analysis of the sort of 'war on terrorism' narrative that Allhoff blindly follows, see Richard Jackson, *Writing the War on Terrorism* (Manchester: Manchester University Press, 2005).

15  Fritz Allhoff, 'A Defense of Torture: Separation of Cases, Ticking Time-Bombs, and Moral Justification', *International Journal of Applied Philosophy* 19, 2 (2005): 261.

16  Ibid., 260–61.

17   Or, at the time of writing his book, he could have attended to Physicians for Human Rights, *Broken Laws, Broken Lives: Medical Evidence of Torture by US Personnel and Its Impact*, A Report by Physicians for Human Rights, Executive Summary, June 2008, accessed 14 May 2017, http://brokenlives.info/?page_id=69.

18   See, for instance, Laleh Khalili, *Time in the Shadows: Confinement in Counterinsurgencies* (Stanford, CA: Stanford University Press, 2012).

19   Darius Rejali, *Torture and Democracy* (Princeton, NJ: Princeton University Press, 2009), 4 and 5. Allhoff apparently thinks he can brush this under the carpet simply by classifying Rejali's research agenda as a different kettle of fish: 'He is deeply concerned with pervasive, institutionalized torture and spends much of the book discussing problems thereof. By contrast, my focus is on exceptional cases rather than normalized ones' (*TTT*, 144).

20   Khalili, *Time in the Shadows*, 4.

21   Jennifer Harbury, *Truth, Torture and the American Way: The History and Consequences of U.S. Involvement in Torture* (Boston, MA: Beacon Press, 2005), 29. Similarly, on Britain's involvement in torture, see Gareth Peirce, *Dispatches from the Dark Side: On Torture and the Death of Justice* (London: Verso, 2012); and Ian Cobain, *Cruel Britannia: A Secret History of Torture* (London: Granta, 2013). Cobain came to understand 'that far from being a nation that doesn't "do" torture, Britain had been employing such cruelties for generations, and for a multitude of reasons' (ibid., 307).

22   For a frightening collection of torture memos and government officials' reports produced by that regime, see Karen Greenberg and Joshua L. Dratel (eds.), *The Torture Papers: The Road to Abu Ghraib* (Cambridge: Cambridge University Press, 2005). Note that this collection was published seven years before Allhoff wrote his defence of torture. For analyses of Bush's torture regime – also published *before* Allhoff set out to write his book – see Philippe Sands, *Torture Team: Uncovering War Crimes in the Land of the Free* (London: Penguin, 2008); and Jane Mayer, *The Dark Side: The Inside Story of How the War on Terror Turned into a War on American Ideals* (New York: Doubleday Books, 2009).

23   Gordon, *Mainstreaming Torture*, 7. Gordon makes the case that 'torture is not an episode but a socially embedded practice' (ibid., 7).

24   Madeleine Albright, quoted in Sheldon Richman, 'Iraqi Sanctions: Were They Worth It?' *Global Policy Forum*, January 2004, accessed 14 May 2017, https://www.globalpolicy.org/component/content/article/170/41952.html.

25   Antonio Taguba, 'Preface', in *Broken Laws, Broken Lives*, viii.

26   Uwe Steinhoff, *On the Ethics of War and Terrorism* (Oxford: Oxford University Press, 2007), 109, emphasis in the original.

27   Ibid., 137.

28   Ibid.

29   Brecher's case against interrogational torture is explicitly *utilitarian* rather than *absolutist*. As Brecher writes, 'I shall restrict myself to utilitarian considerations, despite my conviction that the theory offers a wholly inadequate understanding of morality. Because it is utilitarianism which is so often at the root of public policy, I think that what is centrally important is to show that arguments advocating interrogational torture in the ticking bomb scenario and/or its legalization are spurious even on their own utilitarian terms' – Brecher, *Torture and the Ticking Bomb*, 12.

30   Ibid., 3.

31   Steinhoff also alludes to a third case where an adult was taken hostage (*ET*, 166, footnote 77). See http://law.justia.com/cases/federal/appellate-courts/F2/734/770/365150/, accessed 14 May 2017.

32   This is hardly surprising, because, as Mayerfeld points out, '[I]n the long history of counter-terrorist campaigns there has not been one verified report of a genuine ticking bomb torture scenario. There has not been a verified incident that even comes close to the ticking bomb torture scenario' – Mayerfeld, 'In Defense of the Absolute Prohibition of Torture', 111.

33   Compare Michael Welch, 'Book Review: Uwe Steinhoff, *On the Ethics of Torture*', *Punishment & Society* 17, 2 (2015): 261.

34   The second real-world example to be encountered in Steinhoff's book is 'the famous Daschner case', where 'the mere *threat* of torture (and some think that threatening torture *is* torture) sufficed to make the child kidnapper, Magnus Gäfgen, disclose the location of the child (who, however, had already been murdered by Gäfgen – but that does not speak against the effectiveness of torture for retrieving the truth in some cases)' (*ET*, 58).

35   See also Allhoff on this: 'For example, we could just hand an interrogator a baseball bat and see what happens; the chance of getting actionable intelligence from someone who has it is surely greater than zero' (*TTT*, 152). Having written this, Allhoff then feels the need to clarify that he does not actually propose this way of proceeding (ibid.).

36   And just in case readers doubt the badness of killing, they are, for three pages, 'subjected to a direct quote from a Wikipedia entry on "Decomposition"' – Welch, 'Book Review', 262. I recommend Welch's review highly.

37   When reading the following citation, readers might be reminded of sweatshop defender Powell's invocation of reason one week after the collapse of the Rana Plaza sweatshop that crushed more than 1,100 people.

38   Steinhoff claims that he is not a utilitarian: 'The necessity justification of torture that I defend and endorse . . . is a *threshold deontological* justification that takes rights seriously (without absolutizing them) and is *incompatible* with utilitarianism' (*ET*, 44, emphases in the original). Quoting Larry Alexander and Michael S. Moore affirmatively, he thinks that '[a] threshold deontologist holds that deontological norms govern up to a point despite adverse consequences; but when the consequences become so dire that they cross the stipulated threshold, consequentialism takes over' (*ET*, 44). A different essay would have to be written on the confusions of a threshold deontological position and its alleged incompatibility with utilitarianism. On the confusions of threshold deontology's twin sibling, 'threshold utilitarianism', see Brecher and Neu, 'Intellectual Complicity in Torture'.

39   Steinhoff thinks this because 'there is no evidence that torturing a person by torturing someone he deeply cares for is more effective in retrieving the vital information than torturing himself' (*ET*, 44). This appears to be the only point in his book at which Steinhoff has decided *not* to invent yet another thought experiment to argue *for* torture's justifiability. One wonders why. Fried rightly considers this 'a cop-out, given Steinhoff's argument. He frequently resorts to fantastical thought experiments to demonstrate that certain ethical outcomes are at least conceivable and

therefore undermine absolutist prohibitions. Well, isn't it *conceivable* that a terrorist might have congenital analgia, the inability to feel pain, but still feel deeply about his child?' – Gregory Fried, 'Book Review: Uwe Steinhoff, *On the Ethics of Torture*', *Notre Dame Philosophical Reviews*, 20 May 2014, accessed 14 May 2017, at http://ndpr.nd.edu/news/48412-on-the-ethics-of-torture/ (emphasis in the original).

40 Indeed, in a comment reminiscent of Zwolinski's argument in defence of sweatshops discussed in the previous chapter, Steinhoff insists that we 'should honour' an innocent's assumed 'preference' to be tortured over being killed – Uwe Steinhoff, 'Torture: The Case for Dirty Harry and against Alan Dershowitz', *Journal of Applied Philosophy* 23, 3 (2006): 339.

41 I am not suggesting that this premise ought to be accepted. In fact I think that the question of whether or not killing in self-defence can be morally justified is a deeply misguided one to ask.

42 Brecher, *Torture and the Ticking Bomb*, 72.

43 See also *TTT*, 147–54.

44 Shue, *Fighting Hurt*, 63.

45 Brecher, *Torture and the Ticking Bomb*, 24, emphases in the original.

46 What I mean here is that this is the only point at which his defence goes beyond simply regurgitating standard legal and moral wisdom on matters of self-defence under the astounding banner of defending *torture*.

47 And who should the trainees practise on? Would they be obliged to serve as objects of practice?

48 I owe this observation to Fried, 'Book Review'.

49 Dershowitz, *Why Terrorism Works*, chapter 4.

50 Alternatively, Steinhoff argues, opponents could suggest that it is not that he does not have a *right* to speak his opinion, but that he ought not to do it nonetheless, in which case they 'still bear a burden of proof' (*ET*, 157).

51 Bob Brecher, 'Surrogacy, Liberal Individualism and the Moral Climate', in *Moral Philosophy and Contemporary Problems*, ed. S. D. G. Evans (Cambridge: Cambridge University Press, 1987), 183–97.

52 Laleh Khalili, *Time in the Shadows*.

53 Brecher, 'Surrogacy', 185, emphasis added.

54 See The Guardian, 'Donald Trump: I'd Bring Back "a Hell of a Lot Worse than Waterboarding"', 7 February 2016, accessed 14 May 2017, https://www.theguardian.com/us-news/2016/feb/06/donald-trump-waterboarding-republican-debate-torture.

55 Cobain, *Cruel Britannia*; Peirce, *Dispatches from the Dark Side*; and Rejali, *Torture and Democracy* might all give Steinhoff reasons for hesitation.

56 We are reminded here of Powell's and Zwolinski's case against bans and boycotts discussed in the previous chapter.

57 Luban, *Torture, Power, and Law*, 102. For Luban, 'This is, indeed, a familiar drawback to consequentialism: it always makes morality hostage to evil' (ibid., 102). Again, Steinhoff would deny that he is a utilitarian, but, be that as it may, his threshold deontology suffers from the same drawback.

58 I cannot engage in a theoretical discussion of moral dilemmas here. For a useful volume, see Christopher W. Gowans, ed., *Moral Dilemmas* (Oxford: Oxford University Press, 1987). According to Sinnott-Armstrong, 'A moral dilemma is any

situation where at the same time: (1) there is a moral requirement for an agent to adopt each of two alternatives, (2) neither moral requirement is overridden in any morally relevant way, (3) the agent cannot adopt both alternatives together, and (4) the agent can adopt each alternative separately' – Walter Sinnott-Armstrong, *Moral Dilemmas* (Oxford and New York: Basil Blackwell, 1988), 29.

59   Luban, *Torture, Power, and Law*, 104.

60   Ibid., 104.

61   William Styron, *Sophie's Choice* (London: Vintage, 2005).

62   Luban, *Torture, Power, and Law*, 105.

63   Steinhoff, 'The Case of Dirty Harry', 344, emphasis added. In fact, it might be worth giving the full citation: 'A member of a terrorist group might be liable to torture in the ticking bomb case, even if he does not know were [*sic*] the bomb is' (ibid.).

64   Mayerfeld, 'In Defense of the Absolute Prohibition of Torture', 121.

65   Wolfendale, 'Training Torturers', 285.

66   Mayerfeld, 'In Defense of the Absolute Prohibition of Torture', 121–22.

67   See ibid., 122.

68   Ibid.

69   Ibid.

70   Compare Mayerfeld, who writes that '[t]he liability view gives dangerous scope to fear and anger. Racism (conscious or unconscious) lends further power to these emotions' (ibid., 123).

71   Ibid., 122, emphasis in the original.

72   Luban, *Torture, Power, and Law*, 73.

73   Not every torture defender comments on the question of legalization. Fritz Allhoff does, but is inclusive on this matter: 'I am more concerned with the morality of torture than the legality but, insofar as legality tracks morality, if torture could be shown to be morally permissible then there might be cause for legal reform' – Allhoff, 'Terrorism and Torture', 106.

74   Luban, *Torture, Power, and Law*, 53.

75   On the 'liberal ideology of torture', see ibid., 43–73.

76   Galtung, 'Cultural Violence', 294.


# CHAPTER 5

1   By focussing on liberal contemporary just war theory, I am not suggesting that this is the only just war theory in town. Cheyney Ryan distinguishes between the '*liberal* tradition' as 'identified with Grotius' and the '*republican* tradition' as 'identified with Rousseau', suggesting that 'Walzer and most contemporary political philosophers of war stand within the former' (emphases in the original) – Cheyney Ryan, 'Pacifism(s)', *The Philosophical Forum* 46, 1 (2015): 32, accessed 20 May 2017, http://onlinelibrary.wiley.com/doi/10.1111/phil.12053/epdf. Ryan also provides further references on this matter. The second thing to be pointed out is that the just war tradition is much older than liberalism. For a historical overview – written from *within* the tradition – see, for example, Alex Bellamy, *Just Wars: From Cicero*

*to Iraq* (Malden, MA: Polity Press, 2006). An excellent introduction to the ethics of war and peace more generally is Nigel Dower, *The Ethics of War and Peace: Cosmopolitan and Other Perspectives* (Cambridge: Polity, 2009). Also see A. J. Coates, *The Ethics of War*, 2nd ed. (Manchester: Manchester University Press, 2016).

2  It would be impossible to list all contemporary just war theorists, let alone the countless pieces of writing they have produced during the past few – and particularly the past two – decades. It would also be impossible to analyse all the different twists and turns within contemporary just war theory. But for an overview – written from *within* – see Seth Lazar, 'War', in *The Stanford Encyclopedia of Philosophy* (summer 2016 edition), ed. Edward N. Zalta, accessed 20 May 2017, http://plato.stanford.edu/archives/sum2016/entries/war/. There are many contemporary just war theorists who might – in very different ways, to different degrees, and whatever the merits of some of their works – find themselves liable to at least some of the criticisms articulated in this chapter. Here are some (I also point the reader in the direction of *one* publication per theorist): Saba Bazargan, 'Defensive Wars and the Reprisal Dilemma', *Australasian Journal of Philosophy* 93, 3 (2015): 583–601; C. A. J. Coady, *Morality and Political Violence* (Cambridge: Cambridge University Press, 2008); Mark Evans, 'In Defence of Just War Theory', in *Just War Theory: A Reappraisal*, ed. Mark Evans (Edinburgh: Edinburgh University Press, 2005), 203–22; Cécile Fabre, *Cosmopolitan War* (Oxford: Oxford University Press, 2012); Helen Frowe, *Defensive Killing* (Oxford: Oxford University Press, 2014); Thomas Hurka, 'Proportionality in the Morality of War', *Philosophy & Public Affairs* 33, 1 (2005): 34–66; Frances Kamm, *The Moral Target: Aiming at Right Conduct in War and Other Conflicts* (Oxford: Oxford University Press, 2012); Seth Lazar, *Sparing Civilians* (Oxford: Oxford University Press, 2015); Brian Orend, *The Morality of War*, 2nd ed. (Peterborough: Broadview Press, 2013); David Rodin, 'Justifying Harm', *Ethics* 122, 1 (2011): 74–110; and Bradley Strawser, 'Moral Predators: The Duty to Employ Uninhabited Aerial Vehicles', *Journal of Military Ethics* 9, 4 (2010): 342–68. My criticisms *also* apply to theorists contributing to the 'Responsibility to Protect' discourse, but we shall deal with those in Robin Dunford and Michael Neu, *Just War and the Responsibility to Protect: A Critique* (London: Zed, forthcoming). Steinhoff has also contributed extensively (and in my view more critically than others) to the contemporary just war discourse – see, for instance, Uwe Steinhoff, *On the Ethics of War and Terrorism* (Oxford: Oxford University Press, 2007). But his work would in many ways require a separate and perhaps slightly less damning analysis. I tried to offer such an analysis in 'The Fragility of Justified Warfare: A Comment on Steinhoff', *Theoretical & Applied Ethics* 1, 4 (2012): 45–53. This article is, however, too accepting of the liberal just war framework to be of much worth. I now think that any young academic who finds themselves on their way to becoming a just war theorist should pause for a moment and read Henry Giroud, *The University in Chains: Confronting the Military-Industrial-Academic Complex* (London and New York: Routledge, 2016).

3  I will partially draw on arguments I developed earlier, in Michael Neu, 'The Supreme Emergency of War: A Critique of Walzer', *The Journal of International Political Theory* 10, 1 (2013): 3–19; 'The Tragedy of Justified War', *International Relations* 27, 4 (2013): 461–80; 'Why McMahan's *Just* Wars Are Only *Justified*

and Why that Matters', *Ethical Perspectives* 19, 2 (2012): 235–55; and 'Why There Is No Such Thing as Just War Pacifism and Why Just War Theorists and Pacifists Can Talk Nonetheless', *Social Theory & Practice* 37, 3 (2011): 413–33. By utilizing ideas from my previous work, however, I am not suggesting that I still agree with everything I wrote back then. Specifically, whatever else might have been implied by my previous writings, I do *not* think that wars that kill innocents can be, or ought to be attempted to be, morally justified.

4  Two important philosophical critiques of the just war tradition had a tremendous impact on my views when I first started thinking about these matters: Robert Holmes, *On War and Morality* (Princeton, NJ: Princeton University Press, 1989); and Richard Norman, *Ethics, Killing and War* (Cambridge: Cambridge University Press, 1995). For more recent critiques of just war, see Anthony Burke, 'Just War or Ethical Peace: Moral Discourses of Strategic Violence after 9/11', *International Affairs* 80, 2 (2004): 329–53; Laurie Calhoun, *War and Delusion: A Critical Examination* (Basingstoke: Palgrave Macmillan, 2013); Soran Reader, 'Making Pacifism Plausible', *Journal of Applied Philosophy* 17, 2 (2000): 169–80; and Tarik Kochi, *The Other's War: Recognition and the Violence of Ethics* (Abingdon: Birkbeck Law Press, 2009), especially 23–54. Kimberley Hutchings argues for 'decolonising' just war in 'Cosmopolitan Just War and Coloniality', in *Race, Empire and Global Justice*, ed. Duncan Bell, forthcoming. I also highly recommend Cheyney C. Ryan's critical work on just war theory. See, for instance, Ryan, 'Democratic Duty and the Moral Dilemmas of Soldiers', *Ethics* 122, 1 (2011): 10–42; and Ryan, 'Pacifism(s)'. Also see his earlier essay, 'Self-Defense, Pacifism, and the Possibility of Killing', *Ethics* 93, 3 (1983): 508–24. Ryan is a pacifist, but committed to 'an ongoing dialogue with just war theory' – Ryan, 'Democratic Duty', 42. I admire Ryan for his work, as he clearly offers it with the intention of prompting just war theorists to reconsider some of their views. Whether or not, in so doing, he ends up giving too much credit to just war theory is not a question I can answer here. Finally, an excellent book that greatly influenced my early thinking on these matters was David Rodin, *War and Self-Defense* (Oxford: Oxford University Press, 2002). Not only did Rodin argue in here that 'the right of national self-defense cannot be explained in terms of personal self-defense'; he also expressed his belief that dilemmas are 'real moral possibilities' and that 'aggression, occurring in the world as it currently is, could only face us with a terrible dilemma' (ibid., 5, 67 and 199). Subsequently, however, Rodin seems to have been somewhat absorbed by the just war discourse. For example, in a later piece, he appears to be accepting of the possibility that 'bomber pilots are objectively justified in inflicting incidental harm on the civilians. Their actions are not wrong, all things considered' – despite still insisting that 'the conditions for justifying the collateral harming of civilians are considerably more restrictive than is typically accepted' and continuing to flirt with 'contingent pacifism' – Rodin, 'Justifying Harm, 87, 86 (footnote 14), 109. He also justified the Libya war in 2011, despite knowing that 'using airpower in crowded urban settings will inevitably lead to the accidental killing of civilians', arguing that '[i]t seems reasonable that [the civilians] will bear the risk of accidental air strike, provided that we keep our side of the bargain by doing everything humanly possible to minimise that risk' – Mervyn Frost and David Rodin, 'How to Get Humanitarian Intervention Right: What Libya Teaches Us about Responsibility

to Protect', *Inside Briefing, Oxford Martin Law School*, March 2011, accessed 20 May 2017, http://www.oxfordmartin.ox.ac.uk/downloads/briefings/2011-03-Libya.pdf, 2. Another prominent thinker who I think ought to disentangle himself from the just war web is Lazar. See his, in many ways instructive, imminent critique of McMahan's work on liability in war – Seth Lazar, 'The Responsibility Dilemma for *Killing in War*: A Review Essay', *Philosophy & Public Affairs* 38, 3 (2010): 180–213.

5  I am not suggesting that this is a problem only of *contemporary* just war theory. For example, according to Kochi, 'One major problem with [Francisco de] Vitoria's theory of just war is his scholastic theological approach which relies heavily upon principles that float above, or are disconnected from, the realities of the historical and political situation of his time. His principles are too "abstract" in the sense of not being tied to the practicalities of the colonial experience. . . . Modern just war theorists, which do not pay enough attention to the colonial heritage of the just war tradition and rely merely upon abstract principles, replicate the same problems and difficulties that plague Vitoria's account – they often present a "principled" justification for neo-colonial, ideological or politically motivated violence' – Kochi, *The Other's War*, 39.

6  Michael Walzer, 'Response to McMahan's Paper', *Philosophia* 34, 1 (2006): 43.

7  Michael Walzer, *Arguing about War* (New Haven, CT, and London: Yale University Press, 2004): 22. When I write '(*AW*, page number)' in this chapter, I refer to this book. Unless otherwise indicated, emphases in citations from *AW* are in the original.

8  To A. J. Coates's mind, '*In its authentic form . . . the aim of just war thinking is not justification (and certainly not glorification) of war, but containment*' (emphasis in the original) – Coates, *The Ethics of War*, 22. This reflects Larry May's interpretation too: 'Contrary to what is often thought today, I read the Just War tradition as continuing a tradition of generally condemning war' – Larry May, *Aggression and Crimes against Peace* (Cambridge: Cambridge University Press, 2008), 9.

9  Walzer is, however, aware of a criticism according to which 'just war theory . . . frames wars in the wrong way. It focuses our attention on the immediate issues at stake before the war begins – in the case of the recent Iraq war, for example, on inspections, disarmament, hidden weapons, and so on – and then on the conduct of war, battle by battle; and so it avoid the larger questions about imperial ambition and the global struggle for resources and power' (*AW*, xi). For an exploration of the shortcomings of Walzer's defence against this criticism, see Dunford and Neu, *Just War and the Responsibility to Protect*.

10  For instance, he wrote with regard to the Afghanistan war in 2001: 'Assuming that we correctly identified the terrorist network responsible for the September 11 attacks and that the Taliban government was in fact its patron and protector, the war in Afghanistan is certainly a just one' (*AW*, 137).

11  See Michael Walzer, 'The Case against Our Attack on Libya', *New Republic*, 20 March 2011, accessed 20 May 2017, https://newrepublic.com/article/85509/the-case-against-our-attack-libya.

12  Michael Walzer, 'What a Little War in Iraq Could Do', *The New York Times*, 7 March 2003, accessed 20 May 2017, http://www.nytimes.com/2003/03/07/opinion/what-a-little-war-in-iraq-could-do.html, emphasis added. The piece was reprinted in

*AW*, 157–59. According to Tarik Kochi, Walzer's 'pronouncements about what does or does not constitute a "just cause" resemble little more than the private and dubious opinions given by politicians and so-called media "experts"' – Kochi, *The Other's War*, 23.

13  This is so even though the concrete *substance* of his just war theory is directed against Walzer's work. For an exchange between the two thinkers that illuminates the differences between Walzer's and McMahan's thinking about war, see their various papers in *Philosophia* 34, 1 (2006). Here, I focus on their similarities and shared mistakes.

14  Jeff McMahan, *Killing in War* (Oxford: Clarendon Press, 2009), vii. When I write '(*KW*, page number)' in this chapter, I refer to this book. Unless otherwise indicated, emphases in citations from *KW* are in the original.

15  Jeff McMahan, 'Just War: A Response to Neu', *Ethical Perspectives* 19, 2 (2012): 257–61, 258.

16  Jeff McMahan, 'Duty, Obedience, Desert, and Proportionality in War: A Response', *Ethics* 122, 1 (2011): 136.

17  Ibid.

18  According to Cheyney, 'A problem for this approach . . . is how it *individuates* wars – to be assessed "one at a time." Grotius, and later Walzer, and now some revisionist theorists take this as obvious. But is it?' – Cheyney, 'Pacifism(s)', 33. For an attempt to '[forestall] the criticism that [just war theory] is structurally incapable of looking beyond the "moment of crisis"', see Bazargan, 'Defensive Wars', 600. Bazargan is aware that there might be a 'problem with assessing the morality of resorting to war at the moment of crisis', namely 'that sometimes the state considering the resort to war is partly responsible, by having committed past wrongs, for creating the situation in which the resort to war becomes necessary in the first place', and he argues 'that the wrongs our country has committed in the recent past can affect the stringency of the wide proportionality constraint on the pursuit of just military aims against unjust aggressors' (ibid., 583 and 599). While I applaud Bazargan for attempting to push just war theory beyond 'the moment of crisis', his account remains deeply entrenched in contemporary analytic just war theory. He is not pushing nearly hard enough.

19  Jeff McMahan, 'The Moral Responsibility of Volunteer Soldiers: Should They Say No to Fighting in an Unjust War?' *The Boston Review*, 6 November 2013, accessed 20 May 2017, http://bostonreview.net/forum/jeff-mcmahan-moral-responsibility-volunteer-soldiers. I should emphasize that McMahan supported *only* the initial strikes in Afghanistan, not the ongoing war.

20  He even thinks 'that the reasons that favor humanitarian intervention actually rise to the level of obligation far more often than we intuitively recognize' – Jeff McMahan, 'Humanitarian Intervention, Consent, and Proportionality', in *Ethics and Humanity: Themes from the Philosophy of Jonathan Glover*, ed. N. Ann Davis, Richard Keshen and Jeff McMahan (Oxford: Oxford University Press, 2010), 62.

21  Ibid., 66. I write 'seems to judge' because McMahan's view that the Kosovo war was just and proportionate has a hypothetical bent to it – he articulates it on grounds of certain assumptions, namely that 'the intervention as it was carried out was better for

the Albanian Kosovars than their situation would have been if the United States had not intervened' (ibid., 66). This is a typical manoeuvre for the defender of just liberal violence: the philosopher can always hide behind a veil of epistemic uncertainty, suggesting what the argument *would* be if certain conditions *were* met. So there is a sense in which contemporary just war theorists embrace their epistemic incompetence. Compare Ryan, who points out that '[p]ost-Walzer theory drops [the] presumption for war. It aims to specify what a just war must look like, without assuming one way or another whether actual war ever meets that standard. It is open then to both contingent war-ism (upon inspection, *some* wars are just) and contingent pacifism (upon inspection, *no* wars are just)' – Ryan, 'Pacifism(s)', 26. In embracing epistemic incompetence, however, McMahan gives *carte blanche* to those whom he considers epistemically privileged. We remember from the previous chapter that torture defender Allhoff makes exactly the same move.

22  Jeff McMahan, 'Proportionality in the Afghanistan War', *Ethics & International Affairs* 25, 2 (2011): 154, emphasis added. For a detailed political analysis of this war and its terrible effects, see Dunford and Neu, *Just War and the Responsibility to Protect*.

23  For McMahan's qualified case for military strikes against Syria, see Jeff McMahan, 'The Moral Case for Military Strikes Against Syria', *Al Jazeera*, 4 September 2013, accessed 20 May 2017, http://america.aljazeera.com/articles/2013/9/4/the-moral-case-formilitarystrikesagainstsyria.html, emphasis added. Note once again that McMahan's case for limited military strikes is only *hypothetical*, since he 'lack[s] the information and expertise necessary to be confident that limited strikes against Syria could be effective in deterring or preventing further massacres of civilians' (ibid.).

24  Jeff McMahan, 'On the Moral Equality of Combatants', *The Journal of Political Philosophy* 14, 4 (2006): 390, emphasis added. The 'even' is important here. It reveals McMahan's assumption that liberal regimes, while not perfectly rational, have at least *begun* to be receptive to moral argument.

25  See, for example, his early book: Jeff McMahan, *Reagan and the World: Imperial Policy and the New Cold War* (London: Pluto Press, 1984).

26  Jeff McMahan and Robert McKim, 'The Just War and the Gulf War', *Canadian Journal of Philosophy* 23, 4 (1993): 541.

27  Jeff McMahan, 'The Morality of Occupation', *Loyola of Los Angeles International and Comparative Law Review* 31, 7 (2009): 17. For McMahan, the Iraq war was neither justified as preventive defence nor as a humanitarian intervention (ibid., 15–19).

28  Jeff McMahan, 'Preventive War and Killing of the Innocent', in *The Ethics of War: Shared Problems in Different Traditions*, ed. David Rodin and Richard Sorabji (Aldershot: Ashgate, 2005), 174–75. (To avoid a possible confusion, it should be pointed out that McMahan wrote this in 2005, so he is *not* referring to the 2011 Libya war.)

29  Ibid., 181–82.

30  Michael Walzer, *Just and Unjust Wars: A Moral Argument with Historical Illustrations*, 4th ed. (New York: Basic Books, 2006), 253. When I write '(*JUW*, page number)' in this chapter, I refer to this book. Unless otherwise indicated, emphases in citations from *JUW* are in the original.

31  To Walzer's mind, 'territorial integrity and political sovereignty can be defended in exactly the same way as individual life and liberty' (*JUW*, 54). For a critique of what Rodin refers to as the 'analogical strategy to justify war', see Rodin, 'War and Self-Defense', 141–62.

32  Rodin has also criticized this 'reductive strategy' (ibid., 127–32). McMahan does, however, 'recognize that there may be wrongs that are not entirely reducible to wrongs against individuals because they have a collective as their subject' – Jeff McMahan, 'Just Cause for War', *Ethics & International Affairs* 19, 3 (2005): 12.

33  Jeff McMahan, 'War as Self-Defense', *Ethics & International Affairs* 18, 1 (2004): 75.

34  McMahan, 'Just Cause for War', 8.

35  Ibid., 11–12.

36  The literature on double effect is extensive. For a collection of essays, see P. A. Woodward (ed.), *The Doctrine of Double Effect: Philosophers Debate a Controversial Moral Principle* (Notre Dame, IN: University of Notre Dame Press: 2001). For a defence of double effect in the specific context of *jus in bello*, see Coates, *The Ethics of War*, 254–78. For criticisms, see Jonathan Bennett, *Morality and Consequences: The Tanner Lectures on Human Values*, delivered at Brasenose College, Oxford University, 9, 16 and 23 May 1980, accessed 20 May 2017, http://tannerlectures.utah.edu/_documents/a-to-z/b/bennett81.pdf; David Lefkowitz, 'Collateral Damage', in *War: Essays in Moral Philosophy*, ed. Larry May (Cambridge: Cambridge University Press, 2008), 145–64; Judith Lichtenberg, 'War, Innocence, and the Doctrine of Double Effect', *Philosophical Studies* 74, 3 (1994): 347–68; Alison McIntyre, 'Doing Away with Double Effect', *Ethics*, 111, 2 (2001): 219–55; and Thomas Scanlon, *Moral Dimensions: Permissibility, Meaning, Blame* (Cambridge and London, 2008).

37  I elaborate on this more extensively in Neu, 'The Supreme Emergency of War'.

38  See Neu, 'Why McMahan's Just Wars Are Only Justified'. Also see McMahan, 'Just War'.

39  Jeff McMahan, 'Debate: Justification and Liability in War', *The Journal of Political Philosophy* 16, 2 (2008): 235, footnote 6.

40  McMahan, 'Just War', 259. In the end, McMahan does not think it matters what we call a war that we are right to wage: 'If we know that the harming and killing in a war are morally justified, and if we also know what kinds of justification there are for the different acts of harming and killing, we know the important moral facts. What labels we give to wars that are justified in different ways is mainly a matter of clarity and convenience of classification' – Jeff McMahan, 'Proportionality and Just Cause: A Comment on Kamm', *Journal of Moral Philosophy* 11 (2014), 428–53, 442.

41  I have refrained from counting how often the words intuition(s), intuitive(ly) and counterintuitive(ly) feature in *Killing in War*, let alone in McMahan's entire body of work.

42  Ryan, 'Democratic Duty', 41. Ryan thinks that 'any attempt to make war morally coherent will itself be incoherent' – Ryan, 'Pacifism(s), 25.

43  Michael Walzer, 'Political Action: The Problem of Dirty Hands', *Philosophy & Public Affairs* 2, 2 (1973): 161.

44   See also Graham Parsons, 'On the Incoherence of Walzer's Just War Theory', *Social Theory and Practice* 38, 4 (2012): 663–88. Parson argues that 'rather than operating within an individualist frame, as it originally appeared, Walzer's theory of *jus ad bellum* is based on a strong anti-individualism wherein the interests of irreducibly social entities not only have intrinsic value, but this value trumps the deepest interests of individuals, privately conceived' (ibid., 676–77).

45   This is also Coady's view: 'If we accept that some incidental killing (collateral damage) is morally legitimate in a just war, either because of the [doctrine of double effect] or for some other principled reason, it is then unclear (at least to me) how the non-combatants . . . have been wronged. They have not been done any injustice, though their deaths are a horrible and deeply regrettable outcome of what we are assuming to be right action' – Coady, *Morality and Political Violence*, 84.

46   McMahan, 'The Basis of Moral Liability', 388. If readers thinks that is an outlandish hypothetical, they have not yet read McMahan's later essay on the matter, where he introduces an example in which 'villagers have a remote control device capable of jamming the bomb doors of the bombers' plane' – Jeff McMahan, 'Self-Defense against Justified Threateners', in *How We Fight*, ed. Helen Frowe and Gerald Lang (Oxford: Oxford University Press, 2014), 110.

47   McMahan, 'The Basis of Moral Liability', 388, emphasis added.

48   Ibid., 389.

49   Ibid.

50   Ibid., 399 and 400.

51   Ibid., 400.

52   He reiterated this attempt in 2008. See McMahan, 'Debate: Justification and Liability in War'.

53   McMahan, 'Self-Defense against Justified Threateners', 104–73.

54   Ibid., 106.

55   Ibid., 106, emphasis added.

56   Ibid., 109.

57   Ibid., 114.

58   Ibid., 115.

59   Ibid., 126. I am sparing the reader the technical details of McMahan's case.

60   McMahan, 'Just Cause for War', 3, emphasis added.

61   McMahan, 'Self-Defense against Justified Threateners', 106, emphasis added.

62   Jeff McMahan, 'The Just Distribution of Harm between Combatants and Non-combatants', *Philosophy and Public Affairs* 38, 4 (2010): 378.

63   See John Taurek, 'Should the Numbers Count?' *Philosophy and Public Affairs* 6, 4 (1977): 293–316.

64   Let us just agree that we should resist using McMahan's euphemistic language of 'infringing' rights.

65   Ryan, 'Democratic Duty', 42.

66   Compare Cheyney, 'Pacifism(s)', 33.

67   Calhoun, Laurie, *War and Delusion: A Critical Examination* (Basingstoke: Palgrave MacMillan, 2013), 191.

68   For references, see chapter 2.

69  Frowe, Helen, *The Ethics of War and Peace: An Introduction* (Abingdon: Routledge, 2011), 2. Compare Seth Lazar, who writes that '[a]bstraction forestalls unhelpful disputes over historical details. It also reduces bias – we are inclined to view actual conflicts though the lens of our own political allegiances' – Seth Lazar, 'War'.

70  Helen Frowe and Tony Lang, 'Introduction', in *How We Fight*, ed. Frowe and Lang, xvii.

71  I owe this term to Afxentis Afxentiou.

72  Compare Burke, who argues for '[shifting] the normative ideal from just war to *ethical peace*, an ethics that eschews abstract moral theory in favour of a context-sensitive ethical orientation that is concerned with the *outcomes* of decisions and the *avoidance* of suffering' – Burke, 'Just War or Ethical Peace', 333. Also see Butler, who writes that 'if war is to be opposed, we have to understand how popular assent to war is cultivated and maintained, in other words, how war waging acts upon the senses so that war is thought to be an inevitability, something good, or even a source of moral satisfaction' – Judith Butler, *Frames of War* (London: Verso, 2010), ix.

73  Butler, *Frames of War*, xviii.

## CHAPTER 6

1  Kazuo Ishiguro, *Never Let Me Go* (London: Faber and Faber, 2005), 262–63.

2  Indeed, one could perhaps say that Miss Emily is more like those sweatshop 'critics' who think that sweatshops should be made to improve their conditions by being regulated, but who do not fundamentally question the existence of sweatshops *per se* since they think they are inevitable. More rigorous sweatshops defenders are not even Miss Emily's; they would argue against even these types of reform.

3  Alasdair MacIntyre, 'Social Structures and Their Threats to Moral Agency', *Philosophy* 74, 3 (1999): 328.

# Bibliography

Afxentis Afxentiou, Robin Dunford, and Michael Neu. 'Introducing Complicity'. In *Exploring Complicity: Concept, Cases and Critique*, edited by Afxentis Afxentiou, Robin Dunford and Michael Neu, 1–15. London: Rowman & Littlefield International, 2017.

Allhoff, Fritz. 'A Defense of Torture: Separation of Cases, Ticking Time-Bombs, and Moral Justification'. *International Journal of Applied Philosophy* 19, 2 (2005): 243–64.

Allhoff, Fritz. 'Terrorism and Torture'. *International Journal of Applied Philosophy* 17, 1 (2003): 105–18.

Allhoff, Fritz. *Terrorism, Ticking Time-Bombs, and Torture: A Philosophical Analysis*. Chicago: University of Chicago Press, 2012.

Anghie, Antony. *Imperialism, Sovereignty and the Making of International Law*. Cambridge: Cambridge University Press, 2004.

Arnold, Denis G., and Norman E. Bowie. 'Sweatshops and Respect for Persons'. *Business Ethics Quarterly* 13, 2 (2003): 221–42.

Arnold, Denis G., and Laura P. Hartman. 'Beyond Sweatshops: Positive Deviancy and Global Labour Practices'. *Business Ethics: A European Review* 14, 2 (2005): 206–22.

Arnold, Denis G., and Laura P. Hartman. 'Moral Imagination and the Future of Sweatshops'. *Business and Society Review* 108, 4 (2003): 425–61.

Arnold, Denis G., and Laura P. Hartman. 'Worker Rights and Low Wage Industrialization: How to Avoid Sweatshops'. *Human Rights Quarterly* 28, 3 (2006): 676–700.

Bagaric, Mirko, and Julie Clarke. *Torture: When the Unthinkable Is Permissible*. Albany: State University of New York Press, 2007.

Bales, Keven. *Disposable People: New Slavery in the Global Economy*. Revised ed. Berkeley and Los Angeles: University of California Press, 2004.

Bazargan, Saba. 'Defensive Wars and the Reprisal Dilemma'. *Australasian Journal of Philosophy* 93, 3 (2015): 583–601.

Bellamy, Alex. *Just Wars: From Cicero to Iraq*. Malden, MA: Polity Press, 2006.

Bellamy, Alex. *The Responsibility to Protect: A Defence*. Oxford: Oxford University Press, 2014.

Bennett, Jonathan. *Morality and Consequences: The Tanner Lectures on Human Values*. Delivered at Brasenose College, Oxford University, 9, 16 and 23 May 1980. Accessed 20 May 2017. http://tannerlectures.utah.edu/_documents/a-to-z/b/bennett81.pdf.

Bhagwati, Jagdish. *In Defense of Globalization*. New York: Oxford University Press, 2004.

Boyden, Jo et al. 'Letter: When Work Is Right for Children'. *The Observer*, 18 December 2016. Accessed 10 May 2017. https://www.theguardian.com/theobserver/2016/dec/18/tech-companies-must-take-responsibility-for-algorithms.

Brecher, Bob. 'Surrogacy, Liberal Individualism and the Moral Climate'. In *Moral Philosophy and Contemporary Problems*, edited by S. D. G. Evans, 183–97. Cambridge: Cambridge University Press, 1987.

Brecher, Bob. *Torture and the Ticking Bomb*. Oxford: Wiley-Blackwell, 2007.

Brecher, Bob, and Michael Neu. 'Intellectual Complicity in Torture'. In *Exploring Complicity: Concept, Cases and Critique*, edited by Afxentis Afxentiou, Robin Dunford and Michael Neu, 143–60. London: Rowman & Littlefield International, 2017.

Brown, Garrett Wallace, and Alexandra Bohm. 'Introducing *Jus ad Bellum* as a Cosmopolitan Approach to Humanitarian Intervention'. *European Journal of International Relations* 22, 4 (2016): 897–919.

Bufacchi, Vittorio, and Jean Mario Arrigo. 'Torture, Terrorism and the State: A Refutation of the Ticking-Bomb Argument'. *Journal of Applied Philosophy* 23, 3 (2006): 355–73.

Burke, Anthony. 'Just War or Ethical Peace: Moral Discourses of Strategic Violence after 9/11'. *International Affairs* 80, 2 (2004): 329–53.

Butler, Judith. 'Can One Lead a Good Life in a Bad Life? Adorno Prize Lecture'. *Radical Philosophy* 176 (November/December 2012): 9–18.

Butler, Judith. *Frames of War*. London: Verso, 2010.

Calder, Todd. 'Shared Responsibility, Global Structural Injustice, and Restitution'. *Social Theory and Practice* 36, 2 (2010): 263–90.

Calhoun, Laurie. *War and Delusion: A Critical Examination*. Basingstoke: Palgrave MacMillan, 2013.

Calhoun, Laurie. *We Kill Because We Can: From Soldiering to Assassination*. London: Zed, 2015.

Chamayou, Grégoire. *Drone Theory*. London: Penguin, 2015.

Chang, Ha-Joon. *23 Things They Don't Tell You about Capitalism*. London: Penguin Books, 2011.

Charlesworth, Hilary. 'International Law: A Discipline of Crisis'. *Modern Law Review* 65, 3 (2002): 377–92.

Coady, C. A. J. 'The Idea of Violence'. *Journal of Applied Philosophy* 3, 1 (1986): 3–19.

Coady, C. A. J. *Morality and Political Violence*. Cambridge: Cambridge University Press, 2008.

Coates, A. J. *The Ethics of War*. 2nd ed. Manchester: Manchester University Press, 2016.

Cobain, Ian. *Cruel Britannia: A Secret History of Torture*. London: Granta, 2013.

Cohen, G. A. 'Are Disadvantaged Workers Who Take Hazardous Jobs Forced to Take Hazardous Jobs?' In *Moral Rights in the Workplace*, edited by Gertrude Ezorsky, 61–80. Albany, State University of New York Press, 1987.

Cohen, G. A. 'The Structure of Proletarian Unfreedom'. *Philosophy & Public Affairs* 12, 1 (1983): 3–33.

Davis, Mike. *Planet of Slums*. London and New York: Verso, 2006.

Dershowitz, Alan. 'Tortured Reasoning'. In *Torture: A Collection*, edited by Sanford Levinson, 257–80. Oxford: Oxford University Press, 2004.

Dershowitz, Alan. 'The Torture Warrant: A Response to Professor Strauss'. *New York Law School Legal Review* 48 (2004): 275–94.

Dershowitz, Alan. 'When Torture Is the Least Evil of Terrible Options'. *Times Higher Education Supplement*, 11 June 2004. Accessed 14 May 2017. https://www.timeshighereducation.com/features/when-torture-is-the-least-evil-of-terrible-options/189257.article.

Dershowitz, Alan. *Why Terrorism Works*. New Haven and London: Yale University Press, 2002.

Deveaux, Monique, and Vida Panitch. 'Introduction'. In *Exploitation: From Practice to Theory*, edited by Monique Deveaux and Vida Panitch, 1–11. London: Rowman & Littlefield International, 2017.

Devine, Philip. 'Book Review: Fritz Allhoff, *Terrorism, Time-Bombs, and Torture: A Philosophical Analysis*'. *Ethics* 123, 2 (2013): 346–49.

Docherty, Thomas. *Complicity: Critique between Collaboration and Commitment*. London: Rowman and Littlefield, 2016.

Dower, Nigel. *The Ethics of War and Peace: Cosmopolitan and Other Perspectives*. Cambridge: Polity, 2009.

Dunford, Robin. 'Toward a Decolonial Global Ethics', *Journal of Global Ethics*, DOI: 10.1080/1749626.2017.1373140, 2017.

Dunford, Robin. 'Peasant Activism and the Rise of Food Sovereignty: Decolonizing and Democratising Norm Diffusion'. *European Journal of International Relations* 23, 1 (2017): 145–67.

Dunford, Robin. *The Politics of Transnational Peasant Struggle: Resistance, Rights and Democracy*. London: Rowman & Littlefield International, 2016.

Dunford, Robin, and Michael Neu. *Just War and the Responsibility to Protect: A Critique*. London: Zed, forthcoming.

Eisenstein, Hester. *Feminism Seduced: How Global Elites Use Women's Labor and Ideas to Exploit the World*. London: Taylor & Francis, 2010.

Escobar, Arturo. 'Beyond the Third World: Imperial Globality, Global Coloniality and Anti-Globalisation Global Movements'. *Third World Quarterly* 25, 1 (2004): 207–30.

Evans, Mark. 'In Defence of Just War Theory'. In *Just War Theory: A Reappraisal*, edited by Mark Evans, 203–22. Edinburgh: Edinburgh University Press, 2005.

Fabre, Cécile. *Cosmopolitan War*. Oxford: Oxford University Press, 2015.

Frank, Andre Gunder. 'The Development of Underdevelopment'. *Monthly Review* 18, 4 (1966): 17–31.

Fried, Gregory. 'Book Review: Uwe Steinhoff, *On the Ethics of Torture*'. *Notre Dame Philosophical Reviews*, 20 May 2014. Accessed 14 May 2017. http://ndpr. nd.edu/news/48412-on-the-ethics-of-torture/.

Frost, Mervyn, and David Rodin. 'How to Get Humanitarian Intervention Right: What Libya Teaches Us about Responsibility to Protect'. *Inside Briefing, Oxford Martin Law School*, March 2011. Accessed 20 May 2017. http://www.oxfordmartin. ox.ac.uk/downloads/briefings/2011-03-Libya.pdf.

Frowe, Helen. *Defensive Killing*. Oxford: Oxford University Press, 2014.

Frowe, Helen. *The Ethics of War and Peace: An Introduction*. Abingdon: Routledge, 2011.

Frowe, Helen. 'War and Intervention'. In *Issues in Political Theory*, edited by Catriona McKinnon, 213–35. 3rd ed. Oxford: Oxford University Press, 2015.

Frowe, Helen, and Tony Lang. 'Introduction'. In *How We Fight*, edited by Helen Frowe and Gerald Lang, xiii–xxxii. Oxford: Oxford University Press, 2014.

Galtung, Johan. 'Cultural Violence'. *Journal of Peace Research* 27, 3 (1990): 291–305.

Galtung, Johan. 'Violence, Peace, and Peace Research'. *Journal of Peace Research* 6, 3 (1969): 167–91.

Garver, Newton. 'What Violence Is'. *Nation*, 24 June 1968, 817–22. Reprinted in modified form in Vittorio Bufacchi. *Violence: A Philosophical Anthology*, 170–82. New York and Basingstoke: Palgrave MacMillan, 2009.

Gilligan, James. *Violence: Reflections on a National Epidemic*. New York: Vintage Books, 1997.

Ginbar, Yuval. *Why Not Torture Terrorists? Moral, Practical, and Legal Aspects of the 'Ticking Bomb' Justification for Torture*. Oxford: Oxford University Press, 2010.

Giroud, Henry. *The University in Chains: Confronting the Military-Industrial-Academic Complex*. London and New York: Routledge, 2016.

Gordon, Rebecca. *Mainstreaming Torture: Ethical Approaches in the Post-9/11 United States*. New York: Oxford University Press, 2014.

Gowans, Christopher W., ed. *Moral Dilemmas*. Oxford: Oxford University Press, 1987.

Graubart, Jonathan. 'R2P and Pragmatic Liberal Interventionism: Values in the Service of Interests'. *Human Rights Quarterly* 35, 1 (2013): 69–90.

Greenberg, Karen, and Joshua L. Dratel, eds. *The Torture Papers: The Road to Abu Ghraib*. Cambridge: Cambridge University Press, 2005.

Grosfoguel, Ramón. 'The Epistemic Decolonial Turn'. *Cultural Studies* 21, 2/3 (2007): 211–23.

*The Guardian*. 'Donald Trump: I'd Bring Back "a Hell of a Lot Worse than Waterboarding"', 7 February 2016. Accessed 14 May 2017. https://www.theguardian. com/us-news/2016/feb/06/donald-trump-waterboarding-republican-debate-torture.

Harbury, Jennifer. *Truth, Torture and the American Way: The History and Consequences of U.S. Involvement in Torture*. Boston, MA: Beacon Press, 2005.

Harris, John. 'The Marxist Conception of Violence'. *Philosophy & Public Affairs* 3, 2 (1974): 192–220.

Henderson, David. 'The Case for Sweatshops'. *Hoover Daily Report*, 7 February 2000. Accessed 4 April 2016. www.hoover.org/research/case-sweatshops.

Hickel, Jason. 'The 'Girl Effect': Liberalism, Empowerment, and the Contradictions of Development'. *Third World Quarterly* 35, 8 (2014): 1355–73.

Holmes, Robert. *On War and Morality*. Princeton, NJ: Princeton University Press, 1989.

Hurka, Thomas. 'Proportionality in the Morality of War'. *Philosophy & Public Affairs* 33, 1 (2005): 34–66.

Hutchings, Kimberly. 'Cosmopolitan Just War and Coloniality'. In *Race, Empire and Global Justice*, edited by Duncan Bell, forthcoming.

International Labour Organization. *Forced Labour, Modern Slavery and Human Trafficking*. Accessed 20 May 2016. http://www.ilo.org/global/topics/forced-labour/lang – en/index.htm.

Iraq Body Count. Accessed 14 May 2017. https://www.iraqbodycount.org/.

Iraq Body Count. *A Dossier of Civilian Casualties in Iraq 2003–2005*, 12 July 2005. Accessed 29 April 2017. https://www.iraqbodycount.org/analysis/reference/press-releases/12/.

Ishiguro, Kazuo. *Never Let Me Go*. London: Faber and Faber, 2005.

Jackson, Richard. *Writing the War on Terrorism*. Manchester: Manchester University Press, 2005.

Kamm, Frances. *The Moral Target: Aiming at Right Conduct in War and Other Conflicts*. Oxford: Oxford University Press, 2012.

Kates, Michael. 'The Ethics of Sweatshops and the Limits of Choice'. *Business Ethics Quarterly* 25, 2 (2015): 191–212.

Kershnar, Stephen. *For Torture: A Rights-Based Defence*. Lanham, MD: Lexington Books, 2011.

Khalili, Laleh. *Time in the Shadows: Confinement in Counterinsurgencies*. Stanford, CA: Stanford University Press, 2013.

Kochi, Tarik. *The Other's War: Recognition and the Violence of Ethics*. Abingdon: Birkbeck Law Press, 2009.

Kristoff, Nicholas. 'In Praise of the Maligned Sweatshop'. *The New York Times*, 6 June 2006. Accessed 10 May 2017. http://www.nytimes.com/2006/06/06/opinion/06kristof.html?mcubz=0.

Kristoff, Nicholas. 'My Sweatshop Column'. *The New York Times*, 14 January 2009. Accessed 18 July 2016. http://kristof.blogs.nytimes.com/2009/01/14/my-sweatshop-column/comment-page-1/.

Kristoff, Nicholas. 'Where Sweatshops Are a Dream'. *The New York Times*, 14 January 2009. Accessed 4 April 2016. www.nytimes.com/2009/01/15/opinion/15kristof.html?_r=0.

Kristoff, Nicholas, and Sheryl WuDunn. *Half the Sky: Turning Oppression into Opportunity for Women Worldwide*. New York: Knopf Doubleday, 2010.

Krugman, Paul. 'In Praise of Cheap Labor: Bad Jobs at Bad Wages Are Better than No Jobs at All'. *Slate*, 21 March 1997. Accessed 4 April 2016. www.slate.com/articles/business/the_dismal_science/1997/03/in_praise_of_cheap_labor.html.

Krugman, Paul. 'Safer Sweatshops'. *The New York Times*, 8 July 2013. Accessed 4 April 2016. http://krugman.blogs.nytimes.com/2013/07/08/safer-sweatshops/?_r=0.

Lazar, Seth. 'The Responsibility Dilemma for *Killing in War*: A Review Essay'. *Philosophy & Public Affairs* 38, 3 (2010): 180–213.

Lazar, Seth. *Sparing Civilians*. Oxford: Oxford University Press, 2015.

Lazar, Seth. 'War'. In *The Stanford Encyclopedia of Philosophy*, edited by Edward N. Zalta (summer 2016 ed.). Accessed 20 May 2017. http://plato.stanford.edu/archives/sum2016/entries/war/.

Lee, Steven. 'Poverty and Violence'. *Social Theory and Practice* 22, 1 (1996): 67–82.

Leech, Garry. *Capitalism: A Structural Genocide*. London: Zed, 2012.

Lefkowitz, David. 'Collateral Damage'. In *War: Essays in Moral Philosophy*, edited by Larry May, 145–64. Cambridge: Cambridge University Press, 2008.

Levin, Michael. 'The Case for Torture'. *Newsweek*, 7 June 1982. Accessed 14 May 2017. http://people.brandeis.edu/~teuber/torture.html.

Liberti, Stefano. *Land Grabbing: Journeys in the New Colonialism*, translated by Enda Flannelly. London and New York: Verso, 2013.

Lichtenberg, Judith. 'War, Innocence, and the Doctrine of Double Effect'. *Philosophical Studies* 74, 3 (1994): 347–68.

Lippert-Rasmussen, Kasper. 'Global Justice and Redistributive Wars'. *Law, Ethics and Philosophy* 1, 1 (2013): 65–86.

Losurdo, Domenico. *Liberalism: A Counter-History*. London and New York: Verso, 2014.

Luban, David. *Torture, Power, and Law*. Cambridge: Cambridge University Press, 2014.

MacIntyre, Alasdair. *Dependent Rational Animals: Why Human Beings Need the Virtues*. London: Gerald Duckworth, 1999.

MacIntyre, Alasdair. 'Social Structures and Their Threats to Moral Agency'. *Philosophy* 74, 3 (1999): 311–29.

Maitland, Ian. 'The Great Non-Debate over International Sweatshops'. In *Ethical Theory and Business*, edited by Tom L. Beauchamp, Norman E. Bowie and Denis G. Arnold, 597–608. 8th ed. Upper Saddle River, NJ: Pearson Prentice Hall, 2008.

Malmqvist, Erik. 'Taking Advantage of Injustice'. *Social Theory and Practice* 39, 4 (2013): 557–80.

Mamdani, Mahmood. 'Responsibility to Protect or Right to Punish'. *Journal of Intervention and Statebuilding* 4, 1 (2010): 53–67.

Marantz, Steve. 'Young Fighters Exposed to Exploitation'. *Entertainment and Sports Programming Network (ESPN)*, 5 November 2013. Accessed 10 May 2017. http://www.espn.com/espn/e60/story/_/id/9929399/child-fighters-thailand-vulnerable-exploitation.

May, Larry. *Aggression and Crimes against Peace*. Cambridge: Cambridge University Press, 2008.

May, Todd. *Nonviolent Resistance: A Philosophical Introduction*. Cambridge: Polity Press, 2015.

Mayer, Jane. *The Dark Side: The Inside Story of How the War on Terror Turned into a War on American Ideals*. New York: Doubleday Books, 2009.

Mayer, Robert. 'Sweatshops, Exploitation, and Moral Responsibility'. *The Journal of Social Philosophy* 38, 4 (2007): 605–19.

Mayerfeld, Jamie. 'In Defense of the Absolute Prohibition of Torture'. *Public Affairs Quarterly* 22, 2 (2008): 109–28.

McIntyre, Alison. 'Doing Away with Double Effect'. *Ethics* 111, 2 (2001): 219–55.

McKeown, Maeve. 'Sweatshop Labour as Global Structural Exploitation'. In *Exploitation: From Practice to Theory*, edited by Monique Deveaux and Vida Panitch, 35–57. London: Rowman & Littlefield International, 2017.

McMahan, Jeff. 'The Basis of Moral Liability to Defensive Killing'. *Philosophical Issues* 15, 1 (2005): 386–405.

McMahan, Jeff. 'Debate: Justification and Liability in War'. *The Journal of Political Philosophy* 16, 2 (2008): 227–44.

McMahan, Jeff. 'Duty, Obedience, Desert, and Proportionality in War: A Response'. *Ethics* 122, 1 (2011): 135–67.

McMahan, Jeff. 'Humanitarian Intervention, Consent, and Proportionality'. In *Ethics and Humanity: Themes from the Philosophy of Jonathan Glover*, edited by N. Ann Davis, Richard Keshen and Jeff McMahan, 44–72. Oxford: Oxford University Press, 2010.

McMahan, Jeff. 'Just Cause for War'. *Ethics & International Affairs* 19, 3 (2005): 1–21.

McMahan, Jeff. 'The Just Distribution of Harm between Combatants and Noncombatants'. *Philosophy and Public Affairs* 38, 4 (2010): 342–79.

McMahan, Jeff. 'Just War: A Response to Neu'. *Ethical Perspectives* 19, 2 (2012): 257–61.

McMahan, Jeff. *Killing in War*. Oxford, Clarendon Press, 2009.

McMahan, Jeff. 'The Moral Case for Military Strikes against Syria. *Al Jazeera*, 4 September 2013. Accessed 20 May 2017. http://america.aljazeera.com/articles/2013/9/4/the-moral-case-formilitarystrikesagainstsyria.html.

McMahan, Jeff. 'The Moral Responsibility of Volunteer Soldiers: Should They Say No to Fighting in an Unjust War?' *The Boston Review*, 6 November 2013. Accessed 20 May 2017. http://bostonreview.net/forum/jeff-mcmahan-moral-responsibility-volunteer-soldiers.

McMahan, Jeff. 'The Morality of Occupation'. *Loyola of Los Angeles International and Comparative Law Review* 31, 7 (2009): 7–29.

McMahan, Jeff. 'On the Moral Equality of Combatants'. *The Journal of Political Philosophy* 14, 4 (2006): 377–93.

McMahan, Jeff. 'Preventive War and Killing of the Innocent'. In *The Ethics of War: Shared Problems in Different Traditions*, edited by David Rodin and Richard Sorabji, 169–90. Aldershot: Ashgate, 2005.

McMahan, Jeff. 'Proportionality and Just Cause: A Comment on Kamm'. *Journal of Moral Philosophy* 11 (2014), 428–53.

McMahan, Jeff. 'Proportionality in the Afghanistan War'. *Ethics & International Affairs* 25, 2 (2011): 143–54.

McMahan, Jeff. *Reagan and the World: Imperial Policy and the New Cold War*. London: Pluto Press, 1984.

McMahan, Jeff. 'Self-Defense against Justified Threateners'. In *How We Fight*, edited by Helen Frowe and Gerald Lang, 104–37. Oxford: Oxford University Press, 2014.

McMahan, Jeff. 'Torture in Principle and in Practice'. *Public Affairs Quarterly* 22, 2 (2008): 111–28.

McMahan, Jeff. 'War as Self-Defense'. *Ethics & International Affairs* 18, 1 (2004): 75–80.

McMahan, Jeff, and Robert McKim. 'The Just War and the Gulf War'. *Canadian Journal of Philosophy* 23, 4 (1993): 501–41.

Mehta, Vijay. *The Economics of Killing: How the West Fuels War and Poverty in the Developing World.* London: Pluto, 2012.

Meyers, Chris. 'Wrongful Beneficence: Exploitation and Third World Sweatshops'. *Journal of Social Philosophy* 35, 3 (2004): 319–33.

Mgbeoji, Ikechi. 'The Civilised Self and the Barbaric Other: Imperial Delusions of Order and the Challenges of Human Security'. *Third World Quarterly* 27, 5 (2006): 855–69.

Mignolo, Walter D. *The Darker Side of Western Modernity: Global Futures, Decolonial Options.* Durham, NC: Duke University Press, 2011.

Mill, John Stuart. *On Liberty and Other Essays,* edited by John Gray. Oxford and New York: Oxford University Press, 1991.

Miller, John. 'Why Economists Are Wrong about Sweatshops and the Antisweatshop Movement'. *Challenge* 46, 1 (2003): 93–122.

Miller, Seumas. 'Is Torture Ever Morally Justified?' *International Journal of Applied Philosophy* 19, 2 (2005): 179–92.

Miller, Seumas. *Terrorism and Counter-Terrorism: Ethics and Liberal Democracy.* Oxford: Blackwell, 2009.

Moniruzzaman, Monir. '"Living Cadavers" in Bangladesh: Bioviolence in the Human Organ Bazzar'. *Medical Anthropology Quarterly* 26, 1 (2012): 69–91.

Morgenthau, Hans J. *Politics among Nations: The Struggle for Power and Peace.* 7th ed. Revised by Kenneth W. Thompson and W. David Clinton. New York: McGraw-Hill, 2006.

Müller, Mirjam. 'The Relationship between Exploitation and Structural Injustice: Why Structures Matter in an Account of Exploitation'. *Unpublished Manuscript.*

Neu, Michael. 'The Fragility of Justified Warfare: A Comment on Steinhoff'. *Theoretical & Applied Ethics* 1, 4 (2012): 45–53.

Neu, Michael. 'The Supreme Emergency of War: A Critique of Walzer'. *The Journal of International Political Theory* 10, 1 (2013): 3–19.

Neu, Michael. 'The Tragedy of Justified War'. *International Relations* 27, 4 (2013): 461–80.

Neu, Michael. Why McMahan's *Just* Wars Are Only *Justified* and Why that Matters'. *Ethical Perspectives* 19, 2 (2012): 235–55.

Neu, Michael. 'Why There Is No Such Thing as Just War Pacifism and Why Just War Theorists and Pacifists Can Talk Nonetheless'. *Social Theory & Practice* 37, 3 (2011): 413–33.

Nili, Shmuel. 'Humanitarian Disintervention'. *Journal of Global Ethics* 7, 1 (2011): 33–46.

Noonan, Jeff. *Democratic Society and Human Needs.* Montreal: McGill-Queen's University Press, 2006.

Norman, Richard. *Ethics, Killing and War*. Cambridge: Cambridge University Press, 1995.

Olsaretti, Serena. *Life, Desert and the Market: A Philosophical Study*. Cambridge: Cambridge University Press, 2004.

O'Mane, Shara. *Why Torture Doesn't Work: The Neuroscience of Investigation*. Cambridge, MA: Harvard University Press, 2015.

Orend, Brian. *The Morality of War*. Peterborough: Broadview Press, 2006.

Orend, Brian. *The Morality of War*. 2nd ed. Peterborough: Broadview Press, 2013.

Øverland, Gerhard. '602 and One Dead: On Contribution to Global Poverty and Liability to Defensive Force'. *European Journal of Philosophy* 21, 2 (2013): 279–99.

Parsons, Graham. 'On the Incoherence of Walzer's Just War Theory'. *Social Theory and Practice* 38, 4 (2012): 663–88.

Pearce, Fred. *The Land Grabbers: The New Fight over Who Owns the Earth*. Boston, MA: Beacon Press, 2012.

Peirce, Gareth. *Dispatches from the Dark Side*: *On Torture and the Death of Justice*. London: Verso, 2012.

Peter, Fabienne. 'Choice, Consent, and the Legitimacy of Market Transactions'. *Economics and Philosophy* 20, 1 (2004): 1–18.

Physicians for Human Rights. *Broken Laws, Broken Lives: Medical Evidence of Torture by US Personnel and Its Impact*. A Report by Physicians for Human Rights, Executive Summary, June 2008. Accessed 14 May 2017. http://brokenlives.info/?page_id=69.

Plato. *The Republic*, translated by Desmond Lee. London: Penguin Classics, 2007.

Powell, Benjamin. 'In Reply to Sweatshops Sophistries'. *Human Rights Quarterly* 28, 4 (2006): 1031–42.

Powell, Benjamin. 'Meet the Old Sweatshops: Same as the New'. *The Independent Review* 19, 1 (2014): 109–22.

Powell, Benjamin. *Out of Poverty: Sweatshops in the Global Economy*. Cambridge: Cambridge University Press, 2014.

Powell, Benjamin. 'Sweatshops in Bangladesh Improve the Lives of Their Workers, and Boost Growth'. *Forbes*, 2 May 2013. Accessed 27 February 2017. https://www.forbes.com/sites/realspin/2013/05/02/sweatshops-in-bangladesh-improve-the-lives-of-their-workers-and-boost-growth/#31e6c79c74ce.

Powell, Benjamin, and David Skarbek. 'Sweatshops and Third World Living Standards: Are the Jobs Worth the Sweat?' *Journal of Labor Research* 27, 2 (2006): 263–74.

Powell, Benjamin, and Matt Zwolinski. 'The Ethical and Economic Case against Sweatshop Labor: A Critical Assessment'. *The Journal of Business Ethics* 107, 4 (2012): 449–72.

Preiss, Joshua. 'Global Labor Justice and the Limits of Economic Analysis'. *Business Ethics Quarterly* 24, 1 (2014), 55–83.

Quijano, Anibal. 'Coloniality and Modernity/Rationality'. *Cultural Studies* 21, 2/3 (2007): 168–78.

Reader, Soran. 'Making Pacifism Plausible'. *Journal of Applied Philosophy* 17, 2 (2000): 169–80.

Rejali, Darius. *Torture and Democracy*. Princeton, NJ: Princeton University Press, 2009.

Richman, Sheldon. 'Iraqi Sanctions: Were They Worth It?' *Global Policy Forum*, January 2004. Accessed 7 August 2016. https://www.globalpolicy.org/component/content/article/170/41952.html.

Rodin, David. 'Justifying Harm'. *Ethics* 122, 1 (2011): 74–110.

Rodin, David. *War and Self-Defense*. Oxford: Oxford University Press, 2002.

Rose, David. 'Tortured Reasoning'. *Vanity Fair*, 16 December 2008. Accessed 14 May 2017. http://vanityfair.com/magazine/2008/12/torture200812.

Rosen, Ellen Israel. *Making Sweatshops: The Globalization of the U.S. Apparel Industry*. Berkeley and Los Angeles: University of California Press, 2002.

Ross, Robert J. S. *Slaves to Fashion: Poverty and Abuse in the New Sweatshops*. Ann Arbor: University of Michigan Press, 2004.

Ryan, Cheyney. 'Democratic Duty and the Moral Dilemmas of Soldiers'. *Ethics* 122, 1 (2011): 10–42.

Ryan, Cheyney. 'Pacifism(s)'. *The Philosophical Forum* 46, 1 (2015): 17–39.

Ryan, Cheyney. 'Self-Defense, Pacifism, and the Possibility of Killing'. *Ethics* 93, 3 (1983): 508–24.

Sachs, Jeffrey. *The End of Poverty: Economic Possibilities for Our Time*. New York and London: Penguin, 2006.

Salmi, Jamil. *Violence and Democratic Society*. London: Zed, 1993.

Sands, Philippe. *Torture Team: Uncovering War Crimes in the Land of the Free*. London: Penguin, 2008.

Scanlon, Thomas. *Moral Dimensions: Permissibility, Meaning, Blame*. Cambridge and London: Belknap Press of Harvard University Press, 2008.

Seymour, Richard. *The Liberal Defence of Murder*. London: Verso, 2008.

Shue, Henry. *Fighting Hurt: Rule and Exception in Torture and War*. Oxford: Oxford University Press, 2016.

Sinnott-Armstrong, Walter. *Moral Dilemmas*. Oxford and New York: Basil Blackwell, 1988.

Snyder, Jeremy. 'Exploitation and Demeaning Choices'. *Politics, Philosophy & Economics* 12, 4 (2013): 345–60.

Snyder, Jeremy. 'Needs Exploitation'. *Ethical Theory and Moral Practice* 11, 4 (2008): 389–405.

Steinhoff, Uwe. *On the Ethics of Torture*. Albany, NY: Suny Press, 2013.

Steinhoff, Uwe. *On the Ethics of War and Terrorism*. Oxford: Oxford University Press, 2007.

Steinhoff, Uwe. 'Torture: The Case for Dirty Harry and against Alan Dershowitz'. *Journal of Applied Philosophy* 23, 3 (2006): 337–53.

Strawser, Bradley. 'Moral Predators: The Duty to Employ Uninhabited Aerial Vehicles'. *Journal of Military Ethics* 9, 4 (2010): 342–68.

Styron, William. *Sophie's Choice*. London: Vintage, 2005.

Taguba, Antonio. 'Preface'. In *Broken Laws, Broken Lives: Medical Evidence of Torture by US Personnel and Its Impact*. A Report by Physicians for Human Rights,

Executive Summary, June 2008. Accessed 14 May 2017. http://brokenlives. info/?page_id=69.

Taurek, John. 'Should the Numbers Count?' *Philosophy and Public Affairs* 6, 4 (1977): 293–316.

Tesón, Fernando R. 'Ending Tyranny in Iraq'. *Ethics & International Affairs* 19, 2 (2005): 1–20.

United Nations Human Settlements Programme (UN-Habitat). *The Challenge of Slums: Global Report on Human Settlements 2003*. London and Sterling, VA: Earthscan Publications, 2003.

Veitch, Scott. *Law and Irresponsibility: On the Legitimation of Human Suffering*. Abingdon: Routledge-Cavendish, 2007.

Vorobej, Mark. 'Structural Violence'. *The Canadian Journal of Peace and Conflict Studies* 40, 2 (2008): 84–98.

Waldron, Jeremy. *Torture, Terror, and Trade-Offs: Philosophy for the White House*. Oxford: Oxford University Press, 2010.

Walzer, Michael. *Arguing about War*. New Haven, CT, and London: Yale University Press, 2004.

Walzer, Michael. 'The Case against Our Attack on Libya'. *New Republic*, 20 March 2011. Accessed 20 May 2017. https://newrepublic.com/article/85509/the-case-against-our-attack-libya.

Walzer, Michael. *Just and Unjust Wars*. 4th ed. New York: Basic Books, 2006.

Walzer, Michael. 'Political Action: The Problem of Dirty Hands'. *Philosophy & Public Affairs* 2, 2 (1973): 160–80.

Walzer, Michael. 'Response to McMahan's Paper'. *Philosophia* 34, 1 (2006): 43–5.

Walzer, Michael. 'What a Little War in Iraq Could Do'. *The New York Times*, 7 March 2003. Accessed 20 May 2017. http://www.nytimes.com/2003/03/07/opinion/what-a-little-war-in-iraq-could-do.html.

Welch, Michael. 'Book Review: Uwe Steinhoff, *On the Ethics of Torture*'. *Punishment & Society* 17, 2 (2015): 261–62.

Wolf, Martin. *Why Globalization Works: The Case for the Global Market Economy*. New Haven, CT, and London: Yale Nota Bene, 2005.

Wolfendale, Jessica. 'Training Torturers: A Critique of the "Ticking-Bomb" Argument'. *Social Theory and Practice* 32, 3 (2006): 269–87.

Young, Iris Marion. 'Responsibility and Global Justice: A Social Connection Model'. *Social Philosophy and Policy* 21, 1 (2006): 102–30.

Zwolinski, Matt. 'Structural Exploitation'. *Social Philosophy and Policy* 29, 1 (2012): 154–79.

Zwolinski, Matt. 'Sweatshops, Choice, and Exploitation'. *Business Ethics Quarterly* 17, 4 (2007): 689–727.

# Index

absolutism/absolutist, 56, 59, 91, 119n29, 121n39
abstraction, 13, 26, 108n3
Abu Ghraib, 54–55
action-guiding, 7, 15, 23, 57, 67, 116n1
Afghanistan War, 14, 78–79, 104n25, 115n33, 125n10, 126n19
agency: moral, 2, 11, 26, 47, 49, 68–69, 71–72, 107n47; reactive, 2, 4–5, 11, 25, 71, 75, 99; reduction of, 2, 5, 10–13, 25, 72
aggression/aggressor: crime of, 20, 81; culpable, 58–59; unjust, 2, 8, 11, 75, 81, 93, 95, 126n18
Albright, Madeleine, 9, 54, 103n13, 119n24
analytic atomism, 2, 4, 7, 16, 22, 26, 39, 50, 67, 71, 75, 80
atomization, 18, 38–40
autonomy/autonomous, 12–13, 15, 30–31, 33, 41–43, 104n23, 114n67, 114n74

background conditions, 28, 32, 37, 100
Bangladesh/Bangladeshi, 25, 27, 29, 31, 43
barbaric/barbarians/barbarism, 17, 19–20, 106n43

binary, 4–5, 11–12, 14, 19, 22–23, 28, 45, 67–68, 72, 76, 81, 84, 89, 92–93, 95–96, 100; moral structure, 67, 76, 84, 93, 95, 100
blame/blame-shifting, 5, 37–39, 65, 82, 112n52
Britain. *See* United Kingdom (UK)/Britain
Bush, George W., 51, 54–55, 66, 80, 119n22

Cambodia/Cambodian, 29, 80
capitalism/capitalist, 19, 21, 35, 48, 110n15, 113n57
Cheney, Dick, 52–53
choice: and coercion, 40–46; forced, 13, 49, 68–69; horrible, 12, 69; non-interference with, 27, 39, 42–44; rational, 17, 30; terms of, 28, 33, 42; voluntary, 26–32, 42–46, 90, 108n6, 114n67
CIA (Central Intelligence Agency), 54, 116n1
civilians, 10, 13, 51, 79, 82, 85, 87–89, 91, 124n4, 127n23
civilizational divide, 19, 21, 34, 72
civilized/uncivilized, 16–17, 21, 34, 39, 72, 76, 79, 94, 103n11

# About the Author

**Michael Neu** is a senior lecturer in philosophy, politics and ethics at the University of Brighton. His research addresses moral and political questions pertaining to violence. He has published articles in *Social Theory and Practice, International Relations* and the *Journal of International Political Theory*. He is also the co-author of *Just War and the Responsibility to Protect: A Critique* (forthcoming) and has co-edited *Exploring Complicity: Concept, Cases and Critique*.